Radio Free Europe's
"Crusade for Freedom"

D1562571

ALSO BY RICHARD H. CUMMINGS

Cold War Radio: The Dangerous History of American Broadcasting in Europe, 1950–1989 (McFarland, 2009)

Radio Free Europe's "Crusade for Freedom"

*Rallying Americans Behind
Cold War Broadcasting, 1950–1960*

RICHARD H. CUMMINGS

McFarland & Company, Inc., Publishers
Jefferson, North Carolina, and London

LIBRARY OF CONGRESS CATALOGUING-IN-PUBLICATION DATA

Cummings, Richard H., 1944–
    Radio Free Europe's "Crusade for Freedom" : rallying
Americans behind Cold War broadcasting, 1950–1960 /
Richard H. Cummings.
        p.   cm.
    Includes bibliographical references and index.

    ISBN 978-0-7864-4410-6
    softcover : 50# alkaline paper ∞

    1. Radio Free Europe — History. 2. International broad-
casting — United States. 3. International broadcasting —
Europe, Eastern. 4. Patriotism — United States. I. Title.
HE8697.45.E852C866   2010
384.54094'09045 — dc22   2010022901

British Library cataloguing data are available

Front cover: Replica of Freedom Bell that was distributed to 48 states
for use in local campaigns (courtesy of RFE/RL); background Cold
War Globe (Wikipedia.org)

Manufactured in the United States of America

McFarland & Company, Inc., Publishers
    Box 611, Jefferson, North Carolina 28640
    www.mcfarlandpub.com

Acknowledgments

This book could not have been written without the assistance of others, and I wish to pay homage to their time and effort in helping me complete my manuscript.

In general, I thank the Hoover Institution, Stanford, California, and the Arthur W. Page Center for Integrity in Public Communication, Penn State University, for their generous financial support, which enabled me to travel to and around the United States in search of relevant archival materials.

I thank Dr. A. Ross Johnson, who has been involved with Radio Free Europe and RFE/RL over many years in various roles, for his friendship and taking time away from his own research to advise and assist me during my research and manuscript preparation.

Dr. Anatol Schmelev, Project Archivist, Collection, Hoover Institution, Stanford University provided continuous and valuable assistance and guidance via e-mail and personally at the Hoover Institution archives and deserves my gratitude.

The following persons are thanked for their expertise and knowledge to guide me through the labyrinth of their respective archives: Richard Sousa, Deborah Ventura, and Celeste Szeto, Hoover Institution, Stanford University; Zoe Ann Stolz, Reference Historian, and Rebecca Kohl, Photograph Archivist, Montana Historical Society; Eve Mangurten, Ad Council Archives, University of Illinois at Urbana-Champaign; Simone Munson, Reference Assistant and ARC Coordinator, Wisconsin Historical Society; Cinda Kostyak, Director of Research Administration, Arthur W. Page Center for Integrity in Public Communication, Penn State University; Maerenn Ball, Corporate PR, General Mills, Minneapolis; and Dawn Hugh, Archives Manager, Historical Museum of Southern Florida.

And I thank all those who worked at Radio Free Europe and Radio Liberty for their years of dedicated work, which contributed to the radio's success in the Cold War, including the eventual collapse of Communism in East Europe and in the USSR.

Table of Contents

Preface

Millions of Americans were impacted, directly and indirectly, by the Crusade for Freedom in the United States, beginning in 1950 and ending approximately ten years later. While I was doing research for my book *Cold War Radio: The Dangerous History of American Broadcasting in Europe, 1950–1989*, I realized that there was no single book about the Crusade for Freedom. What little appeared about the Crusade for Freedom in books and articles about Radio Free Europe was inaccurate or incomplete. For example, Jean Edward Smith's tome *Lucius D. Clay: An American Life*, which runs to over 800 pages, has only two pages devoted to the Crusade for Freedom and Radio Free Europe. As I wrote in the preface:

> I grew up in the greater Boston area, never dreaming that I would someday be working in Munich, Germany, in charge of security at an American-sponsored radio station. How I reached that position is a story of fate or luck. I vividly recall watching black and white television commercials on small screens asking for dollars for Radio Free Europe, especially the one where Ronald Reagan asked for support for the Crusade for Freedom. There were posters in the subway and cars traveling in and out of Boston, asking for contributions to be sent to Mt. Vernon, New York. It seemed that every time I went to a Red Sox game, I saw those posters looking down on me. I did not understand what they were for, but I found them fascinating.[1]

I decided to write the book to give the reader a history of a decade-long domestic "propaganda" campaign in the 1950s that appeared on the surface highly visible but was, in fact, developed mostly behind closed doors of the government and corporate worlds.

In the late 1940s, a diverse group of prominent Americans publicly put forth an enterprising agenda to change the American political landscape. Their visions and dedicated efforts resulted in the Crusade for Freedom, which, for more than ten years, was an intense domestic public relations and media campaign. It evolved not only to arouse the "average" American against the Communist threat, real and perceived, but also to morally, politically, and financially support the radio station Radio Free Europe (RFE) in Cold War Germany and, for a few years in the early 1950s, Radio Free Asia (RFA) in San Francisco, California.

There was another side to the Radio Free Europe story, a side hidden to

1

the American and European public for almost 20 years: Radio Free Europe and its sister station Radio Liberty (RL) in Germany were described in a secret 1968 Central Intelligence Agency (CIA) report as that agency's "two largest and most successful covert action projects in the U.S. effort to break the communist monopoly on news and information in the Soviet Union and Eastern Europe.... The two radios have been covered as privately financed, non-profit American corporations. During that time their funds have largely been provided and their policy controlled by the CIA."[2]

Radio Free Asia, a short-lived third "covert action project," is examined in some detail in this book as its fate was directly connected to Radio Free Europe and the Crusade for Freedom. The early 1950s Radio Free Asia had nothing to do with the current overtly U.S. government supported radio network of that same name, which began broadcasting in 1996 and broadcasts today in nine Asian languages.[3]

From 1949 to 1971, thousands of persons worked at Radio Free Europe and Radio Liberty at a cost of over $465 million. The history of Radio Liberty (RL) is not included in this book, as it had little impact on domestic activity in the United States, and there were no fund-raising campaigns.[4]

Had you lived in the United States in the 1950s and early 1960s, read national and local newspapers and magazines, listened to and watched local and national radio and television, ridden in public transportation and read the advertisements in busses and subways, Radio Free Europe (RFE) and the Crusade for Freedom would have been as well known to you as any American consumer icon in that decade. Today the Crusade for Freedom is, for the most part, just a historical reference note, sometimes inaccurate in details, to the linear history of the Cold War between the United States and the Soviet Union.

From 1950 to 1960, millions of Americans throughout the United States willingly and enthusiastically signed "Freedom Scrolls" and "Freedom-Grams," participated in fund-raising dinners and lunches, attended "Crusader" meetings, marched in parades, launched large balloons filled with leaflets, participated in writing contests, bowled in tournaments, and otherwise were active in the belief that they were individually and collectively supporting Radio Free Europe in the battle against Communist aggression in Europe.

Many corporate and government records no longer exist or have yet to be discovered. For example, I could not find a complete set of Crusade for Freedom Newsletters. The Library of Congress has but a few copies of this valuable source that are in the personal archives of persons who were associated in some way with the Crusade.[5] Yet, at one point in the Crusade's history, over 5000 copies of just one edition were printed and distributed. It is possible that a complete set of the newsletters is sitting in someone's attic or cellar, or in a library storage room gathering dust, collecting mildew, deteriorating, or simply fading away.

The goals of Radio Free Europe and the Crusade for Freedom could be seen as fundamentally the same: winning the hearts and minds of Americans in the ideological struggle against Communism. Their targets were different: Radio Free Europe focused on the hearts and minds of those behind the Iron Curtain; the Crusade for Freedom targeted Americans. Their commonality was to keep the true sponsorship of Radio Free Europe hidden from the public.

I was intrigued about the impact the Crusade for Freedom had on grass roots America — the small cities and towns like the one in which I grew up, rather than what happened in America's largest cities. I will show how the decisions and directives made at the national level — CIA, State Department, Advertising Council, Crusade for Freedom, Free Europe Committees, and other government and nongovernmental organizations — played out on the state and local level in the small cities and towns. That is where the Crusade for Freedom really impacted Americans. Thousands of local volunteer "Crusaders" used their imagination, creativity, and willpower to keep the campaigns moving for ten years. If they had not bought into the idea, the Crusade for Freedom would not have succeeded for as long as it did. There are too many local stories of civic duty and activities to be covered in one book. I have selected some that truly represent how the Crusade campaigns played out locally.

The dynamic early Cold War combination of Radio Free Europe and the Crusade for Freedom was a powerful change management tool of the U.S. government. This mobilization tool should not, in my opinion, be seen an evil *deus ex machina* in the government's Cold-War activities but a successful evolutionary process involving the government, private industry, mass media, academia, religious leaders, and, lastly, "your average Joe." The Crusade for Freedom could be termed a "fraud" on Americans, but it was, in my opinion, a benign fraud: it probably gave most Americans what they wanted anyway: pageantry, a feeling of belonging and contributing to a justified cause — a Cold War consensus. I found no evidence that any individual or group financially profited from the contributions paid out in good faith for a good cause.

My intention is to add to the Cold War historiography by correcting some previously published information on both Radio Free Europe and the Crusade for Freedom and by filling in some gaps of knowledge with details that have become available with the release of previously classified U.S. government information. This is the first book to comprehensively look at the Crusade for Freedom and its impact on Americans in the 1950s. Just as there will never be only one book about Radio Free Europe, Radio Liberty and Radio Free Asia, there will never be only one book on the Crusade for Freedom. I think is safe to say that the book you are about to read will not be the last to study the Crusade for Freedom in the United States, 1950–1960.

Introduction

The idea of American radio broadcasting in Russian to the Soviet Union from Germany, rather than from the official Voice of America, was first broached by the U.S. State Department in August 1946. Lieutenant General Lucius D. Clay, Deputy Military Governor in Allied-occupied Berlin, rejected the idea because it was "inimical to the purposes of four-power government."[1] General Clay focused on sustaining a German-language radio station named Radio in the American Sector (RIAS), for all Berlin and the Soviet-military-occupied zone of Germany. RIAS started broadcasting in February 1946, and its successful staff experiences, techniques, and programming became the model for Radio Free Europe (RFE) in Munich.

The origins of Radio Free Europe can be traced to 1947–48: it was a time of the completion of the Soviet Union's step-by-step domination of Eastern Europe, the Berlin airlift, the Marshall Plan, and the Iron Curtain. Eastern, Central, and Western Europe were physically divided by barbed wire, armed patrols, land mines, and guard towers. The Communist Party monopoly and censorship of the domestic media had effectively cut off and prevented the free flow of information to the peoples of Eastern Europe. In response to these unwelcome developments, a combination of United States government officials, Congress, and the American corporate world decided to act in a secret private-government relationship to bring news and information to the "peoples of the captive nations."

On December 17, 1947, the United States National Security Council reported:

> The USSR is conducting an intensive propaganda campaign directed primarily against the U.S. and is employing coordinated psychological, political and economic measures designed to undermine non–Communist elements in all countries. The ultimate objective of this campaign is not merely to undermine the prestige of the U.S. and the effectiveness of its national policy but to weaken and divide world opinion to a point where effective opposition to Soviet designs is no longer attainable by political, economic or military means. In conducting this campaign, the USSR is utilizing all measures available to it through satellite regimes, Communist parties, and organizations susceptible to Communist influence.[2]

The National Security Council then issued directive NSC 4-A, which called for the director of the Central Intelligence Agency (CIA) to "initiate and conduct covert psychological operations designed to counteract Soviet and Soviet inspired activities, which constitute a threat to world peace."[3] One aim of this psychological-war campaign was to create "surrogate" radio stations that would broadcast to countries under the Soviet control yet not be officially connected with the United States government. These stations could broadcast programs and take positions which the U.S.–sponsored Voice of America could not: "all activities ... conducted or sponsored ... against hostile foreign states or groups or in support of friendly foreign states or groups but which are so planned and executed that any U.S. Government responsibility for them is not evident to unauthorized persons and that if uncovered the U.S. Government can plausibly disclaim any responsibility for them."[4]

In 1948 George Kennan was the director of the Department of State's policy planning staff and the prime mover in creating Radio Free Europe. On May 4, 1948, he presented a State Department position paper to the National Security Council entitled "The Inauguration of Organized Political Warfare." Political warfare was described as "the logical application of Clausewitz's doctrine in time of peace."[5] Kennan proposed a program of support for "liberation committees, underground activities behind the Iron Curtain, and support of indigenous anti–Communist elements in threatened countries of the Free World." The purpose of these "liberation committees" was

> To encourage the formation of a public American organization which will sponsor selected political refugee committees so that they may
>
> (a) act as foci of national hope and revive a sense of purpose among political refugees from the Soviet World;
> (b) provide an inspiration for continuing popular resistance within the countries of the Soviet World; and
> (c) serve as a potential nucleus for all-out liberation movements in the event of war.[6]

Kennan further described the "liberation committees" as overt operations that should receive covert guidance and possibly assistance from the government: "It is proposed that trusted private American citizens be encouraged to establish a public committee which would give support and guidance in U.S. interests to national movements (many of them now in existence) publicly led by outstanding political refugees from the Soviet World."[7]

In June 1948, after a lengthy debate among various interested government agencies on the questions of overt and covert propaganda, domestic and international information programs, the National Security Council superseded NSC 4-A with another directive, NSC 10/2. Kennan reportedly drafted this directive, which presented more details of planned psychological war with the Soviet Union:

> The National Security Council, taking cognizance of the vicious covert activities of the USSR, its satellite countries and Communist groups to discredit and defeat

the aims and activities of the United States and other Western powers, has determined that, in the interests of world peace and U.S. national security, the overt foreign activities of the U.S. Government must be supplemented by covert operations.[8]

Covert operations were listed as "Propaganda; economic warfare; preventive direct action, including sabotage, anti-sabotage, demolition and evacuation measures; subversion against hostile states, including assistance to underground resistance movements, guerrillas, and refugee liberation groups, and support of indigenous anti–Communist elements in threatened countries of the free world."[9]

NSC 10/2 specifically dealt with the creation of an Office of Special Projects within the CIA. This new office would, in part, plan and conduct covert operations. The person in charge of this new office would report directly to the director of central intelligence (DCI), and for "purposes of security and of flexibility of operations, and to the maximum degree consistent with efficiency," the Office of Special Projects would "operate independently of other components of Central Intelligence Agency."[10]

On July 16, 1948, U.S. Secretary of State George Marshall sent a telegram to American ambassadors in Eastern Europe and the USSR telling them, "Considerable thought has been given to question whether political refugees in U.S. from Iron Curtain countries should be used over VOUSA broadcasts to these countries."[11] He asked for their opinions. The ambassadors were unanimous in rejecting the plan. The U.S. ambassador in the Soviet Union explained, for example: "In my opinion Soviet or other political refugees from Iron Curtain countries should not be used.... Under present circumstances use of any Soviet refugees on VOUSA would not only be ineffectual but would undoubtedly excite resentment and ridicule against our broadcasts."[12] This was the final bureaucratic rejection of any remaining idea of using refugees over official or overt U.S. radio facilities in the upcoming psychological war. Covert broadcasting became the only alternative available for the Truman administration.

Frank Wisner was a World War II Office of Strategic Services (OSS) veteran and lawyer, and one of the main actors responsible for the development of Radio Free Europe. In September 1944, he was in Bucharest, Romania, where he controlled an OSS operation that evacuated allied airmen downed behind enemy lines. Wisner remained in Bucharest until March 1945, when he witnessed the arrival of Soviet troops and the tragic aftermath of the occupation. After World War II, Frank Wisner returned to private practice in New York and joined the influential Council on Foreign Relations.[13] Former OSS Switzerland chief Allen Dulles was then the Council's president. Allen Dulles was the third major personality in the development of Radio Free Europe.[14]

In 1947, Wisner joined the U.S. State Department as the Deputy Assistant Secretary of State for Occupied Countries. Wisner became involved with the refugees from the USSR and Soviet-dominated countries in Eastern Europe.

Evan Thomas has written, "During their long lunches at the Down Town Association right after the war, Wisner and Dulles had talked about using radio broadcasts as a propaganda tool."[15] George Kennan placed Wisner in June 1948 at the head of his list of candidates for a new CIA position located within the State Department: Director of the Office of Special Projects, based on the "recommendations of people who know him." Kennan wrote, "I personally have no knowledge of his ability, but his qualifications seem reasonably good."[16]

By June 1948, the CIA's Special Operations Group in Europe had acquired a radio transmitter and a printing plant, and began stockpiling meteorological balloons to carry and drop propaganda leaflets and other materials over the Iron Curtain into East European countries, apparently using the code word "Project ULTIMATE."[17] In his new position, Frank Wisner telephoned Director of Central Intelligence Roscoe Hillenkoetter on August 4, 1948, and told him that "project for the clandestine radio transmitter" had been approved in principle. The final approval would follow once the details were determined regarding "who was to operate the transmitter, to whom the transmissions would be directed, and who would set up the raw material to be transmitted."[18]

On June 1, 1949, Wisner met John McCloy, then State Department High Commissioner for Germany, and wrote a memorandum to his staff concerning that meeting:

> Last night I talked for about forty-five minutes with Mr. McCloy.... I explained to Mr. McCloy the general significance and origin of OPC and then I took up with him certain aspects of our present and prospective operations in Germany. In the latter regard I mentioned in particular the conversations and exchange of communications, which I had had with General Clay in regard to the radio broadcasting activity from Germany. In this connection I filled him in on the background and significance of the developments regarding the formation of the various refugee national committees and the New York Committee, pointing out that General Clay had said that he saw no problem in allowing duly authorized representatives of really responsible and broadly representative national committees of refugees to enter Germany and there to arrange for broadcasts.[19]

The philosophical, political, and operational groundwork for the creation of Radio Free Europe, using émigrés as broadcasters, had been set on the government side. The Central Intelligence Agency would provide "confidential or unvouchered funds" to finance Radio Free Europe and provide policy control based upon State Department guidance — all of which was reviewed and approved by appropriate congressional committees. The first half of the state-private broadcasting equation was set. The private side now had to be developed.

ONE

How It All Began

National Committee for Free Europe

The certificate of incorporation of a nonprofit company called the Committee for Free Europe, Inc. was submitted to the State of New York for approval on April 29, 1949. The New York City law firm for which Allen Dulles worked, Sullivan and Cromwell, filed the papers required for incorporation. The Committee for Free Europe was founded, in part, to

> Help the non–Fascist and non–Communist leaders who have fled to the United States from the countries of Eastern Europe to maintain themselves in useful occupations during their enforced stay in the United States.
>
> Assist these leaders in maintaining contact with their fellow citizens in other lands and in keeping alive among them the ideals of individual and national freedom.[1]

One of the most critical incorporation document articles was: "No part of the activities of the corporation shall be the carrying on of propaganda or otherwise attempting to influence legislation."[2]

The first meeting of the Committee for Free Europe (CFE) took place on May 17, 1949, when corporate by-laws were adopted and directors were selected. Directors and officers included future CIA director Allen Dulles and future president Dwight D. Eisenhower. The first president of CFE was Dulles, who resigned this position after a few weeks but took on the position of chairman of the Executive Committee. Other directors included DeWitt Wallace, publisher of *Reader's Digest*, and Henry Luce, publisher of *Time, Fortune*, and *Life* magazines.

DeWitt Clinton Poole, graduate of Princeton University, succeeded Dulles as president of the committee for Free Europe. DeWitt Poole's illustrious experience included that of United States Consul General in Russia during the Bolshevik Revolution. The *New York Times* September 13, 1918, wrote that he "is an American citizen to be noted and remembered. When the Americans left Moscow, Poole refused to go. He stayed there to stand by the French and British, who are in danger of their lives." After his diplomatic career, Poole joined the board of directors of *Public Opinion Quarterly*, printed by Princeton University Press, and was editor from 1937 to 1939. In World War II, DeWitt Poole headed the Foreign Nationalities Branch of the Office of Strategic Services.

Former U.S. ambassador to Japan, Joseph C. Grew, became CFE chairman of the board. He announced at a press conference on June 1, 1949, that the new corporation will

> Put the voices of these exiled leaders on the air, addressed to their own peoples back in Europe, in their own languages, in the familiar tones. We shall help them also, if we can, to get their messages back by the printed word.... Of course we are not going to compete with the Voice of America, for the Voice is under restrictions by reason of its official character. It is our American habit not to leave everything to government. In the field of the contest of ideas there is much which private initiative can accomplish best.
>
> The Committee will rally popular support in the United States for the cause of Free Europe, and, in this way, will aid in the cause of freedom everywhere.
>
> It will raise and dispense funds in behalf of this cause.[3]

The next day, on June 2, 1949, the corporate name was changed to National Committee for Free Europe (NCFE). Over the next weeks and months, there was general editorial praise for the NCFE in various newspapers throughout the United States:

> ...The National Committee for Free Europe has shaped an imaginative and flexible program.... It may be taken as a sign of our maturity that we are dealing seriously with a situation which before this has been treated haphazardly and frequently misunderstood [New York *Herald Tribune*, June 5, 1949].
>
> ...if real self-determination ever shall come to Eastern Europe, vigorous native leadership for democracy will be needed and may be furnished by the kind of men the (NCFE) purposes to assist. Much good can be done that way which is out of State Department's official province, and the Committee should be able to attract the popular support it is seeking. No effort should be shirked to keep hope alive among America's friends behind the Iron Curtain [San Antonio, Texas *Express*, June 8, 1949].
>
> ...The Committee is performing an important service to the refugees, to their peoples, to the United States—and to the cause of freedom throughout the world [*New York Times*, August 19, 1949].
>
> ...(the NCFE's radio programs) show real promise of aiding the democratic values in the war of ideologies.... It seems to us that the best way to combat distorted propaganda is to use propaganda of our own, based on truth [Sherman, Texas *Democrat*, November 20, 1949].
>
> a freedom offensive was launched by the National Committee for Free Europe.... Its weapons are chiefly moral and psychological. But these are the weapons on which we must rely to save the world from the long-range dangers of the present uncertain truce. In our opinion, they need to be greatly strengthened. Indeed, only a society dynamically devoted to freedom is likely to remain free in this revolutionary age [*Washington Post*, December 14, 1949].
>
> There is no point in attempting to outline all the things that these men are now doing. Sufficient to say that they form a core of highly resourceful and determined psychological warriors. The spoken and written word is their weapon. Their goal is to keep hope alive among the millions who live against their will under commu-

nism and who, in the case of all too many, have concluded that the outlook is hopeless and that they have been abandoned by the West [Baltimore, Maryland *Sun*, December 14, 1949].

On June 21, 1949, Acting Secretary of State James Webb sent a cable to 24 embassies, legations, and missions in Europe and the Middle East giving some details of the new organization:

> This Committee is a private organization concerning itself with democratic leaders and scholars who are exiled.... The Committee will be financed by private contributions.
>
> For your information, the Department has been continually informed of the process of formation of the Committee, Although the Department has no active concern with the Committee's activities, it has given its unofficial approval to the Committees objectives. Because of the implicitly political nature of the Committee's work, there will be coordination between it and the Department. We expect that the Committee will cooperate in every way toward the accomplishment of our objectives in Eastern Europe and the general aims of our foreign policy.[4]

During his press conference on June 23, 1949, Secretary of State Acheson said that the State Department "was very happy to see the formation of the distinguished group" and "the Department felt the purpose of the organization was excellent and was glad to welcome its entrance in the field and give it hearty endorsement."[5]

Fund-Raising

The evolving fund-raising concept quickly followed the creation of the NCFE, when on May 27, 1949, Joseph Grew wrote a letter to potential members of the Committee that included the fund-raising concept:

> Concurrently with the announcement, an advertising campaign of a suitable tone and dignity will start. From this campaign, it is hoped, private contributions will come to support the work of the Committee. The enterprise touches so closely upon the instinct of survival, and the need is so clear, that substantial contributions have already been assured from a number of sources, and adequate funds are in hand for some time to come.[6]

The financial books of the NCFE were set up for five committees:

1. General Administrative
2. Committee on Intellectual Activities
3. Committee on Radio and Press
4. Committee on American Contacts
5. National Committees (Bulgarian, Czechoslovak, Hungarian, Romanian).

Allen Dulles on July 14, 1949, sent a memorandum to NCFE Directors Poole, Altschul, Page, and Spofford that included a "Memorandum on Organization Operations" that read, in part:

In reply to the Committee's application to the Treasury Department for Federal income tax exemption, the Treasury ruled favorably and has also held that contributions to the National Committee for Free Europe, Inc. will be deductible by the donors for income tax purposes as provided in the income tax law.

A Finance Committee is in course of being organized to give attention to fund raising: an advertising campaign is being planned: and attention is being directed to the formation in various centers throughout the country of small committees or groups which will assist in making known the objectives and work of the National Committee and aid in the raising of funds.[7]

On August 4, 1949, at a "special meeting," the Directors of NCFE passed a comprehensive resolution on the operations of the NCFE. The Committee on Radio and the Press, known as Committee II, was under the chairmanship of Frank Altschul with one other member, Edward Barrett, who would later resign from the NCFE after being named Assistant Secretary of State. In his new position, Edward Barrett would continue his close relationship with Radio Free Europe.

Congressional Concerns

United States Senator Ralph Flanders of Vermont wrote to Allen Dulles on August 10, 1949,

Your letter of August 5 has been received and Mr. Poole has made a call on me, which I found to be very interesting. I did not find from the conversation with him that he had the same sense of urgency that I have with regard to rather more dramatic measures in the propaganda line such as that illustrated in the material sent you. If he has the feeling or urgency, I judge that it is dampened by the attitude of Mr. Kennan ... who feels that undertakings of this sort are unconventional and irregular — as of course they are.[8]

Dulles wrote another letter to Senator Flanders on August 30, 1949, in which he stated, "After the Labor Day holiday we plan a real campaign to broadcast the objectives of the National Committee to get financial and other support and to carry out what I hope will be a constructive and practical program."[9]

Beginning of the Public Relations– Advertising Connection

Decisions and directives made at the state-private level, i.e., CIA, State Department, Advertising Council, Crusade for Freedom, Free Europe Committees, and other government and nongovernmental organizations concerning international broadcasting, affected many small cities and towns of the United States. That is where the Crusade for Freedom really impacted ordinary Americans: thousands of grass-roots volunteer "Crusaders" used their imagination, creativity and willpower to keep the campaigns moving for ten years. If the volunteers had not bought into the idea, the Crusade for Freedom would not have succeeded for as long as it did.

In June 1949, the NCFE formed an advertising committee with Howard M. Chapin as its advisor. Chapin, a director of advertising of General Foods Corporation,[10] was a former World War II OSS colonel responsible for Czechoslovakia.[11] On August 11, 1949, DeWitt Poole lunched with Chapin and they discussed the proposed financing of NCFE. The same day Poole wrote to Allen Dulles giving him some details of the lunch discussion. Poole recommended that Dulles and Chapin meet to discuss fund raising. Poole then explained that "Chapin anticipates that the advertising series which is now proposed to begin at mid–September may very well of itself bring in $100,000. He thinks it not at all impossible that well organized fund raising, in conjunction with advertising, would yield us a half-million dollars a year, year after year."[12]

On August 26, 1949, Erwin Tuthill, vice-president of the public relations firm John Price Jones Company, wrote a letter to Charles Taft, NCFE director, whom he personally knew, in which he explained how he understood NCFE activities. He then asked Taft, "If this Committee now is, or shortly will be, contemplating a fund-raising effort to support its planned activities, it is possible that we might be of service to the Committee." Tuthill went on, "I am writing to you to inquire whether you know the immediate plans of the Committee, whether they now may be considering an early campaign for funds, and if so, who may be responsible for such planning."[13]

The answer to Tuthill was not long in coming: at their August 1949 meeting, the NCFE's Directors authorized DeWitt Poole to negotiate with the public relations firm John Price Jones, and he thereafter met with Messrs Jones and Tuthill, who later would become advisor to NCFE on public relations.[14]

DeWitt Poole and Allen Dulles discussed fund-raising at a luncheon at the Downtown Association club in September 1949. Poole followed up the discussion with a letter to Dulles on September 13, 1949, where he enclosed a list of prospective and influential donors who would be "urgently" approached by NCFE members on an individual basis in order to reach a goal of "first hundred thousand."[15]

Poole wrote to Allen Dulles on October 13, 1949 asking for the consent of the NCFE Executive Committee in order to enter into a contract with the John Price Jones Company regarding the NCFE's fund-raising campaign:

> John Price Jones ... proposes a study, which it would require some five weeks to complete. The cost would be $5,000.00 plus travel expense. I recommend that we ask the John Price Jones Company to undertake this study on the terms proposed.
>
> It seems to me imperative that we get on with this business of fund-raising, and it seems that we have made about all the progress we can short of a survey such as Jones proposes.[16]

Emotion, Reason, and Action

DeWitt Poole wrote to Allen Dulles on November 16, 1949, further giving his thoughts on fund-raising:

> Our fund-raising campaign can be thought of in two ways. The objective can be simply to raise money. If it is restricted to this scope we are interested only in sizable donors. Donations of one dollar or even of five dollars cost as much as or more than the sum received.
>
> The alternative conception thinks not only of bringing in money but also of arousing a still livelier and broader public concern than already exists over the Communist threat, and so to obtain a wide democratic support for the particular work of defense and counterattack upon which the National Committee for Free Europe is embarked. If this larger purpose is our goal, contributions of one dollar are welcome, even if each would be found upon analysis to cost us more than one dollar.
>
> Of the two conceptions, I personally prefer the second. I believe that it has an appeal much more cogent than the plain businesslike idea of getting in some money on the most economical basis.
>
> You will be better able to judge than I, but I also surmise that the second conception is the one, which is the more likely to move General Clay, or any other such as he, to lend us his name and support. If you put the project before him as a characteristically American movement of a characteristically democratic type, I should think that he would find it warm-blooded, congenial and moving.
>
> The foregoing are just personal ideas. Since the choice between the two conceptions will affect our public relations throughout, I am taking the liberty of sending a copy of this letter directly to Arthur Page and Howard Chapin, and also to Mr. Tuthill at the John Price Jones Company, since he is our professional adviser.[17]

In January 1950, John Price Jones sent the NCFE the company's report written in December 1949 that was entitled *Analysis and Plan of Fund Raising*, in which plans were listed for public relations and publicity for the NCFE in the United States:

> Purpose. The public relations and publicity program will be two-fold in its objectives: to further support for a free Europe, and to develop financial and working support. The purpose may be broken down as follows:
>
> 1. To arouse the American public to dangers of Communism, and the urgent necessity for checking it at point of origin.
> 2. To demonstrate why a Free Europe is essential to our own freedom — national and individual.
> 3. To describe the NCFE and what it is doing to check Communism at home by defeating it in Europe.
> 4. To inspire support for NCFE.
> 5. To stimulate both group and individual action to increase the number of persona who are individually doing something to stem Communism.
>
> Method. Every known method of publicity should be utilized, but the weight of effort should be localized publicity, where a Committee is soliciting. Only by bringing the publicity down to the local level will it have the effect of stirring the greatest number of individuals into action. A background of national publicity is essential, but the greatest action will accrue when individuals are reached in their own communities by the community media.[18]

The advertising campaign was "specifically written to meet the need of the fund-raising campaign ... extensive study of the needs of the National Committee for Free Europe" by the company of Hewitt, Ogilvy, Benson and Mather. One of the listed advertising aims was "To capitalize on the public's anti-communist sentiment, beat the drum of immediate danger, and paint a bold picture of the personal loss that is bound to follow Communism."[19] The advertising structure was to be based on three major appeals: Emotion, Reason and Action:

Emotion

To create emotion, personalized dramatic headlines ... will be written in terse simple words that speak directly to the average man.

Reason

Point-by-point listings of the concrete things NCFE is doing and will do to achieve its goal of halting and destroying World Communism. Once the emotions are aroused, the immediate danger is stated, and tangible "what can you do" ... it is felt that the reader will be motivated to the action he is next exhorted to take.

Action

To get action, end copy will emphasize urgency and utilize the "act now before it's too late" technique.[20]

NCFE Board of Directors Special Meeting

The NCFE Board of Directors convened a special meeting on January 19, 1950. Joseph Grew told the Board that General Lucius D. Clay had "manifested a deep interest in all phases of the work" of the NCFE and would be moving to New York City in March. The Board then unanimously approved Clay's election to the Board. Grew went on to report on the fund-raising question with the idea of setting up a special committee of the NCFE to organize and conduct the fund-raising campaign. General Clay, Allen Dulles, Arthur Page, Frank Altschul, and DeWitt Poole were then appointed as the Executive Committee for fund-raising. The NCFE had previously set aside $80,961.18 for advertising. The Executive Committee was empowered additionally to use up to $100,000 from the NCFE general funds for the initial campaign expenses, for a total of just over $180,000.[21]

The Birth of the Crusade for Freedom

The John Price Jones fund plan, written in 1949, called for a symbol to be used in fund raising. In January 1950, DeWitt Poole called his friend Harry Bullis, then Chairman of General Mills Corporation in Minneapolis, Minnesota, and asked him for assistance in fulfilling the plan. Bullis agreed and contacted Abbott Washburn, World War II OSS veteran and public relations expert at the General Mills Corporation, who consented to cooperate with the Crusade team.

Washburn, in turn, asked Nate Crabtree, who handled the General Mills account for the public relations firm of Batten, Barton, Durstine, and Osborn, to accompany him on his trip to New York. At the end of January 1950, they met with Poole, who explained how the NCFE had thought up the idea of a nation-wide support drive, including the need of a symbol for the fund-raising campaign. Washburn and Crabtree agreed to help and on January 26, 1950, they drew up a list of first steps to develop a public relations plan of the NCFE for the fund-raising campaign with the name "Crusade for Freedom."[22]

After returning the Minneapolis, Washburn met with the General Mills president Leslie Perrin and vice president Sam Gale. On February 1, 1950, Washburn wrote to DeWitt Poole of the NCFE advising him that both Perrin and Gale had endorsed the NCFE and he was convinced that he had the agreement from both to actively participate in the developments of the NCFE.

Washburn and Crabtree had by February 1, 1950, developed this initial plan, which "we think holds considerable possibility of enlisting tremendous interest and support from the American public. However it will require a high degree of cooperation from Washington ... in building this kind of broad national interest." The suggested plan included an overview of a fund-raising campaign that remained valid for the life of the Crusade for Freedom:

> The fist thing that must be accomplished, before any financial campaign can be successful, is the building of broad public understanding of the work of NCFE and Radio Free Europe. This implies enlisting the support of some ten to twelve million Americans. To accomplish will require the active help of the men who control the mass media. We must have a program so dramatic and forceful that these men will want to help implement it by making free time and space available to us.[23]

Abbott Washburn further advised DeWitt Poole that General Mills vice president Sam Gale had just been elected Chairman of the Board of Directors of the Advertising Council: "This is a stroke of good fortune, as the Advertising Council can be extremely helpful to us at the time of the CRUSADE campaign." Washburn went on to explain the role of the Advertising Council, which, indeed, would later become extremely important and vital to both Radio Free Europe and the Crusade for Freedom:

> As you doubtless know, the Council is a group of the foremost advertisers, publishers, radio people, and advertising agency men, who screen the hundreds of national causes and select those which will be given free time and space in media of all kinds throughout the country. The Council was developed during the war and proved very successful in coordinating the conveying of public services messages to the masses.[24]

Birth of the Freedom Bell

Abbott Washburn and Nate Crabtree also came up with idea of a bell as a symbol for the Crusade: a Freedom Bell, based on the Liberty Bell, housed in Independence Hall in Philadelphia. New York industrial designer Walter Dorwin

Figure 1. Replica of Freedom Bell that was distributed to 48 states for use in local campaign. This photograph was used in newspaper releases to announce arrival of state Freedom Bell in local communities (courtesy RFE/RL).

Teague was chosen by the Crusade directors to design the bell. Teague decided on the inscription based on a statement by Abraham Lincoln, "That this World, Under God, shall have a new birth of freedom." At the May 18, 1950 meeting, the Crusade directors approved the Freedom Bell and its inscription as its symbol and approved a contract for its construction.[25] The result is shown in Figure 1.

DeWitt Poole wrote to General Clay on February 24, 1950, giving him details of the planned fund-raising crusade, with Clay as its chairman. Arthur

Page was identified as the Chairman of the Policy Committee with Abbott Washburn as the Vice-Chairman. Poole asked Clay for his blessings:

> Naturally we foresee that this will be your operation, and I am sure that I speak for all the directors when I say that we shall wish to make any changes in our present ideas, which you may care to recommend to us. I hope that you will find the present conception good in the main.[26]

Questions of Contribution Handling

John R. Burton, Jr., the legal counsel of the NCFE wrote a memorandum to DeWitt Poole, Frank Altschul, and Theodore Augustine, in which he outlined the legal foundation of the upcoming fund raising campaign. He assumed that the name would be "Crusade for Freedom" of the NCFE. The "Crusade for Freedom" committee would be part of the NCFE and "empowered to conduct the fund drive and to accept contributions" on behalf of the NCFE, "as well as to disburse funds." He explained how the financial books and accounting procedures, including the depositing of checks received in a special account in both names, would be set up.[27]

American Heritage Foundation

The American Heritage Foundation would be an important factor in the life of the Crusade for Freedom in the 1950s. On March 10, 1950, as a precursor of the future relationship, Allen Dulles wrote to his brother John Foster Dulles, U.S. senator and a director of the American Heritage Foundation:

> The National Committee for Free Europe in connection with its fund raising program was thinking of approaching the American Heritage Foundation with a view possibly both to getting a contribution and also getting the backing of the foundation in connection with this campaign.
>
> I note that you are a director and, if this comes to your attention, I would appreciate any push you can give it.[28]

Board of Directors Meeting March 16, 1950

On March 16, 1950, there was a regular monthly meeting of the NCFE board of directors at which the directors approved a six-month budget of $250,000 for the fund-raising campaign. Also approved was a revised budget for Radio Free Europe of $899,386.00, which was a capital expenditure increase of over $400,000 but with the decrease in operating expenditures of almost $200,000, there was a net overall increase of $214,000. Robert Lang of the Free Europe division was scheduled to leave to Germany to purchase and set up the necessary equipment for broadcasting and to hire local personnel. The Board agreed to give Lang up to $200,000 for that purpose. Total NCFE budget allotments up to June 30, 1950, for all projects amounted to $1,893,526: $613,447 for capital expenses and $1,280,079 for operating expenses.[29]

NCFE Annual Meeting

On April 3, 1959, the NCFE held its annual meeting. The Committee passed a resolution changing the National Committee's name from "for Free Europe, Inc." to National Committee "for a Free Europe, Inc." Joseph Grew reported in detail on the events and developments of the previous ten months. He was optimistic that Radio Free Europe would begin broadcasting in the near future, with the transmitter ready as early as April 19, 1950:

> We are well started toward setting up an instrumentality which, at work along-side of the official Voice of America, following the American tradition of peoples talking freely to peoples, enabling the exiled democratic leaders to be heard in their homelands after all, may very seriously help in the end to turn in our favor the battle of ideas and save us from having to defend freedom once more with blood.[30]

Grew finished his annual report to the directors with an update of developments in the "campaign for funds":

> Meanwhile plans have matured for arousing the American people to the danger in which freedom stands, and to move them to support the National Committee for Free Europe as the handy instrument through which in the spirit of American individual initiative each can throw his weight into the fight. Obviously our money needs are large and we hope broad public support will be forthcoming.[31]

Truman's Campaign of Truth

On April 20, 1950, President Truman spoke at a luncheon of the American Society of Newspaper Editors on American foreign policy. President Truman called for a "campaign of truth" in the United States information programs:

> The cause of freedom is being challenged throughout the world today by the forces of imperialistic communism. This is a struggle, above all else, for the minds of men. Propaganda is one of the most powerful weapons the Communists have in this struggle. Deceit, distortion and lies are systematically used by them as a matter of deliberate policy.
> This propaganda can be overcome by the truth — plain, simple, unvarnished truth — presented by the newspapers, radio, newsreels, and other sources that the people trust. If the people are not told the truth, or if they do not have confidence in the accuracy and fairness of the press, they have no defense against falsehoods. But if they are given the true facts, these falsehoods become laughable instead of dangerous.
> We must make ourselves known as we really are — not as Communist propaganda pictures us. We must pool our efforts with those of other free peoples in a sustained, intensified program to promote the cause of freedom against the propa-

ganda of slavery. We must make ourselves heard round the world in a great campaign of truth.[32]

Crusade for Freedom Announcement

On April 26, 1950, DeWitt C. Poole announced that retired General Clay accepted the position of Chairman of the Crusade for Freedom. In Clay's name, an emotional statement of purpose of the Crusade was issued to the press, which, in part, read:

> The soul of the world is sick, and the peoples of the world are looking to the United States for leadership and hope.... They are looking to us for leadership in a great moral crusade — a crusade for freedom, friendship and faith throughout the earth.... If we to prove equal to this desperate need, each U.S. citizen must feel a personal responsibility. We cannot leave the job to government alone.
>
> We have suffered serious setbacks in the contest of ideas between our way of life and totalitarianism.
>
> It is with a great deal of humility that I have accepted responsibility as national chairman of this Crusade, for I am convinced that upon its success could very well depend the prevention of World War III.[33]

On the same day, the National Committee for a Free Europe sent a telegram, under the names of General Clay and Joseph Grew, NCFE Board Chairman, to president Truman advising him of the new Crusade for Freedom and its future plans:

> In your speech of April 20, you urged private initiative in expressing the voice of freedom. The National Committee for a Free Europe was organized for this purpose, and particularly to help those who love freedom and, as a result, have been exiled to continue to fight for the restoration of freedom in their countries. We believe that the American people are ready for a crusade for freedom which will not only support the voices of those from behind the Iron Curtain who have lost freedom and home but will augment their voices with an overwhelming expression from free people in this country and everywhere of their faith and confidence that there will yet be a free world.
>
> We recognize the additional responsibility which has been thrust upon us by your challenging words, and we want to assure you that we are proceeding immediately with every resource at our disposal to organize in this country a crusade for freedom which will be a genuine expression of the will of the American people and which, through Radio Free Europe and other facilities, will be carried throughout the world. We have every confidence that the American people will join enthusiastically in this crusade to preserve their heritage, and thus respond fully and promptly to your expression of faith.[34]

President Truman responded with letters to General Clay and Joseph Grew:

> Your telegram of April twenty-sixth, advising me that the National Committee for a Free Europe is launching a nationwide crusade for freedom, meets with my heartiest approval. I hope that all Americans will join with you in dedicating themselves to this critical struggle for men's minds. I am deeply gratified by your

prompt response to my appeal of April twentieth, in which I emphasized the important role of private groups and organizations in this great endeavor.[35]

Crusade Campaign Letter Number One

On May 1, 1950, the Crusade for Freedom's *Campaign Letter Number One* was sent to the regional and state chairmen in the United States, under General Clay's name, with details of the bell symbol:

> The long range, broad-gauge objectives of the Crusade for Freedom are to enlist several million Americans in a Crusade for Freedom and Friendship to put the lie to Kremlin propaganda that our goal is world domino and war to affirm our resolution that America is in the Crusade to stay.
>
> The ideal of the *Crusade for Freedom* is to feed human souls.
>
> Compelling symbol of the Crusade will be a great new Freedom Bell.... Throughout history the struggle toward human freedom has been one of the noblest achievements of man. The Freedom Bell will become a permanent memorial to all the men and women, of all periods, who gave their lives to the cause of freedom.
>
> The first clap of the Freedom Bell will be carried to the peoples of the earth by the most extensive network of radio power ever assembled — spearheaded by Radio Free Europe. Simultaneously, bells will ring out all over America: church bells, city hall bells, school bells.
>
> Contributions on a broad basis—from nickels and dimes from school children on up — will be sought to underwrite the Bell and the rest of the Crusade program, via radio and newspaper publicity. The assistance of the Advertising Council will be very helpful in this regard.[36]

The letter went on to list the various functions of the regional and state chairmen regarding city and state activities. Among them were

- Appoint bell-ringing committees in every community.
- Stimulate and organize the sending of printed matter overseas— to show how we live in America.
- Develop contests among both groups and individuals for the best ideas on how to get our message and freedom and friendship to people abroad.[37]

Governmental Relationships

On May 4, 1950, there was a meeting in the office of Robert Joyce of the State Department's Police Planning Staff to discuss the relationship to be established between RFE and the Department of State. Carmel Offie of the CIA participated in the meeting and presented the origins, personnel, and mission of RFE. Those who attended the meeting agreed that the Department of State would prepare regular policy guidance for American managers at Radio Free Europe. They also agreed that

A man at a working desk level who will be responsible that there will be no deviation from overall policy.... As presently conceived, the vast bulk of the material will come from unclassified (including wire services) and underground services. However, a small but spicy percentage will be culled from official sources.

The Department of State is recognized as the senior clearance agency and, when the item is carried by State and one or more other government agencies; the item will be submitted to State for clearance.[38]

May 1950 Progress Reports

Major General C.L. Adcock, chosen by Lucius Clay as his Executive Vice Chairman, sent Clay a progress report for the period ending May 18, 1950, indicating that John McCloy, U.S. High Commissioner for Germany, had been informed of a tower requirement for the erection of the Freedom Bell and "whole-heartedly" approved the West Berlin site for the dedication ceremony planned for October or November 1950. He mentioned that Abbott Washburn held discussions with the Advertising Council about the allocation of free time and space but because it was unclear of any relationship with the American Heritage Foundation (absorption or partnership), no specific time and space could be allocated. Adcock finished the progress report with the warning that the budget estimates were too low due to preparation and reproduction of press releases, rental of larger office space, the full-time employment of a public relations expert, and $25,000 for the planned "indoctrination" trip to Germany.[39]

Adcock sent a separate progress report to Allen Grover of Time, Inc., and Harry Harper of *Reader's Digest* magazine, on May 23, 1950, in which he identified five regional chairmen, and General Clay was waiting for the acceptance of a sixth regional chairman before he would go to the radio networks and the American Heritage Foundation and Advertising Council with the idea of taking over "the AHF space and time allotments." In this progress report, Adcock mentioned two ideas of Abbott Washburn that would have a major impact on the Crusade for Freedom for the 1950s:

1. That we invite millions of people to sign their names to a document —
perhaps a Declaration of World Freedom — such signatures to be placed in some permanent form at the site of the Freedom Bell

2. To invite suggestions from all the American people on how best to sell the idea of Freedom (perhaps the device of a nationwide essay or statement contest).[40]

Crusade Campaign Letter No. 3

Letter No. 3 was sent out on June 2, 1950, and was the first with detailed instructions to regional, state, and city chairmen with "organization, financial methods for handling contributions, measures suggested for arousing and maintaining interest in the Crusade by local programs...." The "first responsibility" of each regional chairman was to "line up" an advisory council representing all groups in his region. To accomplish this, the regional chairman was to select

- Two principal labor organizations
- Three principal faiths
- Educators
- Women's organization leader
- Agriculture leader
- Prominent Negro
- Industrialist
- Retailer.[41]

Preparations for Berlin

Abbot Washburn met with General Adcock and Nate Crabtree and wrote a letter on June 20, 1950, to General Clay, wherein he outlined the agreed-upon tactical plan for the upcoming delivery of the Freedom Bell to Berlin.

> The Crusade is of sufficient importance in the world picture to justify calling in representatives of all the papers and wire services, as well as some of the radio news editors. Since this will be a P.M. release for July 10, the press conference should be held at 9:15 A.M., at some convenient location — the Ambassador Hotel might be suitable since the tour group will meet there for luncheon that day.
>
> We should have glossy photographs of the Freedom Bell replica to distribute along with the news release. It is going to be difficult, in any case, to keep the project alive in the press between July 10 and the kickoff of the Airlift Cavalcade, tentatively set for Labor Day, September 4.
>
> As discussed with General Adcock today, I feel it is absolutely essential to have National Crusade Council set up representing all of the major segments of the American public before any details of the Crusade are released. Failing to set up this Council first would be a fatal mistake.[42]

There was some fiduciary concern among the Crusade directors about the fund-raising for Radio Free Europe, when Frank Altschul, Treasurer of the NCFE, wrote to Allan Dulles, then chairman of the executive committee, on June 24, 1950:

> If there is any risk in the public campaign for funds maybe we had better consider incorporating the crusade as a separate organization and getting its tax-exempt status properly established. I imagine there is still time to do this.[43]

Radio Free Europe Goes on the Air

In the late 1940s, the CIA's Special Procedures Group (SPG) had small short-wave transmitters from the American military for broadcasting to the Soviet Union and Eastern Europe from the U.S. zone of Germany, under the code name "Project UMPIRE."[44] A 7.5-kilowatt, short wave transmitter (studio and transmitter vans, fuel supply truck and a truck for antennas) nicknamed "Barbara" was positioned near Lampertheim, Germany.

On July 4, 1950, Radio Free Europe transmitted its first program from "Barbara," only thirty minutes in length, to Czechoslovakia as an "audience building broadcast." The press release the day before outlined not only the ideological basis for the programming, but also the cover-up of the true sponsorship of RFE: "Owned and operated by the National Committee for a Free Europe, Inc., a group of private American citizens, Radio Free Europe will broadcast the true story of freedom and democracy to the eighty million people living in Communist slavery between Germany and Russia. Freed of diplomatic limitations, the broadcasts will be hard-hitting."[45]

Broadcasts to Romania followed on July 14, 1950, to Poland and Hungary on August 4, 1950, and to Bulgaria on August 11, 1950. RFE also broadcast to Albania from June 1, 1951, to September 30, 1953. The first broadcasts were prepared in New York and air transported to Germany, but soon the entire broadcast operation was moved to Munich, Germany. *Time* reported on July 17, 1950, under the rubric "Urgent Whisper":

> This week Czech and Rumanian radio listeners could hear music, plays and satires forbidden by their Communist masters—as well as the voices of men long exiled. These forbidden broadcasts came from a Radio Free Europe transmitter deep in Western Germany.
>
> RFE's lone 7½ kilowatt transmitter is only a whisper compared to the worldwide 58-station network of Voice of America. But RFE, a branch of the National Committee for a Free Europe founded last year by a group of private U.S. citizens, expects to make up in pungency for its lack of volume. Explains Banker Frank Altschul, chairman of RFE: "Unhampered by diplomatic restrictions, we can slant our programs in a more definitely anti–Soviet way than the Voice."
>
> Welcomed by the State Department as a freewheeling, free-speaking ally in the propaganda war, RFE plans to boost its power with five transmitters now on order. It intends, eventually, to speak strongly to every Communist satellite from the Baltic to the Black Sea.[46]

One local newspaper in the United States printed this editorial about Radio Free Europe:

> Many wise statesmen have been appealing insistently to the free world to exert greater effort to the grimy "struggle for men's minds." They have pounded repeatedly on the idea that it isn't enough to combat Russian Communism with economic and military measures: that freedom must be shown to be the great cause it really is—a way of life eminently superior to the slavery imposed by Moscow. The first Imaginative stride in this direction has now been taken. From a secret radio transmitter in Europe, a new series of programs is being beamed to the countries behind the Iron Curtain.... Radio Free Europe, as the new transmitter is called, is the product of the National Committee for Free Europe, which was organized about a year ago by outstanding American citizens.
>
> We must make plain to decent people everywhere that the language of Communism is the language of falsehood, that Russia's words can never be believed because words to the Soviet Union are simply weapons in the psychological theater of war.[47]

Cord Meyer, the CIA official directly responsible for RFE policy and programming, has written in his autobiography:

> At the start, the somewhat naïve notion existed that all that was necessary was to build some radio transmitters and to hand the microphones to exiles to say what they wished. It quickly became evident that the exile leaders were so divided among themselves on ideological lines and the different political groups were so prone to infighting, that a tower of Babel would be erected if they were left to their own devices.[48]

Paul B. Henze was one of the early American managers of Radio Free Europe in Munich. He would later join the U.S. State Department and National Security Council. At a conference at the Hoover Institution in Stanford, California, in 2004 examining the role of international broadcasting, Henze succinctly summed up the radio station's genesis:

> Radio Free Europe was an experiment. It was jerrybuilt. Its success was far from foreordained. The early years of its operation were never trouble-free. It faced many difficulties, some inherent in the operation itself, some the result of bureaucratic factors, many caused by doubts about — even strong opposition to— the notion of radio broadcasts as a means of communicating with peoples who had been forcibly incorporated into the Soviet Empire and isolated from the outer world with no immediate prospect of improvement of their situation.
>
> Almost all the planning that went into the creation of Radio Free Europe was an improvised response to the sense of urgency that prevailed in the early 1950s about the threat, which Stalinist aggressive expansionism represented for the United States and the Free World. The notion that Radio Free Europe resulted from a coherent concept of what needed to be done has become widespread in recent years, but it remains an illusion.[49]

The real target audience of the first RFE broadcast was not intended for listeners behind the Iron Curtain but for the nascent anti–Communist domestic activities in the United States in behalf of the Crusade for Freedom. Radio Free Europe became the focal point of the fund raising campaign.

The Advertising Campaign

The domestic advertising campaign picked up steam in July 1950,when, for example, the Crusade for Freedom Committee on July 7, 1950, approved the design for the lapel button and sent out bids to three companies for an order of 500,000 buttons. On July 13, 1950, General Lucius Clay met with the Advertising Council and gave details of the upcoming Crusade for Freedom campaign. Also, he presented a two-minute excerpt from first program of Radio Free Europe transmitted on July 4, 1950. The Advertising Council agreed at this meeting to place the Crusade's problem in the appropriate Advertising Council committee for its consideration and necessary action. By then the Advertising

Council had already approved the necessary art work for billboard and street car advertising in behalf of the Crusade for Freedom.

On July 18, 1950, DeWitt Poole gave Joseph Grew an updated status report of developments within the Crusade for Freedom:

> The primary objective of the Crusade is to enlist the aid of at least twenty million Americans, and to make them fully conscious of the extent of the dangers confronting them. The Korean crisis has made this ever more imperative. They will, we hope, symbolize their adherence to the Crusade by wearing in their lapels small replicas of the Freedom Bell. The Crusade is not primarily intended to be a fund raising operation. We are, nevertheless, conscious of the need for additional financial support, particularly for the greatly expanding operations of Radio Free Europe.... Consequently we hope to obtain small contributions on a broad basis from many individuals and trust that the sum thus raised will be sufficiently large to enable us to continue expansion of our activities which the present critical world situation makes even more imperative.
>
> We intend to utilize all possible means to carry this message throughout the country: radio broadcast, a documentary film now being prepared (which we hope to show in every moving picture theater in the country), phonograph records, and as many local meetings and local drives, sponsored by local organizations, as we can arrange for.[50]

At the July 20, 1950, regular monthly meeting of the NCFE, General Adcock reported on the progress of the Crusade for Freedom. He submitted a study by the company Baldwin and Mermey, the Crusade for Freedom's public relations consultants, regarding the allotments of the funds to the regional, state, and city chairmen. Adcock then reported on the conclusion of the public relations contract with Nate Crabtree on July 31, 1950, and asked for and received approval of a contract with the firm of Baldwin and Mermey as public relations consultants at a cost of $2,500 per month, not to exceed three and one half months.

Adcock advised the NCFE that the planned charter flight to Europe for a tour by the Crusade local chairmen was cancelled because of the intensified fighting in Korea. Instead, the Crusade staff decided to hold a meeting in Chicago on July 27, 1950, to have a "full dress press conference" and discuss the launching of the Freedom Bell in Berlin at which the executive committee would attend. Adcock asked that the budget for the European tour be reallocated to cover the expenses of the July 27th meeting in Chicago. The NCFE then approved the re-allocation of $17,429.60 from the 1950-1951 budget for that purpose.[51]

General Eisenhower and the Crusade for Freedom

On July 27, 1950, there was a campaign kickoff meeting in Chicago's Blackstone Hotel of the national Crusade directors from New York with the regional and state chairmen to discuss the upcoming Crusade campaign. Seventy-one persons attended the meeting in an atmosphere where a "full exchange of views helped develop a high degree of teamwork and desire to make the Crusade a success."[52] Dwight Eisenhower did not attend the meeting but sent an inspirational message to General Clay, for him to relay to the Regional and State Chairman:

> One effective way of combating communistic projects in Korea and of advancing America's peaceful purposes is to insure an understanding abroad of American strength, aspirations and determination. Because of the vital importance of the European area it is especially necessary that the facts of American integrity and decency and of communistic double-dealing and ruthlessness are constantly publicized on both sides of the curtain. Where this can be done by respected nationals of the affected countries, it will be doubly effective. Consequently I earnestly believe that everyone who assists in the program of the CRUSADE FOR FREEDOM is doing our country a real service.[53]

Frank Altschul Report: Whither RFE?

Frank Altschul, Chairman of the Radio Committee for NCFE, wrote a letter to Allen Dulles on August 21, 1950, in which he told Dulles, "It occurred to me that after over a year's association with Radio Free Europe, my reflections on its present position and prospects might be of interest to you — and possibly to other members of the Board." He attached a copy of his lengthy report dated August 15, 1950, wherein he voiced some concerns about the future of RFE:

> The time now has come, however, in the light of a year's experience to consider whether and under what circumstances Radio Free Europe is likely to justify its continuing existence. This is a matter of obvious concern to those who have assumed the responsibility of meeting our budgetary requirements.
> It must be stated in all frankness that Radio Free Europe as an instrument of propaganda is under a handicap inherent in its structure. It is a creature of the National Committee for a Free Europe, and is closely allied with the National Councils set up under the auspices of the Committee. The staff at the desk level has been largely recruited with the advice and assistance of these National Councils.
> Yet to a considerable extent these Councils represent the past, and in measure the unpalatable past, of the peoples whom we wish to influence.
> Whether in light of all the foregoing the experiment will seem to continue to justify the very considerable capital and current expenditure involved is primarily a question for those who decide who have assumed the responsibility for defraying up to now our budgetary requirements.[54]

August 1950 Status Report on the Crusade for Freedom

By August 24, 1950, all regional chairmen had been appointed; 45 as state chairmen (out of 48 who had been asked to participate); and 17 out of 35 persons, who had been asked to participate as Key City Chairmen, had accepted. Funding had been allocated to all 95 field locations. Contributions had begun to trickle in, although the campaign had not officially started.

The Advertising Council had prepared 3,000 outdoor billboards, and posters for street and subway cars. Additionally, the Advertising Council prepared 25,000 window posters measuring 17 × 22 inches and newspaper mats. Artwork, printing and mailing charges were paid for by the Crusade.

Departure of Freedom Bell

After weeks of casting, testing, tuning and mounting, on August 27, 1950, the Freedom Bell was loaded on to the merchant ship *American Clipper*, which departed England and headed to New York, where it would arrive on September 6, 1950, and begin its nation-wide tour to grassroots America.

Expand RFE?

There was a discussion within NCFE on expanding the broadcasting beyond East Europe: and on August 28, 1950, Allen Dulles wrote to Joseph Grew:

> In general, I have felt that in the long run our Committee should not have a geographic limitation. The problem is worldwide. At the moment I doubt whether we could profitably take on anything in addition to what we have and very possibly our next concrete step is to expand Radio Free Europe so as to cover, in addition to the satellite countries, East Germany and eventually Russia. When we have done this, I do not see any reason why we should not consider further expansion to the Far East if we can find the finances and the personnel to do it. Quite frankly, at the moment we have all we can tackle and more.[55]

CHAPTER TWO

A Roll Call of All Americans
Who Love Freedom

Eisenhower's Labor Day Speech

General Dwight D. Eisenhower passionately called for an American Crusade for Freedom in a nation-wide radio broadcast, covered by the four major radio networks, from Denver City Auditorium, Denver, Colorado, on Labor Day, September 4, 1950. That evening's entertainment leading up to the speech was provided by famed opera singer Laurence Melchior. For the day following, Eisenhower's speech was printed in various newspapers throughout the Untied States. In part, Eisenhower said,

I speak tonight about the Crusade for Freedom.
This Crusade is a campaign sponsored by private American citizens to fight the big lie with the big truth. It is a program that has been hailed by President Truman, and others, as an essential step in getting the case for freedom heard by the world's multitudes.
Powerful Communist radio stations incessantly tell the world that we Americans are physically soft and morally corrupt; that we are disunited and confused; that we are selfish and cowardly; that we have nothing to offer the world but imperialism and exploitation.
To combat these evil broadcasts the government has established a radio program called the Voice of America, which has brilliantly served the cause of freedom, but the Communist stations overpower it and outflank it with a daily coverage that neglects no wavelength or dialect, no prejudice or local aspiration. Weaving a fantastic pattern of lies and twisted fact, they confound the listener into believing that we are warmongers, that America invaded North Korea, that Russia invented the airplane, that the Soviets, unaided won World War II; and that the secret police and slave camps of Communism offer humanity brighter hope than do self government and free enterprise.
We need powerful radio stations abroad, operated without government restrictions, to tell in vivid and convincing form about the decency and essential fairness of democracy These stations must tell of our aspirations for peace, our hatred of war, our support of the United Nations and our constant readiness to cooperate with any and all who have these same desires.
One such private station — Radio Free Europe — is now in operation in Western

29

Germany. It daily brings a message of hope and encouragement to a small part of the European masses.

In this battle for Truth, you and I have a definite part to play during the Crusade. Each of us will have the opportunity to sign the Freedom Scroll. It bears a declaration of our faith in Freedom, and of our belief in the dignity of the individual who derives the right of Freedom from God. Each of us, by signing the Scroll, pledges to resist aggression and tyranny wherever they appear on the earth. Its words express what is in all our hearts. Your signature on it will be a blow for liberty.[1]

Freedom Scroll

The "Freedom Scroll," to which Eisenhower was referring, as in Figure 2, contained a "Declaration of Freedom" to be signed:

I believe in the sacredness and dignity of the individual.
I believe that all men derive the right to freedom equally from God.
I pledge to resist aggression and tyranny wherever they appear on earth.
I am proud to enlist in the Crusade for Freedom.
I am proud to help make the freedom Bell possible, to be a signer of this Declaration of Freedom, to have my name included as a permanent part of the Freedom Shrine in Berlin, and to join with the millions of men and women throughout the world who hold the cause of freedom sacred.

Historian Martin Medhurst has analyzed Eisenhower's September 4, 1950, address as an archetypal example of Cold War discourse, inasmuch as it features:

- Stark polarizations (truth vs. lies, peace vs. war, democracy vs. communism, liberty vs. slavery, death vs. life);
- Fear appeals (secret police, slave camps, blackout, executed, blank page in history, cold blooded betrayal);
- Biblical allusions (birthright, venom, hissing, faith, God, devilish, bondage, sacrifice, doctrine);
- Images of death (dying, poison, mastery of life and soul, lose American birthright, mortal fear);
- Use of ultimate terms (freedom, God, democracy, progress, liberty, truth);
- Savagery of the enemy (hissing, hating tirade, godless depravity, aggression and tyranny, predatory military force, ruthless men);
- Righteousness of America (freedom, readiness to cooperate, opportunity, human happiness, hope, encouragement, peaceful intent, decent motives, decency and essential fairness);
- Fragility of liberty (take up arms in defense of liberty, defense of freedom, destroy free government, destroy our system, destroy human liberty, overpower it and outflank it, defense of our way of life, guard it with vigilance and defend it with fortitude and faith).[2]

Opposite: **Figure 2. Newspaper advertisement with photograph of Dwight D. Eisenhower used in 1950 Crusade campaign (courtesy Advertising Council).**

Join the Crusade for Freedom and Back your Country's Cause!

"THE Crusade for Freedom is a roll-call of all Americans who love freedom. Millions of signatures on the Freedom Scroll will give warning to aggressors and encouragement to the oppressed.

"Your name on the Freedom Scroll will be enshrined with the Freedom Bell behind the Iron Curtain in Berlin, proclaiming your faith in God and your devotion to the cause of liberty everywhere.

"Your contribution to the Crusade for Freedom will help Radio Free Europe

pierce the Iron Curtain . . . give hope and courage to 80 million people now living in Eastern Europe, who keep alive in their hearts the hope of freedom and self-government.

"I urge every American to join with the leader of the Crusade for Freedom, General Lucius D. Clay. By doing so, you will strengthen your country's cause and comfort your country's friends on both sides of the Iron Curtain."

Dwight D Eisenhower
DWIGHT D. EISENHOWER

Help lift the Iron Curtain Everywhere

If you cannot sign the actual Freedom Scroll, fill out this coupon and mail it to General Clay, together with whatever contribution you care to make.

Gen. Lucius D. Clay, Nat'l Chairman
Crusade for Freedom
National Committee for a Free Europe, Inc.
Empire State Bldg., New York 1, N. Y.

Please accept my contribution and place my name on the Freedom Scroll.

Signed _____

Address _____

Contributions to the Crusade will help Radio Free Europe pierce the Iron Curtain with daily messages to 80 million victims of Communist tyranny.

SIGN THE FREEDOM SCROLL

SPONSOR'S NAME

FREE MATS OF THIS AD ARE AVAILABLE IN THE FOLLOWING SIZES:

Ad No. CF-1   1000 lines
Ad No. CF-2   600 lines

Becoming "Honest Women"

On September 6, 1950, while vacationing in Bar Harbor, Maine, NCFE president DeWitt Poole wrote to Allen Dulles expressing concerns about the continuing financial cover for the National Committee for a Free Europe:

> Haskins & Sells' audit for the year ended June 30 — a semi-public statement — will disclose the magnitude of our operations, and the figures in the 1951 Audit will be very striking. Our position grows more difficult to explain, unless somehow we are rescued by the Crusade for Freedom.
>
> Might we not make ourselves into a "mixed corporation" in which the Government has frankly a part? It is not a question to be answered quickly, but I know you'll agree that we must keep alive to any possibility of clarifying our position and becoming "honest women."
>
> I sense positively a crisis approaching in which we shall be asked about ourselves in a way we can't evade.[3]

Freedom Bell Tour

After the "Freedom Bell's" arrival in New York City, it was placed on a trailer and exhibited to the public. General Clay and New York City Mayor Vincent Impellitteri were photographed tolling the bell for the first time in the United States. Another publicity photograph showed Walter Dorwin Teague, the designer of the bell, signing a Freedom Scroll as General Clay looked on. A large poster of the Crusade for Freedom was on the trailer behind of the "Freedom Bell" that showed people pulling on a large chain and lifting a metal wall with the words "Help Lift the Iron Curtain Everywhere." Afterwards, the "Freedom Bell" was the center of a large ticker-tape parade on September 8, 1950, that wound down Broadway from the City Hall to the Eternal Light. Mounted police escorted the "Freedom Bell" and marching bands accompanied it to the delight of onlookers on both sides of the streets. (See Figure 3.)

During the Crusade for Freedom's nationwide publicity trip, the Freedom Bell was placed on a flatbed trailer and first transported by truck to Chicago, where it was placed on a "Freedom Train" for the rest of the tour. In total, the "Freedom Bell" was transported to 26 major cities. On September 16, 1950, for example, two thousand persons in Denver went to see the Freedom Bell that had arrived from Kansas City. Dwight Eisenhower was one of the speakers at the rally. In his remarks, he said, "Since the beginning of our republic, a bell has been a symbol of liberty and freedom. The Freedom Bell is designed to spread the truth about America. Every time the bell tolls, we hope new facts and new understandings will go out to the world."[4] The "Freedom Bell" was on display for two hours before leaving for Salt Lake City.

A short film "The Bell," almost ten minutes long, about the Freedom Bell and Radio Free Europe, featured General Clay and was narrated by Hollywood actor Henry Fonda. The film, shown in movie theaters, contained footage of

Figure 3. Welcome Freedom Bell Parade on Broadway in New York City on September 6, 1950 (courtesy RFE/RL).

the new "freedom radio station" that "pits the truth of freedom against the lies of Communism." The film ended with this emotional appeal:

> The American people have been crying out for a chance to do something about the menace of Communism.... Now they have that chance.... By joining the Crusade for Freedom you can make your voice pierce the Iron Curtain.... You counterattack Kremlin propaganda.... You bring the hope of freedom to all the prisoners behind the Iron Curtain. Your name will help ring the Freedom Bell. Join the Crusade for Freedom.[5]

The "Freedom Bell" returned to New York on October 8, 1950, and preparations were made for its departure to Schoeneberg City Hall in West Berlin. More than 16 million Americans eventually joined the Crusade by signing the Freedom Scroll and making contributions. Crusade national headquarters sent a "note" to local Crusade chairmen about a planned "Crusade Airlift." It was termed a "spiritual airlift" operation when completed Freedom Scrolls with one million signatures from each of the 48 states would be flown to New York by the six major airline companies on October 20, 1950, as a show of solidarity. These scrolls were scheduled to be on the same plane as General Lucius D. Clay when he flew to West Berlin on October 22, 1950. The "note, " which was to be used in any local publicity efforts, read, in part:

> A token consignment of the many millions of signatures, which will be taken to Berlin for permanent enshrinement after the conclusion of the Crusade, according

Figure 4. General Clay and other dignitaries at Freedom Bell dedication in Berlin on October 24, 1950 (courtesy RFE/RL, Inc.).

to General Lucius D. Clay, former leader of the Berlin airlift and national Crusade chairman.[6]

Grass-Roots Activities

In September 1950, the Crusade campaign in Onondaga County, New York, collected $50,000 and had a unique contest for junior and senior high school students: write an essay on the them, "Why I Want to Participate in the Crusade for Freedom." Three hundred students sent in their essays for a U.S. savings bond prize. Seven winners were announced and their photographs, along with their teachers, appeared in local newspapers. One of the winners was Joyce Hall, a senior student at Central High School, who wrote:

> As an American, I am endowed with rights and privileges denied the people behind the Iron Curtain. The Crusade for Freedom affords me the opportunity to strike a crushing blow to Communistic propaganda. The light of truth shall penetrate the Iron Curtain thru the combined efforts of Crusading Americans.[7]

In a newspaper advertisement on Friday, September 29, 1950, Boyles Furniture and Carpet Company in Ogden, Utah, "the store with the friendly doors," showed true entrepreneurship by combining sponsorship of the Crusade for Freedom with one promoting its store items on sale: "Saturday Special — We're selling FREEDOM. A Real Bargain! You name your own price. Sign the Freedom Scroll at Boyles Saturday."[8]

Freedom Roll Call

The *Greensburg Daily News* in Indiana carried a full-page advertisement with photographs of Lucius Clay and Dwight Eisenhower, along with a graphic display of a "Freedom Roll Call" being carried by an eagle:

JOIN THE CRUSADE FOR FREEDOM
A Roll Call of All Americans Who Love Freedom
Help Lift the Iron Curtain with Truth Everywhere
What This Crusade Means to You

The CRUSADE FOR FREEDOM offers every American an opportunity to play a personal part in a great moral crusade for freedom, faith and peace throughout the earth.

1. You are invited to sign the Freedom Scroll, with millions of your fellow countrymen, as an individual participant in the CRUSADE FOR FREEDOM. YOUR SIGNATURE — AND EVERY SIGNATURE ON THE FREEDOM SCROLL — WILL BE PERMANENTLY ENSHRINED IN THE BASE OF THE FREEDOM BELL IN BERLIN.

2. You may back up your signature with a voluntary contribution to Radio Free Europe, the American people's broadcasting station in Western Germany. Radio Free Europe daily pierces the Iron Curtain, answering Communist propaganda.

Deposit Your Contribution in the Sealed Coin Box Carried by the Student Solicitor or Leave it at Your Bank.

THE VOICE OF TRUTH[9]

Bonfires and Freedom Belles in Syracuse

The Syracuse Journal reported that on Tuesday night, September 24, 1950, beginning at 9 P.M. "Freedom Fires" were lit in 13 parks in Syracuse, New York, symbolic of the 13 original American colonies. The next evening, the newspaper reported that factory sirens and church bells sounded out at 6 P.M. for two minutes in Syracuse. Also, during the evening more than 3,000 volunteer "Freedom Belles," Minutemen, and volunteer firemen began a house-to house canvass carrying Freedom Scrolls to sign, asking for contributions, and handing out lapel insignias and window stickers of the Freedom Bell replicas to those who did so.

Butte, Montana, Campaign

One example of how America earnestly responded to the Eisenhower speech and the Crusade for Freedom can be illustrated with the example of what happened in Butte, Montana. On October 11, 1950, the newspaper *Montana Standard* carried a full-page advertisement for the Crusade for Freedom, including a relatively large photograph of Dwight Eisenhower. The Freedom Scroll's text with names and signatures of prominent personalities such as General Clay, Eleanor Roosevelt, Drew Pearson, and Douglas Fairbanks, Jr., were displayed under Eisenhower's photograph. The headline read: Add YOUR Name to the Scroll! Join the Crusade for Freedom and back your Country's Cause!"

The goal of the Butte campaign was 5,000 signatures and $2,000 in contributions. Freedom scrolls were sent to local schools to be signed by seventh grade, eighth grade, and high school students. A "Freedom Week" was proclaimed during which time signatures and contributions were to be sought at booths set up in the business district of Butte, e.g. Montana Power Company, Woolworth's, and the Colonial Bakeshop on Harrison Avenue. Each day was allocated to specific groups to man the booths:

- Monday — City and County Officers
- Tuesday — Veteran's Organizations
- Wednesday — Women's Clubs
- Thursday — Service Groups
- Friday — Fraternal Organizations
- Saturday — Labor Groups.

Wednesday, October 14, 1950, was a "Lights-on" night, in Butte, when Boy Scouts, Girl Scouts, and Camp Fire Girls were to go house-to-house seeking contributions and signatures on the Freedom Scrolls. Those who wished to participate were to leave their porch lights on between 6 P.M. and 8 P.M. to signal their willingness. "Freedom Buttons" with a reproduction of the Freedom Bell and the words "WEAR YOUR FREEDOM BELL" would be given to those who contributed. At the bottom of the page, there was a list of firms and individuals who sponsored the newspaper advertisement.

The Crusade and Entertainment

The Billboard, "The World's Foremost Amusement Weekly," on October 21, 1950 carried a full-page article, with photographs, about Radio Free Europe and the Crusade for Freedom:

> Slowly but surely as demonstrated by the lead story on this page, show business is stirring into full life in the fight against Communism. It is heartening and typical of show business and its people that mobilization efforts, like the Crusade for Freedom and Theater for Freedom, are in the making.
>
> It is nice to have *The Billboard* singled out for mention, as it was by Alan Corelli at the Crusade for Freedom Meeting, for having contributed in some small measure of helping in the anti–Commie action. But most gratifying of all is the manner in which Jean Muir and Mady Christians, to name just two, took forceful, all-out

stands against their accusers, and reaffirmed their eagerness to join the pro–American, anti–Communist Crusade for Freedom drive. They, and all of show business, are demonstrating once again that, when the chips are down, the amusement industry can be counted upon for full support.[10]

Walter Wanger, Hollywood, and the Crusade for Freedom

Movie giants Darryl Zanuck and Cecil B. DeMille were two of NCFE's early directors and remained active in behalf of Radio Free Europe in the 1950s. Famed Hollywood actor John Wayne was then president of the Motion Picture Alliance and made speeches at many Crusade meetings around Hollywood. Independent Hollywood producer Walter Wanger was the 1950 Los Angeles Crusade chairman. His 1949 movie *Joan of Arc* was the first film to receive a citation award by the Christian group The Christophers, which acclaimed the movie "for its inspiring demonstration that a motion picture which stresses the spiritual ideal, goodness and decency, can be a popular success."[11]

Lucius Clay wrote to Walter Wanger on July 11, 1950, asking him to join the National Crusade Council, described "as an advisory group of distinguished leaders from all segments of American Life." Wanger answered on July 18, 1950, when he wrote, "For more years than I care to say I have been advocating a crusade to make individual citizens realize their responsibility and realize what could be accomplished if we would mobilize ourselves for intelligence and liberty in a practical way." On July 21, 1950, Lucius Clay wrote to Wanger thanking him for joining the Crusade for Freedom Council and supplying his speeches in support of the Crusade campaign:

> Thank you for your whole-hearted response to our invitation to join the Crusade Council, and also for the copies of your speeches. I know from them that you understand what we are trying to do. Moreover, it is in a field in which your work has made you an expert. I shall look forward to obtaining your wise counsel as the Crusade progresses, and I hope we may meet soon.[12]

Walter Wanger became Crusade chairman of the city and county of Los Angeles and gave a speech about the Crusade for Freedom to the Greater Los Angeles Press Club on August 30, 1950. Crusade headquarters sent Wanger a check on August 29, 1950, for $3,750, which was half of the city's operating budget for the Crusade campaign. Included in the accompanying letter were instructions on account procedures for contributions into the operating account.[13]

On September 28, 1950, more than 3,000 college students in Los Angeles attended a Crusade for Freedom rally. The Dave Brubeck Trio and students provided music and the faculty gave short speeches. Walter Wanger then came on the stage as the "chief speaker" and spoke about the Crusade for Freedom: "The thing we are trying to tell the world, through radio stations we are building as an important part of this Freedom Crusade, is a thing we could show them far more clearly if it was possible to broadcast a television picture of the scene here today to the nations behind the Iron Curtain." He then exhorted the students to sign the Freedom Scrolls:

> We all have a chance, here and now — today, to add our signatures to those who believe as we do, that our system works and works well for our best interests. If you do not believe that, then do not sign. But if you like this scene spread out here today and want to assure that it will not be replaced by something far different, far uglier, then sign the Freedom Scrolls. Make yourself heard. Do not lose this opportunity by default.[14]

The *Los Angeles Times* the next day carried a story about the rally entitled, "Campus Thronged at Crusade Rally. Hundreds of Students Sign Scrolls as Wanger Explains Freedom Movement."

Three hundred eighty thousand Los Angeles citizens eventually responded to the Crusade activities by signing the Freedom Scroll and contributing $59,000.[15] Wanger was not without controversy, however, and had to publicly defended himself because of his alleged "leftist sympathies." He even was denounced as using the Crusade to cover up his political past, and the FBI looked into his background. Wanger made a public disavowal of his past associations and newspapers carried his response.[16]

Life with Luigi

One of the most supportive directors of the National Committee for a Free Europe was Frank Stanton, who was president of the television and radio network Columbia Broadcast System (CBS). A very popular weekly radio program from 1948 to 1953 was a situation-comedy show *Life with Luigi*, with famed Hollywood actor J. Carrol Naish, who, as Luigi Basco, feigned a heavy Italian accent. The show aired before a live audience on the CBS radio network Tuesday evenings from 9 to 9:30 P.M. The fictional Luigi Basco was a new immigrant from Italy, who had recently arrived in the United States. The show's premise was that Luigi wrote a letter to his mother, who remained in Italy, about his continuing experiences in the United States.

On September 19, 1950, the weekly half-hour long radio program was entitled "Crusade for Freedom Speech" and sponsored by the Wrigley Chewing Gum Company. Luigi was visited by a Crusade for Freedom volunteer who not only had Luigi sign the Freedom Scroll but also convinced him to put a Crusade poster in his shop's window and to seek out others to sign the Freedom Scroll. The Crusade volunteer also told Luigi that the scrolls would be collected and "enshrined at the base of a huge Freedom Bell in Berlin." Luigi was unsuccessful as the people he asked to sign ignored him because they were too busy, were in a hurry, or had other reasons not to listen to him about the Crusade for Freedom.

The teacher of his night-school citizenship class, Miss Spaulding, selected Luigi to give a speech about freedom before a meeting of 10,000 other immigrants. The topic selected by Luigi's teacher was "What Freedom Means to Me." At the meeting he told the assembly not only about his failure to gather signatures but also what the Crusade for Freedom meant to him. The results were successful and those 10,000 persons who had listened to him signed the Freedom Scrolls and $300 was collected.

Near the end of the radio program, listeners heard a recorded statement by General Lucius D. Clay in New York:

> Luigi, you give me a great hope. And you also fill me with considerable pride. It has not taken you long to learn what America really stands for. You have also found that because you believe in its ideals, you can reach the hearts and minds of its peoples. Thank you very much, Luigi, and the many thousands of other volunteers who are undertaking the Crusade for Freedom. But thank you especially Luigi for your faith in your new country and your belief in freedom.

Luigi concluded the show with by reading from his letter to his mother:

> Yes, Mama Mia, now you see why America is a wonderful country and is worth fighting for. Because only here is it possible for a little immigrant like your son to hear from a great general and a great American like General Clay. It is like I once wrote to you, in America: everything is possible. Your loving son Luigi Basco.

The radio series ended in on March 3, 1953. *Life with Luigi* was also broadcast as a television series that started on September 22, 1952, but never reached the popularity of the radio show and went off the air in June 1953.

Our Miss Brooks

Another popular radio situation-comedy show on the CBS radio network was *Our Miss Brooks*, starring Eve Arden. The radio show aired from 1948 to 1957 and was adapted to television from 1952 to 1956. At the conclusion of one of the programs entitled "Radio Bombay" that was aired on October 8, 1950, Eve Arden returned to the radio stage to announce to the live audience:

> If you are concerned about the threat of Communism, you should know this fact: The Crusade for Freedom, an organization headed by General Lucius Clay, needs your financial and moral assistance in the support of Radio Free Europe. This is a private radio station now working to bring to communist-dominated European countries the voices of their exiled leaders. Help Radio Free Europe by joining the Crusade for Freedom in your town.

30-Second Spot Announcements

Spot announcement texts were sent to radio stations, one of which was 30 seconds long:

A bitter war is being waged throughout the world ... a war that may will determine the fate of the world ... the war for the minds and hearts of men everywhere...

On one side there are those of us who believe in truth and freedom. On the other side there are the Communists who use the Big Lie to suppress individual liberty...

All American citizens can now help the cause of truth and freedom by joining the CRUSADE FOR FREEDOM ... by signing the FREEDOM SCROLL ... and making a voluntary contribution that will be used to stop Communist aggression and make the world free for peoples everywhere.[17]

African American Leaders

The Crusade for Freedom issued a press release on September 8, 1950, with the title: "Negro Leaders Supporting the Crusade for Freedom." According to the press release, "Top Negro leaders in a variety of fields have joined with other prominent Americans to make the Crusade for Freedom a convincing demonstration to the world of American solidarity against Communist aggression abroad." Dr. Dorothy S. Ferebee, president of the National Council of Negro Women; Lester Granger, executive director of the National Urban League; Jackie Robinson, baseball star; Bishop William Wallis, Zion Church Chicago; and Dr. Charles S. Johnson, president of Fisk University, joined the Crusade National Council.[18]

Dr. Dorothy Ferebee was quoted in newspapers as she "felt prejudice against her race in America." She reportedly said,

Russian propaganda is an engaging form of propaganda for my people. It promises equality. But from the past acts of the Soviet, it's obvious the propaganda can't be trusted. What I am trying to do is show them that it's up to minority groups like us to stick and point out these flaws that the minority groups can see best. Then democracy will be the complete democracy it was set up to be and Russia will have nothing to spout off about. I hope that I can enlist every American of my race to sign the Freedom Scroll. It will be a powerful step to destroy the propaganda of the Soviet regime when they call us "aggressors" and "imperialistic" and "capitalist war-mongers."[19]

Crusade Incorporated

On October 5, 1950, The National Committee for a Free Europe Executive Committee approved the incorporation of the Crusade for Freedom as a separate organization of the NCFE. During the meeting, Allen Dulles said that large individual donations were not precluded and in fact were considered to be urgent. Dulles agreed to meet Generals Clay and Adcock to discuss the issue of large donations.[20]

The New York State Supreme Court approved the incorporation papers filed by Allen Dulles and two office associates of the law firm for which Dulles worked on October 14, 1950. In addition to Dulles, NCFE Directors who signed the papers were Lucius D. Clay, Adolph A. Berle, Frank Altschul, and DeWitt C. Poole. The certificate of incorporation was sent to the New York Secretary of State for filing on October 25, 1950. The stated purpose of the new corporation was

> To voluntarily aid the cause of freedom and liberty in Europe and elsewhere by furthering and promoting the dissemination of information designed to alert public opinion in the United States and abroad to the perils faced by freedom and liberty from aggressive and imperialistic Communism and Totalitarianism in their various forms
> To solicit and obtain funds for these general purposes
> To give financial support for activities and organizations dedicated to the same cause.[21]

One interesting paragraph of the certificate of incorporation that would later be amended was, "No part of the activities of the corporation shall be the carrying on of propaganda or otherwise attempting to influence legislation."

More Promotion

Ronald Reagan

On September 16, 1960, actor Ronald Reagan, president of the Screen Actors Guild Board of Directors, sent a telegram to Lucius Clay:

> Dear General Clay: the more than 8,000 members of the Screen Actors Guild are proud to enlist in the Crusade for Freedom and to take as active part in the battle for men's minds now being waged around the world. We offer you our complete support in this great counter-offensive against Communist lies and treachery. Please call on us.[22]

Walter Wanger wrote to Ronald Reagan on September 21, 1950:

> Dear Ronnie:
> Thank you very much for sending me a copy of the wire.... It is very gratifying to me, as a member of the Motion Picture Industry, to know that the entire industry is willing and anxious to aid in the CRUSADE and on behalf of the entire committee for the CRUSADE FOR FREEDOM I want to thank you and the Guild for pledging your wholehearted support to our drive.[23]

Newsreel Trailer

All five newsreel companies agreed to add a two-minute trailer on the Crusade for Freedom to the regular weekly newsreel shown in movie theaters starting on September 21, 1950. The film ended with the words, "Join now. Sign one of the Freedom Scrolls available in your community. Send your name to Berlin with the Freedom Bell." In a telegram from Lucius Clay to all Crusade chairmen and executive officers dated September 15, 1950, advising them of the newsreel trailer, Clay requested, "Whenever possible, please arrange to have enrollment stations in the lobbies of motion picture theaters, in order to take full advantage of this opportunity to secure signatures and contributions. If time prevents covering all theaters, suggest pick out few of largest ones. The film will play in second-run theaters the following week."[24]

Balloons Over New York City

Fred Osborn, New York City Crusade chairman, sent a memorandum, conceived and set up by the public relations firm of Baldwin and Mermey, to DeWitt Poole September 28, 1950, proposing

> as an attention-catching symbol of the New York City Crusade a ceremony in the tower of the Empire State Building at which 500 helium-filled balloons bearing small Freedom Scrolls would be launched after speeches by various dignitaries. One speaker would be a representative of the ECA to tell how balloons from the Marshall Plan Mobile Exhibit in Western Europe have sailed over the Iron Curtain with messages of hope to the prisoner peoples and their replies.[25]

The scheduled balloon launching had to be postponed to October 10, 1950, due to a photo shoot at the Empire State Building on the original day planned. On October 10, one thousand helium-filled balloons, each carrying small Freedom Scrolls to be signed and returned, were released to demonstrate a method being used by the United States to reach the prisoner peoples behind the Iron Curtain. The next day, the *New York Times* carried a photograph of the balloon launching from atop the Empire State Building with the caption "Crusade for Freedom takes to the Air." The New York Daily Mirror carried the same photograph, with the caption: "Filling the Air with 'Freedom' Notes."

Campus Newspapers

Crusade National Headquarters send out a "note" to campus newspaper editors on October 4, 1950, giving information about the Freedom Bell ceremony in Berlin on October 24, 1950, with a blank news item for the newspaper headlined

> *CAMPUS BELLS RINGING WITH OTHERS*
> *IN NATION ON UNITED NATIONS DAY*
>
> At _____ M. , _____ Standard Time on October 24, United Nations Day, over all principal radio networks will be broadcast from Berlin the beginning of an impressive ceremony dedicating the new Freedom Bell, symbol of CRUSADE FOR FREEDOM, with a two-minute prayerful dedication to world freedom and peace.

The college newspaper note went on to give details of the Crusade for Freedom and Freedom Scrolls and summarized the appeal to college and university presidents to empower students to organize individual crusade activities on their respective campuses. The results were praised as "a fine example of our democratic way of accomplishing things. Left free to devise their own methods, these patriotic young Americans, along with millions of other individual Americans, are speaking up loudly for democracy, thus helping materially in nailing down the Communist lies about our way of life."

The Racquet was a campus newspaper published by and for the students at La Crosse State Teachers College in Wisconsin. The October 11, 1950, edition carried an article about the Crusade for Freedom, "Students to Join Drive Against Communism; Support 'Crusade for Freedom' with Donations." A picture of the Freedom Bell accompanied the article with the caption "Let Freedom Ring." The article began, "Opportunity will come next week for students at La Crosse College to join the Crusade for Freedom which has been launched throughout the nation as a new method of psychological warfare against communism."

> Signatures for the Freedom Scroll and contributions will be collected outside the social room by the campus Crusade for Freedom committee, headed by Phyllis Melby. It is hoped that students will want to contribute as they sign — even if they give up a pack of cigarettes, a milkshake or a movie in order to speak out for freedom.

Freedom Bell Departure Ceremony

The Freedom Bell was loaded on the "freedom ship" USNS *Gen. R. M. Blatchford* at the Brooklyn Army Base in a ceremony on October 9, 1950. The *Blatchford*, a World War II transport ship, was one of the ships charted to the International Refugee Organization (IRO) to carry displaced persons from Europe to the United States. Prior to the Freedom Bell ceremony, the ship had made 12 trips and carried 13,833 persons to the United States. Selected to begin the ceremony was an eight-year-old girl name Ewa Zandler, listed as a refugee from Poland, who "had spent half her life in concentration camp." Ewa Zandler presented a Freedom Scroll to Fred Osborn, chairman of the New York City Crusade. Ewa reportedly said, "Every day my parents talk to me about freedom. And every day I learn more about it just by living here. My mother and father love freedom so much because they had it once and it was stolen. We have it back now and we will take care of it. I pray the IRO ship, which brought DPs like us to this wonderful country, will take this freedom message back to Europe."[26] Nineteen displaced persons participated in the ceremony and wore native costumes of Poland, Russia, Ukraine, Latvia, Estonia, and East Germany.

DeWitt Poole, president of NCFE, also spoke at the ceremony: "As this Freedom Bell has gone back and forth across the country, it has brought again to all of us the realization that, as ever, our freedom can only be preserved by constant struggle against the forces of tyranny."[27] The ceremony ended with a benediction by Commander J.C. Canty of the Chaplin's Corps and the playing of the National Anthem by the Army Band.

Freedom Bell Dedication in Berlin

The Freedom Bell was unloaded at Bremerhaven and traveled via train through the Soviet Zone of Germany to the Schoenberg Town Hall, where it arrived on October 21, 1950. General Clay arrived the next day. Abbott Washington, who with Nate Crabtree came up with the idea of the "Freedom Bell," was in the group that accompanied Clay. It was officially dedicated by Clay, with extensive press coverage, before hundreds of thousands of Berliners on October 24, 1950, when it rang out for the first time shortly after noon. General Clay's speech was broadcast around the world, including East Europe over Radio Free Europe. (See figure 4.) Clay pushed the button that was supposed to electronically ring the bell, but a fuse blew and it had to be first rung by hand.[28]

Advertising Council Continues Support

The Advertising Council sent out suggestions released to in-house magazines for use from Labor Day to October 16, 1950. The suggestions included a quote from General Clay: "Every factory, every business office and every public meeting place should have a freedom station where loyal Americans may sign the Freedom Scrolls. General Clay, who as military governor of Germany directed the Berlin airlift, is asking millions of citizens to join with him in this 'spiritual airlift.'" On October 17, 1950, Abbott Washburn wrote to DeWitt Poole, saying

> Georg Ludlam, vice-president of the Advertising Council in charge of the New York office, talked to me on the phone today about the continuing activities of the Crusade for Freedom and about the possibilities of providing us with Advertising Council support on a permanent basis. We would be, as he put it, their "continuing agency" for coordinating the many requests for help on "campaigns of truth" they are receiving.[29]

The Advertising Council's in-house publication for October 1950, in a small article "Crusade for Freedom Speeds; Gains Advertising Industry Aid," gave some details of the extent of the Ad Council's support of the Crusade for Freedom:

- The nation's press has ordered almost 11,000 newspaper ad mats
- 3000 house magazine editors received copies of the full-page ads
- 37,000 car cards have been displayed.
- The Outdoor Advertising Industry has posted 24 sheets in more than 2,500 locations.[30]

NCFE and CIA at Odds, October 1950

At the end of September 1950, DeWitt Poole, president of the NCFE, had a telephone conversation with Allen Dulles in which he expressed concerns about the NCFE and the Frank Wisner. Allen Dulles said that it was time to "re-examine" the position of the NCFE, in particular "policy guidance" from the Office of Policy Coordination.[31] As a follow-up, on September 28, 1959, Poole wrote to Dulles giving details of his displeasure with the existing relationship. He quoted from a "fundamental memorandum" in October 1949, in which he, Allen Dulles, and Frank Altschul had agreed with Frank Wisner (FW):

> All activities directly or indirectly affecting (governmental or State Department policy) official policy guidance will be given or confirmed through (FW's office) and (FW's office) shall be the sole channel for the purpose.
> On the programming side of the radio we have received scattered "directives" from FW's staff, but the directives, or some of them, don't make too much sense, and here the situation cannot be said to be satisfactory at all. Nor has the coordination between the Voice and us been worked out as it should be and I think can be.
> Relations with the exiles and the national councils constitute obviously a most important area in which close working contact with Washington is essential. Experience so far has been anything but satisfactory.
> The whole NCFE operation has outgrown by far its original conception and arrangement. As this marks the success of the original idea, everybody ought to be happy about it and join gladly in the readjustments consequently needed. I am glad you are opening the way for the needed top-level discussions.[32]

DeWitt Poole went on to write:

> Suffice it to say that the amount is so large it is timely to consider whether this expenditure is likely to prove justified by the potential accomplishments of Radio Free Europe in the field of propaganda.
>
> *Essential Requirements.*
> To adequately discharge the task assigned to Radio Free Europe in the field of propaganda there are certain essential requirements: We must have available to us a regular flow of lively topical information from behind the Iron Curtain. We must be sufficiently familiar, on a day to day basis, with the over-all policies of government to permit of the preparation of concise and intelligible directives for guidance of the staff.[33]

For the six months that he had been actively involved with the NCFE, Abbot Washburn had not been paid. On October 18, 1950, he sent a letter to the NCFE advising them that his expenses for the six months' maintenance of two residences (New York and Minneapolis) had exceeded his budget by $1,800. During the NCFE monthly meeting on October 19, 1950, the NCFE agreed to reimburse him for his over-budget expenditures.[34]

On October 23, 1950, W.H. Jackson, Deputy Director Central Intelligence, DeWitt Poole, and Joseph Grew met at Joseph Grew's house in Washington for two hours in a "very constructive session" to discuss CIA, NCFE, and Radio

Free Europe.[35] The next day, DeWitt Poole reported to the NCFE directors the results of the meeting and told them that the NCFE was "entering a new chapter. How can consultation and coordination be more closely organized than they have been in the past?"[36]

Frank Wisner and W.H. Jackson, met with Radio Free Europe directors at the Union Club in New York on November 2, 1950. RFE's directors were asked to "reexamine its radio activities and prepare a statement of the aims and objectives of Radio Free Europe for study by the Deputy Director of Central Intelligence." Frank Wisner wrote to W.H. Jackson on November 22, 1950:

> As a result of five month's experience, emphasis has shifted from the use of distinguished political and intellectual exiles, whose personal prejudices and protracted absence from their native lands render them of questionable current value, to timely news items and commentary slanted to accomplish Radio Free Europe's purposes.[37]

On December 20, 1950, General Clay wrote a report to Crusade chairmen, giving details of the Crusade to that point. Most of the contributions were less than one dollar, with a few over $1,000, and the largest was $2,500. He went on:

> Since all expenses on conducting the campaign were met by a special contribution to the National Committee for a Free Europe, the entire amount contributed by the public is now being used for the purpose intended — namely, the expansion of the operations of Radio Free Europe.
>
> There is no way, of course, in which we can accurately estimate the intangible values of the CRUSADE.
>
> Without question, also, the campaign served to strengthen our own people's basic understanding and appreciation of the freedoms we enjoy.
>
> It is my personal belief that recent world events make an intensified effort in this field of idea warfare even more important. We must build up our strength in this psychological field just as we are doing militarily and economically — in order that we can meet and turn back the menace of world communist aggression. Speed is of the utmost importance. If we are able to do these things fast enough, we may be able to avoid full-scale war. The next two to three years, in my opinion, will tell the story.[38]

Results of Crusade Campaign

For the first Crusade, Americans contributed $1,317,000 to the expansion of Radio Free Europe. However, expenses for the National Committee for a Free Europe amounted to $2,300,000, including administrative costs and the acquisition of the radio equipment for RFE.[39] Any vision that the Crusade for Freedom alone would be able to fully finance Radio Free Europe started to fade.

CHAPTER THREE

Help Truth Fight Communism: Join the Crusade for Freedom

The year 1951 was a busy one for both NCFE and the Crusade for Freedom. General Lucius Clay remained the National Chairman and Harold E. Stassen, president of the University of Pennsylvania, was 1951 Crusade Drive Chairman. The national effort of the Crusade for Freedom officially began Labor Day, September 3, 1951, and ended in February 1952, but in the months leading up to the official opening of the Crusade, there were many local activities that previewed the upcoming Crusade for Freedom campaign.

Developments in Early 1951

Dulles and Poole Resign from the NCFE

On December 30, 1950, Allen Dulles resigned as Chairman of the Executive Committee and as a director of National Committee for a Free Europe, effective the next day:

> I wish to assure you of my continuing interest in the Committee and of my desire to do everything possible to promote its work. I am tendering my resignation solely because of the fact that I shall in the immediate future be working in Washington for the Government and under these conditions consider it preferable to resign as an officer and director of the Committee.[1]

In truth, Allen Dulles resigned from NCFE to become the CIA's Deputy Director for Plans and was in charge of covert operations, including Radio Free Europe and Radio Liberty. DeWitt Poole resigned as President of NCFE on January 16, 1951, to become vice-chairman of the Board of Directors of NCFE. C.D. Jackson, publisher of *Fortune* magazine, replaced Poole as president of NCFE. On January 25, 1951, Undersecretary of State for Public Affairs Edward Barrett wrote a memorandum on Radio Free Europe to the deputy secretary of state:

It is inevitable that some people must know the full background of the Committee, this number should be kept to the absolute minimum as one of its principal advantages will be lost if the general public, particularly in Europe, has grounds for belief that RFE has any official or semi-official connection with the United States government.

I believe that Mr. Jackson, as an experienced propaganda warfare expert, will give the Committee and RFE the leadership and drive which has been needed.[2]

The CIA approved the capital budget for RFE in January and, in his new role as the CIA's Deputy Director, Plans, Allen Dulles sent a memorandum to Frank Wisner advising him of the approval. He also told Wisner that the operating budget would be presented to the Director, CIA, once C.D. Jackson, as the new president of NCFE, had the opportunity to review it.[3]

Committee for a Free Asia and Radio Free Asia Established

The second "covert operation" of the CIA of interest to be formed was Radio Free Asia, when on March 12, 1951 the articles of incorporation of the Committee for a Free Asia, Inc. (CFA), were filed with the California Office of Secretary of State. Brayton Wilbur, an import-export executive, was the first chairman of Committee for a Free Asia. In announcing the creation of the Committee for a Free Asia, Wilbur said, "The people of Asia must have more of the facts about the suffering that follows Communist aggression. They must also be shown alternative to communism."[4]

In the forward to CFA's "Prospectus" issued in May 1951, Brayton Wilbur wrote, "The purpose of this Committee is to establish channels of direct communication between the people of Asia and the people of the free world everywhere. Through those channels an exchange of thoughts, the hopes and the inspirations of the people of Asia with the people of America and Europe can weld a union of free men which will roll back the dark forces of Soviet imperialism."[5] The Statement of Purposes in the "Prospectus" included the following:

> To promote, aid and assist the cause of individual and national freedom in Asia, as opposed to Communist and other totalitarian doctrines.
> To initiate, assist and conduct, directly or indirectly, investigations and studies relating to such cause; and to obtain, collect, analyze, publish, broadcast, disseminate and distribute information relating thereto through any and all media of communication.
> To assist non–Communist and nontotalitarian elements in the countries of Asia in realizing and maintaining the ideals of individual and national freedom.
> To assist non–Communist and nontotalitarian travelers, refugees and exiles from the countries of Asia in maintaining contact with their fellow citizens for the purpose of keeping alive and promoting the ideals of individual and national freedom; and to make available facilities whereby these travelers, refugees and exiles can contribute to the cause of the maintenance of freedom under law.

To solicit and receive funds for the objects and purposes herein set forth and to administer and use such funds for the promotion of such objects and purposes; or to grant, allocate and appropriate such funds, or any part thereof, to any other organization or organizations for the promotion of such objects and purposes.[6]

The Committee for a Free Asia offices were set up in San Francisco and New York. Similar to the National Committee for a Free Europe, the Committee for a Free Asia would not "engage in carrying out propaganda or otherwise attempting to influence legislation."

Radio Free Europe Begins Broadcasting from Munich

In addition to the 7½ hours per day of short-wave broadcasts, Radio Free Europe began broadcasting to Czechoslovakia, as the Voice of Free Czechoslovakia, on medium wave (AM band) frequencies on May 1, 1951, from the newly constructed transmitter station nicknamed "Carola" at Holzkirchen, about 20 miles south of Munich, Germany. The new transmitter station had four antenna towers, which reached a height of 400 feet, and was, at that time with 135,000 watts of power, three times more powerful than any medium wave transmitter in the United States. The broadcast schedule was increased to 12 hours a day to Czechoslovakia.[7]

"THEY ARE TELLING LIES"

The new Radio Free Europe transmitter site was dedicated on May 1, 1951, at 10 A.M., in Munich's Bayerische Hof Hotel. C.D. Jackson, shown in Figure 5, was one of the speakers. Ferdinand Peroutka, a Czech journalist who had been imprisoned in the Nazi prison camps Dachau and Buchenwald, fled Czechoslovakia in 1948 to the United States. Peroutka, who helped found the Council of Free Czechoslovakia, followed C.D. Jackson and read the following message to those in attendance:

> The Communist government in our country is the biggest attempt, which has ever been undertaken to turn things upside down to deprive words of their meaning. Jailers sing songs of freedom and officials of the secret police lecture on humanity.
> The loss of freedom is officially called independence in our country, aggression is called peace action, plunder of the country "benefits," forced exports to Russia "building up of Czechoslovakia," enslavement of women in heavy industry is called their liberation.
> We know how much effort the Communists stake on reforming your souls.... But we also know that in the evening when you return home from the daily drudgery between your four walls you say to yourself: "They are telling lies."[8]

The inauguration broadcast message read by exile Pavel (Paul) Tigrid was aired at 11 A.M. from a studio in the RFE building. C.D. Jackson also gave a speech in front of the new RFE headquarters building under construction at which time a plaque with this inscription was unveiled to the invited guests:

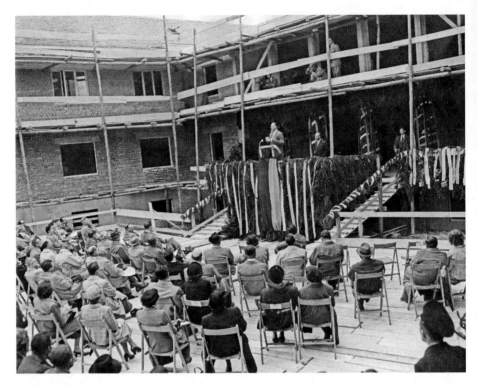

Figure 5. C.D. Jackson speaking at Radio Free Europe headquarters on May 1, 1951 (courtesy RFE/RL).

THIS
VOICE OF FREEDOM
MADE POSSIBLE BY THE CONTRIBUTIONS
OF 16 MILLION AMERICAN CITIZENS TO THE
1950 CRUSADE FOR FREEDOM

Local newspapers in the United States also covered the operation of the transmitter site dedication and first program. For example, *The Chronicle-Express* in Pann Van, New York, began a May 17, 1951, article entitled "Freedom Bell Rings Out Over New Radio Station," with "May 1 was a great day for the 16,000,000 men, women and children who joined the Crusade for Freedom last fall and bucked up their belief in freedom with their nickels, dimes and dollars." Yates County in upper New York contributed $360.33 and 4,000 persons signed the Freedom Scrolls. Moviegoers in the United States would later see a newsreel of the dedication of the new building as well as the building, antennas, and equipment of the new transmitting site.

C.D. JACKSON MESSAGE TO CRUSADERS

After C.D. Jackson visited Munich, a report dated May 15, 1951, under his name was airmailed to "Crusaders" in the United States. The envelopes airmailed from Munich carried four German postage stamps with the image of the Freedom Bell in Berlin. The C.D. Jackson report read in part:

There are many hazards ahead, including enemy jamming and various other countermeasures such as confiscation of radio sets. But as of today there exists a superb and powerful radio instrument, programmed as no such station has ever been programmed before and staffed by an extraordinarily imaginative, capable and dedicated group of individuals.

I am convinced that in the new Munich transmitter we have in our hands a mighty weapon in the struggle for freedom. It is already hitting the Communists hard, and in the months ahead as it reaches full effectiveness it will hit them still harder. With the help of the American people, through the Crusade for Freedom, we can build similar powerful freedom stations for each of the Iron Curtain countries. The success of the Crusade for Freedom next fall will largely determine our ability to carry out these plans. I want you to know that your personal help is deeply appreciated by General Clay, General Eisenhower, Ambassador Grew and all the others associated with us in this undertaking.[9]

Goals for 1951 Crusade

On May 2, 1951, General Clay announced the goals for the 1951 campaign: 25 million Americans enrolled in the Crusade for Freedom, with $3,500,000 in contributions to build two more "freedom" stations in Europe and begin the construction of another CIA covert radio broadcasting station: Radio Free Asia. The Advertising Council was very active during the second Crusade. Advertising Council films was distributed to the five newsreel agencies showed the Freedom Bell and dedication of Radio Free Europe's headquarters. The Advertising Council made Crusade-related materials available for the 1951 campaign, a summary of which is:

Newspaper Kit, Television Kit, House Organ Kit and Radio Kit
POSTERS Mounted and unmounted. 1-sheet posters and 24-sheet posters.
MASS DISTRIBUTION LEAFLETS The basic campaign leaflet. Can be distributed at over-the-counter display points, to employees, through the mail, etc.
WINDOW STICKERS given to all contributors. Can be displayed on store and home windows, automobile windshields, and company bulletin boards.
FILMS
"THE BELL" narrated by Henry Fonda, explains the origin and function of Radio Free Europe, climaxed by a request for support of 1950 Crusade for Freedom. Runs for 9 minutes, 44 seconds; available in 16 mm and 35 mm, black and white, sound.
"CRUSADE REPORT, 1951." Narrated by Ralph Bellamy. Progress report of Crusade for Freedom and Radio Free Europe. Shows casting of World Freedom Bell, its trip across U.S., dedication ceremonies in Berlin. Last part of film covers dedication and initial broadcast of Radio Free Europe's new 135,000-watt transmitter in Munich on May 1 of this year. Runs for 9 minutes, 44 seconds; available in 16 mm and 35 mm, black and white, sound.
"THE BIG TRUTH" (available after August 20). Through its dramatization of an actual case history of an escapee from behind the Iron Curtain, this film portrays the work of Radio Free Europe, and shows what RFE's broadcasts mean to captive

people. Runs for 9 minutes, 44 seconds; available in 16 mm and 35 mm, black and white, sound.[10]

Radio Free Asia Begins Broadcasting

Radio Free Asia (RFA) was included with Radio Free Europe in the fund solicitation activities of the 1951 Crusade campaign. For example, one Advertising Council newspaper advertisement in September 1951 included this appeal: "RADIO FREE ASIA, too, needs your dollars to help start similar truth broadcasts in the Far East ... to halt the spread of Communism in Asia."

A goal of 1,000,000 signatures of Californians in support of Radio Free Asia, to be enshrined in a future RFA transmitter site, was announced by California Southern Chapter chairman C.B. Tibbets: "Like the scrolls set in place last year with the opening of Radio Free Europe, the 1951 freedom pledges— signed, sealed and delivered — will serve as propaganda springboards from which American truths will hurdle the Communist curtain."[11]

On September 4, 1951, at 6:30 A.M., Radio Free Asia (RFA) began live broadcasting on a test basis from a studio rented in the commercial radio station KNBC in downtown San Francisco. After the sound of a gong and music from Mahler's "Song of the Earth," the first broadcast began with these words in Mandarin Chinese, "This is Radio Free Asia ... the voice of free men speaking to the people of Asia." On September 1, 1951, *Time* magazine told its readers, "Like its sister organization, Radio Free Europe, R.F.A. was founded by a group of private U.S. citizens who feel that the Voice of America, though effective in its way, is sometimes hampered because of "good & sufficient reasons of national policy." John W. Elwood, director of RFA, told the press, "Because we have no government ties, we can say anything we damn please."[12]

The initial programs of news and commentary were at first 90 minutes long and divided into three segments in Mandarin, Cantonese, and English languages. The programs were broadcast via a short-wave transmitter to Manila, Philippines and from there to China. Committee for a Free Asia, Brayton Wilbur, told the press, "The fundamental purpose of the broadcasting efforts of Radio Free Asia will be to pierce the Iron Curtain of Communism in Asia with factual, accurate and truthful news." He added,

> Eventually Radio Free Asia will beam towards the various parts of Asia programs on agriculture, health and other topics designed to assist the people of Asia and to maintain their courage and will to resist Communism.[13]

The symbol chosen for Radio Free Asia was a replica of a wooden Asian bell with the slogan "Let Freedom Ring." Radio Free Asia broadcasts were expanded to three hours in December 1951 and a third Chinese dialect, Hakka, was added.

Informers and Quislings

In the summer of 1951 one of the most popular RFE broadcasts to Czechoslovakia was "All This We Know," which broadcast names of "known informers and spies" in that country. Three examples of this type of programming that were used by the Advertising Council in its Crusade for Freedom newspaper advertisements were:

> THE FIGHT IS ON! Already *Truth* ... Communism's deadliest enemy ... is winning major victories behind the Iron Curtain. Radio Free Europe is sowing fear and confusion among the Red rulers and their collaborators ... identifying informers and quislings by name ... and bringing a message of hope to millions of captive people.
>
> Hello Bratislava! In the office of the Resettlement Bureau and the National Reconstruction Fund is employed one Comrade Absolonova. We warn you against her. She is a dangerous agent for the Communist police. Her task is to recruit for the State Security Police new agents and informers from among you people. Absolonova is tall and blonde. She concentrates her attention to young men whom she seduces and then blackmails into collaborating with the police.
>
> Attention! Radio Free Europe calls on Presov! In your town the manager of the Cafe Cergov, Stefan Stupinsky, is a dangerous agent of the State Security Police. Stupinsky is about 33 years old, dark haired and always well dressed. Do not be misled by his simulated friendliness, by his anti–Communist talk. Stupinsky and his helpers take advantage of the people who are intoxicated and try to draw things out of them to report to the police.
>
> Communist Deputy Frano was personally responsible for the murder of the Catholic Priest of Nemsova. Frano's agents called this priest to administer the last sacrament. When he came, they stabbed him to death on the road.[13]

My Name Is Ronald Reagan

In preparing the American public for the Second Annual Crusade for Freedom, in August 1951, the Advertising Council used the services of actor, and future U.S. President, Ronald Reagan in a Hearst Corporation movie newsreel and a televised public service appeal for contributions. Reagan was the star and narrator of the short film entitled *The Big Truth*, which was written by Otis Carney and directed by Seymour Friedman. Carney would receive a Freedom Foundation award in 1952 for his screenplay. Outtakes of the film, including Lucius Clay speaking in Berlin, were then used for a television film appeal for the 1951 Crusade campaign:

> My name is Ronald Reagan. Last year the contributions of 16 million Americans to the Crusade for Freedom made possible the World Freedom Bell — symbol of hope and freedom to the communist-dominated peoples of Eastern Europe. And built this powerful 135,000 Watt Radio Free Europe transmitter in Western Germany.
>
> This station daily pierces the iron curtain with the truth, answering the lies of

the Kremlin and bringing a message of hope to millions trapped behind the iron curtain. Grateful letters from listeners smuggled past the secret police express thanks to Radio Free Europe for identifying Communist Quislings and informers by name.

General Lucius D. Clay now asks you to join with him in a second great Crusade for Freedom to build two more powerful Freedom Stations that will send more messages of hope of truth and hope through the Iron Curtain. And, to establish Radio Free Asia to stop the spread of Communism in the Far East.

The Crusade for Freedom is your chance, and mine, to fight Communism. Join now by sending your contributions to

> General Clay
> Crusade for Freedom
> Empire State Building
> New York City

Or, join in your local community.[14]

"Winds of Freedom"

The National Committee for a Free Europe's Research and Publications Division was abolished in August 1951 and its publishing and pamphlet operations were transferred to the Division of Intellectual Cooperation (DIC).[15] The NCFE then created the Free Europe Press (FEP), which was used not only for the printing of various publications in the United States and Europe but also for the printing of leaflets and launching of balloons to carry them to the countries in Czechoslovakia, Poland, and Hungary. The leaflets contained such slogans as "A new hope is stirring," and "Friends of Freedom in other lands have found a new way to reach you." The schedule and frequencies of Radio Free Europe's broadcasts to Czechoslovakia were on the reverse side of the leaflets. The first leaflets were signed by the CIO-AFL of Canada, the equivalent labor groups of Latin America, the Free Writers Association of Europe, the General Federation of Women's Clubs, and the International Federation of Free Journalists and Confederation Internationale des Anciens Prisonniers de Guerre (more than 1,200,000 war veterans and prisoners of war from Belgium, France, Holland, and Italy).[16]

The first balloons, about 4 feet in diameter, with the Czech word "Svoboda" (freedom) written on the side in red letters as shown in Figure 6, were launched on August 13, 1951, after midnight, in an open field near Tirschenreuth, only 3 miles from the Czechoslovak border. This two-week test operation, known as the "Winds of Freedom," was on an experimental stand-alone basis; i.e., the launching of balloon carrying leaflets was not part of a coordinated programming effort with Radio Free Europe broadcasts.

Participating in the launching were famed American newspaper syndicated columnist Drew Pearson, a major proponent of the balloon launching program in his widely-read U.S. newspaper column "The Washington Merry-Go-

Figure 6. Balloons being prepared for use in Winds of Freedom launching August 1951, with the Czech word "svoboda," which means freedom (courtesy RFE/RL).

Round," C.D. Jackson, president of the NCFE, and prominent Republican Party leader Harold Stassen, former Governor of Minnesota, president of the University of Pennsylvania and the National Chairman of the 1951 Crusade for Freedom campaign. The three of them, "looking like three Statues of Liberty, held high above their heads big rubber balloons. At signal they solemnly let go."[17] After the launching, Harold Stassen was quoted as saying, "We tore a big hole in the Iron Curtain."[18]

On August 14, 1951, the General Mills public relations department posted on bulletin boards at the corporate headquarters in Minneapolis the following information bulletin:

COMPANY-MADE BALLOONS CARRY
FREEDOM MESSAGES BEHIND IRON CURTAIN

MINNEAPOLIS— Tens of thousands of General Mills–made freedom balloons are now landing in Czechoslovakia and Poland, carrying messages of hope to peoples behind the Iron Curtain. Called pillow balloons because of their 54" square size, they were developed at company research laboratories in 1949. The balloons are made of polyethylene, a substance commonly used in food saver bags. The company is one of two manufacturers making balloons for the Crusade For Freedom National Committee for Free Europe, sponsors of this project.[19]

Drew Pearson wrote in his August 15, 1951, nationally syndicated column:

> Freedom-friendship balloons floated across the iron curtain are not, of course, going to change the people of Russia, Czechoslovakia, and Hungary overnight. But they can help, and added to the Voice of America and other propaganda, some of which cannot be written about, they can hit the Kremlin in the Achilles' heel, which Stalin is worried most about — the fear that the peoples behind the iron curtain may get to know that we are a friendly, peaceful people who will fight if necessary, but who, contrary to the Russian radio, do not want war.
> However, this balloon barrage is merely a test — a test of what individual Americans working separately from their government can do to promote people-to-people friendship and to make the Iron Curtain a lace curtain.[20]

In his column dated August 17, 1951, Drew Pearson wrote:

> Near the Czechoslovak border, the current experiment in penetrating the iron curtain by balloons may be a great success or it may fail. It is too early yet to say. But the important thing is that it's an attempt by private individuals under the free-enterprise system to try out certain methods of psychological propaganda — or call it psychological warfare if you will — which governments will not — and perhaps cannot tackle.[21]

In his August 25, 1951, column, Pearson gave credit for the balloon operation to C.D. Jackson, when he wrote: "It is now possible to tell some of the inside facts as to how operation Winds of Freedom was conceived and executed. Chief credit belongs to C.D. Jackson, dynamic executive of *Time*, *Life* and *Fortune*, now on loan to the Committee for Free Europe. Jackson and I first conferred regarding Friendship Balloons on April 13. Four months later, Aug. 13, 1951, the first balloon was launched over Czechoslovakia." In his published diaries, Pearson later wrote, "June 26: Flew to Lennox, Massachusetts, to confer with C.D. Jackson and the Committee for Free Europe. It's apparently definite that we will release balloons at the rate of about 2,000 a day to Poland beginning the latter part of August. The State Department hasn't given its o.k. yet on Czechoslovakia."[22]

Ballooncasting

Abbott Washburn, now executive vice-president of the Crusade for Freedom, witnessed the launching and wrote a first-person account that appeared in American newspapers:

> Here at Radio Free Europe they've begun calling them "ballooncasts." The new Freedom Balloon operations are being quickly integrated with the regular broadcasting schedule. On ballooncasting days, like yesterday, the station stays on the air 20 hours — 9 hours more than usual — in order to report and background the event for its listeners inside Czechoslovakia.

In its present early stage development, "ballooncasting" is a lot more strenuous than broadcasting.... Some day ballooncasting will be as easy as broadcasting. But not for now.[23]

Washburn detailed the balloon program for the American newspaper reader. The Czechoslovak government seemingly ignored the leaflets, and the effect, if any, of the leaflets on the general population was not known. Though apparently not politically successful, the Free Europe Press (and the CIA) gained valuable practical experience in balloon launching. Ballooning had become a cost-effective means of delivering printed propaganda. Each balloon carried about 2000 leaflets, and when the weather was favorable, about 2000 balloon were launched each night. In total, over 11,000,000 leaflets were carried over the Iron Curtain and dropped on the other side.[24] Final Crusade for Freedom expenditures for the Winds of Freedom project were $233,041.89.[25]

On September 24, 1951, Harold Stassen attended a Crusade rally in Kansas City and told his audience, "The American people will tear down the Iron Curtain by using truth as a weapon. The day will come with the people of Russia themselves will tear down the walls of the Kremlin. These injections of truth are making the whole Balkan peninsula a power keg of resistance, which one day will blow the Communists out of the Kremlin and out of the capital of these countries." After he spoke, 50 balloons were launched containing leaflets asking for contributions to the Crusade.[26]

On August 17, 1951, Howland Sargeant, Deputy Assistant Secretary of State for Public Affairs (and future Radio Liberty President), sent a memorandum to James Webb, Under Secretary of State, advising him of the balloon project:

> For several months the Department has been following with interest certain privately sponsored plans to use balloons as vehicles for the delivery of propaganda. The Department felt that such projects had sufficient merit to warrant experimentation on a test basis, and consequently encouraged the private interests involved to proceed.[27]

CIA Director Turns Down Personal Crusade Support

In August 1951, Director of the CIA, Walter Bedell Smith, wrote a letter to Crusade chairman Harold Stassen in which he declined direct participation in the Crusade campaign:

> Though your Crusade has no more faithful a believer than I, my desire to take to the stump in this year's campaign for funds is unfortunately restrained by the prudence I must exercise in this job. The theory persists that the best intelligence officer is also the most anonymous one. And thus while I am part of this trade I must observe these conventions. You know, of course, how much we value your tremendously important good work, how grateful we are that citizens like you should devote so much time and effort to it.[28]

Marathon for Freedom

Over ten million homes were with television sets in the United States in September 1951—about 24 percent of all American households.[29] A 12-hour TV marathon, with viewers calling in contributions on behalf of the Crusade for Freedom, sponsored by the television network CBS and pooled with the other networks, took place on Sunday, September 23, 1951. The marathon featured top names in politics, business, theater, films, and broadcasting. This was the first "live" television fund appeal on a nation-wide basis, with telephone contributions coming from those areas where the program was aired live nationally for four-and-a-half hours and locally for 12 hours.

The live television transmission was over the American Telephone and Telegraph Co.'s recently finished $40,000,000 nationwide microwave relay system that spread from New York to Oakland, California. This was the first time that viewers on the West Coast saw New York and Washington live, and viewers on the East Coast could see Hollywood live.[30] The NBC and ABC television networks also aired special Crusade appeals on all its network programs on Sunday.

The purpose of the marathon was to gain moral and financial support Americans for the Crusade's drive against communism. Viewers could pledge donations via telephone or telegrams, or mail their contributions. In New York, $150,000 was raised through the marathon.

Ed Sullivan, who was once described as television's "best all around product spokesman," was scheduled to emcee the live entertainment program, but at the last minute television personality Steve Allen replaced him due to Sullivan's illness.[31] From 4:30 P.M. to midnight, Steve Allen cut in on network programming, introducing national figures who were supporting the Crusade.

Entertainers who were seen taking telephone calls and contributions from viewers included Ken Murray, Constance Moore, Jan Murray, Robert Merrill, Delores Gray, Mimi Benzell, Earl Wrightson, Joe E. Lewis, the Copacabana girls and the Latin Quarter show. Political personalities included Vice President and Mrs. Alben W. Barkley, former President Herbert Hoover, columnist Drew Pearson, and Ambassador Joseph Grew of NCFE.

From Hollywood, Art Linkletter emceed special half-hour segments that were relayed to the east coast to wind up the huge outdoor rally in Los Angeles. In Hollywood during the evening show, entertainers who manned the telephones included Bob Crosby, Rosemary Clooney, William Bendix, Jack Smith, Vincent Price, Marie Wilson, Ginny Simms, and J. Carrol Naish of the 1950 *Life with Luigi* radio program. One newspaper columnist proclaimed, "It was a successful day all around and for West coast television it was the day we've been waiting three years for. West coast television has taken on a new dress."[32]

Bing Crosby Radio Program

Famed singer, entertainer, television, radio and movie star Bing Crosby also was seen in movie theaters during the 1951-52 campaign, appealing in a short advertising film for support of the Crusade for Freedom:

> I want to tell you something I found out over in Europe: we've got plenty of good friends behind the Iron Curtain. Probably fifty or sixty million of them.
>
> Naturally they're not Russians, they're not Communists. They're freedom-loving peoples in the captive countries, who refuse to believe the big Red lies the Commies tell them. And you know why they don't believe those lies?
>
> It is because we, yes, you and I, and millions of other private U.S. citizens have found a way to pierce the Iron Curtain with the truth. And that way is Radio Free Europe, the most powerful weapon in the Crusade for Freedom.

Bing Crosby and his four sons, Gary, Dennis, Michael, and Lindsay, were featured in a nationwide half-hour radio program on NBC on Friday, September 28, 1951, entitled "Youth Crusade with the Crosbys." The theme of the show was "What is life really like behind the Iron Curtain? What is being done and what can be done to fight Communism throughout the world?"

The Crosby family show was a combination entertainment and solicitation program. Bing Crosby asked his youthful listeners, "Are you willing to give up three pieces of bubble gum?" He explained that "three cents will buy one brick for a new Radio Free Europe station to carry the truth behind the Iron Curtain." He urged them to sign the Freedom Scrolls, which had been sent to schools throughout the country, and to contribute a few cents to the Crusade for Freedom.

A young Czech boy living in Munich, Germany, was interviewed for broadcast during the Crosby show. Newspapers carried a photograph of Bing and three of his sons signing the Freedom Scroll in San Francisco. Included was a poster asking Americans to join the Crusade for Freedom with a man in front of a microphone that carried the word "Truth"—the same one that was seen in the Ronald Reagan television appeal. The show was repeated over the NBC radio network on Saturday, September 29, 1951.

Wednesday, October 3, 1951, was designated as "Youth Crusade Day" in the United States, and the Bing Crosby radio program was rebroadcast for "in-school" listening by students in various schools around the country.

Crusade Radio Broadcast

The 1951 national campaign started on Labor Day, September 3, 1951, with a nationwide radio broadcast carried by CBS and featuring General Dwight D. Eisenhower, Crusade National Chairman Lucius D. Clay, 1951 Crusade Chairman Harold E. Stassen, and others. The broadcast, narrated by Edward R.

Murrow, was also carried by Radio Free Europe. Eisenhower in Paris, as SHAPE commander, said,

> They (citizens of iron curtain countries) hunger also for the truth, to sustain them under the crushing weight of a godless dictatorship. You can help bring them the truth through the Crusade for Freedom. I trust every American will support wholeheartedly its campaign to use truth as a weapon against Communistic domination of the world."[33]

General Clay's Radio Appeal

General Clay gave a nation-wide radio address that was broadcast by radio station WNBC at 10:15 P.M., September 8, 1951. *The New York Times* headlined the speech on September 9, 1951: "CLAY OPENS APPEAL TO AID RED 'SLAVES.'" There was also a newspaper appeal, in the best Cold-war rhetoric, to the women of the United States to support the Crusade:

> This struggle (against Communism) reaches into every American home. It involves you and me. It affects the way of life of our children and our grandchildren.
> The Crusade for Freedom and Radio Free Europe are one of the means, one of the powerful weapons that can be brought into play against the forces of tyranny — powerful because through them American citizens can dispel the chill blackness of evil ideas with the clear warmth and light of truth.
> That is the primary reason why it is urgent for every woman to enroll in the Crusade for Freedom.
> If we truly want a free world, then each and every one of us must be willing to play a part in bringing it about. It is not our way to leave our problems entirely resolved by government. It is our way as a people to join together in doing those things, which we believe worthwhile. The Crusade for Freedom presents the opportunity to each American to take a personal part in the struggle for freedom.[34]

Crusade for Freedom Motorcade

The Ford Motor Company donated 1951 model trucks for the Crusade campaign in the 48 states and the District of Columbia and the Chevrolet Division of General Motors donated the same number of 1951 model station wagon cars. The trucks and cars were identical in every state and each truck (see Figure 7) was clearly marked Crusade for Freedom and numbered as part of the fleet around the nation and that became known as the Freedom Motorcade. The station wagon had a sign Crusade for Freedom in the shape of a flag and two loud speakers on the roof. Advance publicity, times, and locations where the vehicles would be parked were common in each of the states.

The Ford truck carried a replica of the Freedom Bell in Berlin, a Radio Free Europe transmitter tower, with the words Radio Free Europe, Radio Free

Figure 7. Freedom Motorcade truck in front of state capital building, Helena, Montana. Pictured above, left to right, are Sgt. Paul Wirick, Jr.; Montana Attorney General (and future U.S. Congressman) Arnold Olsen; Howard Ellsworth, State Crusade for Freedom Chairman; Walter H. Marshall, Coordinator (Montana Historical Society Research Center Photograph Archives, Helena, Montana).

Asia. An arrow of Truth pierced the symbolic Iron Curtain, as in Figure 8. Transcripts of RFE programs were also available to those interested in reading them and spectators could hear recordings of the programs coming from the Chevrolet's sound system. Local contributors and celebrities often launched helium-filled replicas of the "Winds of Freedom" balloons from the side of the Ford truck parked in pre-announced strategic locations. The Freedom Motorcade provided an excellent backdrop for publicity photographs for the Crusade campaign.

Oklahoma Campaign

The Crusade national goals for the state of Oklahoma were 275,000 signatures and $40,000 in contributions. The Freedom Motorcade started out from

Oklahoma City on Monday, September 17, 1951, for a 19-city tour, including a symbolic "Winds of Freedom" balloon launching demonstrations and handing out of Crusade campaign literature. The two-vehicle Freedom Motorcade arrived back in Oklahoma City on Saturday, September 29, 1951.

Schools, civic groups, and businesses were sent the Freedom Scrolls and other materials for use in the state campaign. The first school to respond with over 90 percent student signatures was the Choteau public school. For that the school superintendent received the certificate of honor signed by Chairman Lucius D. Clay. Oklahoma City chairman, E.K. Gaylord, recommended that local businesses conduct individual campaigns. "We believe it will be easier for each firm to have its own private campaign than to organize on a big manpower basis. If everyone will cooperate we can do a tremendous job."[35]

The big event for Oklahoma City was the annual State Fair at which C.D. Jackson addressed the Crusade Jubilee Saturday night September 29, 1951. The headline for the Oklahoma City newspaper *The Daily Oklahoman* was "Join Freedom's Crusade at the Fair Tonight — Free Show, Free Gate." The fair grounds opened at 6 P.M., with free admission for the first time in the history of the State Fair. The festivities included a grandstand variety show, with an appearance by Miss Oklahoma 1951, on the final night of the fair. The variety show entertained the crowd with patriotic themes before Jackson's address to the crowd, estimated to be over 20,000. C.D. Jackson flew from New York Saturday morning to make the 30-minute address at the fair, which was also broadcast on local radio station WKY. The next stops for C.D. Jackson were San Francisco, California, and then to Reno, Nevada, for a gala event.

The 1951 Crusade for Freedom in Nevada

Nevada, the "Silver State," had the highest percentage of signatures on the Freedom Scrolls in 1950, when approximately 70,000 persons (44.6 percent of the population) signed up for the Crusade for Freedom and contributed over $5,000. The nationwide goal for the 1951 Crusade campaign was 25,000,000 signatures with a goal for Nevada of 73,000. Activities in Nevada in 1951 illustrate not only the pageantry Americans enjoy but also the enthusiasm state and local chairmen brought to the campaign. The regional director was Don Martin, editor of the *Denver Post*. Young students signed the Freedom Scroll. The Manague school system in Nevada was the first to reach 100 percent student participation and won the Crusade's "Award for Merit."

On August 15, 1951, 50 invited guests attended a luncheon in the Nevada room of the Mapes Hotel in Reno. This was a preview of the 1951 Crusade campaign that started on Labor Day, September 3, 1951. The invited guests heard a recording of the Freedom Bell in Berlin and looked at photographs of the Bell and of Radio Free Europe in Munich.

Figure 8. Rear of Motorcade truck showing symbol of Iron Curtain. Shown in photograph are Sgt. Paul Wirick, Jr., left and Prc. William Wirick (Montana Historical Society Research Center Photograph Archives, Helena, Montana).

In July Nevada State Chairman Merrill Inch had traveled to Chicago, where he met state chairmen from the other 47 states and from the territories of Alaska and Hawaii. Merrill Inch told the assembled guests that "The Crusade for Freedom is completely financed, that none of the voluntary contributions received in Nevada will be used for anything but the building of additional radio stations with which to penetrate the Iron Curtain, and that the Crusade for Freedom is a reiteration of the faith in a free world of the people of Nevada."[36]

On September 15, 1951, Harold Stassen, 1951 campaign chairman, sent a telegraph message to Merrill Inch, Nevada state chairman and general manager of Reno Newspapers, Inc., giving some details of the Freedom Train and letters for Radio Free Europe. President Truman also sent a telegram message to Merrill Inch, which read:

As you open the 1951 drive of the Crusade for Freedom which sixteen million Americans have voluntarily joined, I send you greetings and best wishes in your dramatic action as free citizens to carry the message of truth to millions of your fellow men who are struggling against oppression and whose news is poisoned by lies. This joint action of millions of free citizens regardless of party or occupation, race or religion, is an inspiring and effective attack against Red tyranny.[37]

The front page of the newspaper *Nevada State Journal* Sunday edition, September 23, 1951, carried a small notice: "Sign the Crusade for Freedom Roll" and displayed photographs of Radio Free Europe president C.D. Jackson with the headline, "Giant Rally to Open Freedom Crusade Here." Two 24-sheet billboards calling for support of the Crusade for Freedom and Radio Free Europe and Radio Asia were placed on the roads approaching Reno in preparation of Jackson's visit.

Sunday night, September 30, 1951, RFE President C.D. Jackson spoke in Reno, Nevada, at a large rally for the Crusade for Freedom and RFE. There were 1,500 persons in the new Reno high school gymnasium. Jackson's speech was carried over radio station KATO in Reno. In part, he said,

> Truth is Communism's deadliest enemy. If the United States can win the cold war against Communism in Europe, the world stands a good chance of avoiding a shooting war. America's chief hopes for winning the cold war must be pinned on such innovations as radio networks and balloons, which carry messages of truth behind the Iron Curtain.

Three local hotels, Mapes, Riverside, and Golden, provided entertainment for the crowd. That evening, during the three-hour entertainment show, movie star Clark Gable acted as an auctioneer. The item was a silver brick with the words "Nevada 1951" engraved on one side. The brick was reported to be part of the cornerstone of the RFE building in Munich. It was auctioned off for $800 dollars and film actress Ida Lupino presented the brick to the Charles W. Mapes, Jr., the happy auction winner. In keeping with the good spirit of the evening, Mapes returned the silver brick, which was taken the next day to Las Vegas, where it was auctioned off before 2,000 spectators at the Elks Stadium for $1,000.[38] Afterwards it was returned to Crusade organizers so it could be used again in future auctions in Nevada. C.D. Jackson flew on to Las Vegas for the rally there.

Ida Lupino and Clark Gable, described in the newspapers as "Hollywood luminaries, active in the fight against subversive influences in the film capital," had launched balloons earlier in the day that carried messages from Reno and Sparks merchants with instructions to return them to Reno and state when and where they were found. Contributions for each balloon message returned were to come from the merchants and businessmen. Many of the balloons were prepared by the First National Bank of Nevada and were launched in front of one of the 14 branches in the state. One launched balloon later was found after floating hundreds of miles to Nebraska.

The silver brick was transported for auctioning in other cities by the Crusade for Freedom motorcade. The Freedom Motorcade for Nevada had arrived earlier in the month and was then outfitted with sound systems. By the middle of October the silver brick had been successively auctioned off to the sum of

$2,500, including one winning bid of $21.75 from the Smith Valley Rotary Club in Wellington, Nevada. The Freedom Motorcade traveled to over 50 cities and logged over 7,500 miles so citizens could contribute and sign the Freedom Scrolls and launch balloons. The motorcade ended when children at the "Sunny Acres" children's home in Carson City signed the Freedom Scroll on Friday, November 2, 1951. Fifty small Crusade balloons and three large ones were given to the children's home in appreciation of the school's help.

November 1 is Nevada Day (Admissions Day) when entrance of Nevada into the United States is celebrated. The Carson City parade in 1951 lasted 1½ hours before an estimated 25,000 onlookers and marked the 87th anniversary of Nevada's admission into statehood. Fifty floats, 25 marching bands, and a total of 125 separate groups participated. The Crusade for Freedom truck was decked out with small colorful balloons and won second prize in the general float category — the Nevada state prison won the first prize for a float that demonstrated the chiseling of brown stone blocks.

Crusade state chairman Inch went to Munich in November at the expense of the Crusade to visit RFE. Also in November, Catholic Bishop Thomas K. Gorman sent a letter to all parishes in Nevada asking Catholics to sign the Freedom Scroll as a "solid front against Communism." All Catholic churches participated in Crusade for Freedom week, which ended on November 11, 1951. Five thousand Catholics signed in response to Bishop Gorman's appeal and he received a "Certificate of Appreciation" from the Crusade for Freedom for his support.

1951 Crusade for Freedom and the Freedom Train

On September 11, 1951, a passenger train carrying 108 persons and crew was "hijacked" and deliberately driven across the Czechoslovak-German border into the town of Wildenau in the American military sector. Thirty-one persons, including Jaroslav Konvalinka, the train's engineer, Karel Truxa, and their respective families, asked for and received permission to stay in the West. Those remaining passengers who did not request political asylum were returned the same day, but there was a delay in sending the train back.

Karel Truxa was the railroad stationmaster as the Czech town of Cheb. He had been sent to a labor camp for five months for giving refuge to two men who were hiding from the Communist secret police. The day before the escape, he rode his motorcycle to the Asch freight yards and, unseen, threw a switch so that any train that came over that particular track would be diverted onto a spur leading to the Czech border that had not been used since before the Communist coup d'état in 1948. Then Truxa went to Pilsen to wait for the next morning's Prague-Asch express, which he knew would be piloted by Konvalinka.

As the train approached Asch, it did not slow down. Instead, Konvalinka pushed the throttle all the way forward and the train sped past the station platform, through the freight yards and onto the unused track, whose switch Truxa had set the day before.

One of the lucky passengers not privy to the escape plan was a 16-year-old girl, Zdena Hybleva, who had previously escaped to the West. But then she returned to Czechoslovakia. Because of being on that train, she accidentally succeeded in bringing her 16-year-old boyfriend, Kvapil Kamil, to the west. Their story, along with a photograph, appeared in some newspapers in the United States. Konvalinka was given the sobriquet "Freedom's Casey Jones and Czech Casey Jones."[39]

Czech Government Protest

The Czechoslovak government then officially protested to the American Embassy for alleged American complicity in the incident by sending two protest notes on September 20, 1951, to U.S. Ambassador Ellis O. Briggs, who then requested assistance from Washington for a reply. The same day, the State Department sent back a "top-secret, priority, needs immediate action" telegram asking for the Ambassador Briggs's views of a draft propaganda leaflet message intended for Czechoslovakia. The original text, including misspellings of names and abbeviations, read as follows:

> Balloons wld carry unsigned msg providing factual account train episode and reception and handling of passengers aboard. Leaflet wld also contain fol message "31 of the passengers choose to remain in the West. 77 chose to return to their homes, wives and husband and children and have been freely permitted to go back. These 77 chose to defer personal freedom until the day when their country and their people together regain freedom for all. It will take time, just as Engineer Konbalinka's plans did, to switch the track that will shunt Czecho off its present road to Moscow and on to the main line that leads to freedom and justice for all.
>
> Reverse of leaflet bearing pictures of trains, engineer and fireman wld have fol msg from Konbalinka stating: "People of Czecho, I beg you, for your own good, not to believe that 'Amer agents' were involved in freedom train episode. It is just one more of the many lies spread by the Muscovites. Mr. Trusa and I planned the project entirely alone because conditions as so many of you know them at home have become unbearable for us."[40]

The State Department in Washington notified the American Embassy of the balloon launchings. As Konvalinka launched his first balloon at approximately 2 A.M., he reportedly said, "I am happy to know that these messages will reach my friends." Truxa said, " We would prefer to send you freedom instead of freedom balloons. That the time will come when that is possible." The photograph that accompanied many American newspapers articles carried the caption:

> MESSAGE IN THE SKY— Karel Truxa and Jaroslav Konvalinka, leaders the "freedom train" escape from Czechoslovakia, get ready to inform their countrymen still behind the Iron Curtain that "unbearable" conditions spurred their flight to the West and to freedom. The balloons that they hope will carry their message, printed two and one-half million copies, are being launched from a secret point five miles from the Czech frontier.[41]

Newspapers in the United States reported the text of Konvalinka's balloon message to Czechoslovakia, with slight variations, e.g.:

> Dear people at home, please don't believe anybody who tried to link our escape with American agents. It is only a lie of many lies spread by the communists. Truxa and I alone made the plan and carried it out because the conditions at 'home were unbearable. The communists' have undertaken the most insane attempt to hide the truth and are making up fantastic stories involving terrorists and foreign agents.
> The leaflets also contained this message from the Free Europe Press:
> We are coming to you from the free sky again to tell you the truth about the Escape of the Czech train...
> Mr. Konvalinka, Mr. Truxa, and Dr. Svec had planned the escape for months. It was a careful plan, and it involved risks. They moved cautiously, waiting for the right moment.
> The feeling of all those who escaped is summed up in what one young mechanic said in a message over Radio Free Europe: "In Czechoslovakia we felt we were always being shadowed. This and the lack of freedom were the reasons for our flight." His wife added: "I don't want my children to grow up slaves. We are ready to go anywhere people can live their own lives."
> (signed) "Winds of Freedom"[42]

Comrade Beb Takes a Trip

Time magazine published details of the train escape in the September 24, 1951, issue under the headline "Comrade Beb Takes a Trip":

> The train lurched through the Asch station and raced on through the crowded freight yards. Comrade Conductor Beb rushed for the emergency brake and pulled it. Nothing happened: Engineer Konvalinka had done his job well. Beb ran to one of the hand brakes, but the tight-lipped men who had been watching the brakes elbowed him away.
> At the tiny town of Wildenau, half a mile inside Germany, the train panted to a stop. Conductor Beb jumped out and ran toward the locomotive, screaming insults. Said Konvalinka evenly: "You've got nothing more to tell me."

The September 24, 1951, edition of *Life* magazine carried a photo essay, including a photograph of unhappy train conductor August Beb, entitled, "A Red Train Jumps Off Party Line."

State Department Answers Protest Note

On October 1, 1951, the American Embassy in Prague sent the official reply to the Czechoslovakian Foreign Ministry, which in part read:

> The ministry's note employs this fiction apparently with the purpose to conceal, if possible the fact that the direction and departure of the train from Czechoslovakia was an unaided undertaking of certain citizens of that country who adopted this somewhat unconventional method of leaving the country and simultaneously indicated their attitude.
>
> According to such information as has come to the knowledge of the United States Government, recent departures from Czechoslovakia have been effected among other means by such vehicles as bicycles, automobiles and trucks, as well as a considerable assortment of air-planes and even a glider whereof the train is merely the latest and largest conveyance to be employed.[43]

"Windborne Message"

On October 8, 1951, *Time* magazine reported on the balloon launchings and Radio Free Europe under the rubric "Windborne Message" and gave details of the train episode, but the message in the leaflet as reported by *Time* and the spellings of the train's engineer differed from the text in the telegram from the State Department to the U.S. Ambassador in Prague:

> Over hilly Sudetenland and the spires of Prague, thousands of white paper leaflets fluttered down. Each night for four nights, 2,000 plastic balloons spilled out 2,000,000 leaflets. That was the way the people of Red Czechoslovakia got the real story last week of how Locomotive Engineer Jaroslav Konvalinka raced his Prague-Asch "freedom train" across the Czech border into Germany (*Time*, September 24).
>
> Konvalinka himself helped the West's new private and enterprising propaganda agency, Winds of Freedom, launch its balloons at the German town of Selb, where the train, with 108 people aboard, had ended its escapade. The leaflets carried pictures of Konvalinka, the train, and a group of 18 of the 31 Czechs who did not go back to Czechoslovakia.
>
> They also carried a message from Konvalinka scotching the Reds' late, lame explanation that the train had been "kidnapped by U.S agents." Wrote Konvalinka: "My countrymen, I beg you not to believe Americans were involved. It is just one more of the many lies.... No, there were no terrorists, no secret foreign plot. The only terrorists are the Communists; the only foreigners are those from Russia.

Harold Stassen, the 1951 Crusade for Freedom campaign chairman, told the press, "The Communists have concocted a wholly false version of the escape and are pumping it out over their controlled press and radio." Chairman Stassen also sent out telegraph messages to the Crusade state chairman that were in turn given to local newspapers:

One of the passengers aboard the runaway Czechoslovak train had with him several letters for Radio Free Europe, which had been given to him by Prague listeners. He said it was primarily through Radio Free Europe Broadcasts that he finally decided to escape the country. As a special service, Radio Free Europe has been broadcasting personal messages from all passengers to their relatives and friends in Czechoslovakia.[44]

The train was returned intact to Czechoslovakia on October 10, 1951, nearly a month after the incident.

Television Docudrama

On Tuesday night, October 23, at 9:30 P.M., television viewers tuned into the CBS network watched a 30-minute drama in the *Suspense* series that was entitled "The Train from Czechoslovakia." Actor Richard Kiley played the role of Jaroslov Konvalinka and John McGovern played that of Karel Truxa. The television drama began by quoting an RFE message translated into English as follows:

This is Radio Free Europe, the Voice of Free Czechoslovakia, bringing from our station in Munich, message of hope out to fellow Czechoslovakians imprisoned in their homeland behind the Iron Curtain.

At the program's mid-break, Royce G. Martin, President of Auto-Lite, the sponsor of the program, and General Lucius Clay appeared on the television screen with a copy of the 1951 Crusade for Freedom poster in the background. Martin introduced Clay who said:

Well, it was last year's Crusade that built the powerful Munich radio station of Radio Free Europe. That is what the Crusade for Freedom is now doing, a voice which each day penetrates deeper through the Iron Curtain.

Rex Marshall, the narrator of the television program finished the television program with this advice:

Gentlemen, you can join the 1951 Crusade for Freedom by sending your contribution, large or small, to General Lucius D. Clay. Remember you can help fight Communism by joining the Crusade for Freedom.

The Konvalinka and Truxa families were given visas and were flown to the United States, under sponsorship of the International Refugee Organization, accompanied by Joseph Kolarek, special State Department representative. Eleven of the passengers were granted political asylum in Canada and arrived there on October 24, 1951.[45]

On November 19, 1951, Konvalinka, Truxa, and their families, arrived at Idlewild airport in New York, where Lawrence Cohen, president of the Lionel

Electric Train Corporation, met them. The families settled in New Jersey, where the two men were given jobs at the Lionel Electric Train (model) factory. The December 3, 1951, issue of *Life* magazine carried a photograph of Truxa, Konvalinka, his wife and their two children at the Lionel factory looking at a model railroad tabletop display. Afterwards, the two men were sent on a 14-state journey to tell their escape story in support of the Crusade for Freedom campaign for Radio Free Europe.

American Magazine

The February 1952 issue of *American Magazine* had a front-page story entitled "We Stole a Train for Freedom," written by Konvalinka and Truxa, that was later printed in *Reader's Digest* in May 1952. The name of the train conductor was now written as "Alois Bohn, a paunchy, ardent Communist." In this article, the men listed eight reasons why they decided to escape with their families, including

- We were sick and tired of being pushed around, spied upon, and watched.
- Instead of a "worker's paradise," we found our working conditions getting worse and worse.
- We couldn't feed and clothe our families under Communism.
- We were frightened by what the Communists were trying to do to our children.

The *American Magazine* article concluded with

> In America, we have found a life rich in what seem to us luxuries—good food, fine clothes, refrigerators, washing machines. We don't want to presume to give you advice. One thing, however, has worried us with our talks with neighbors and as we have appeared before groups in many of your great cities. You Americans seem to us to take your wonderful free life too much for granted. We hope and pray you will guard your freedom well in America. The millions of decent people who are still behind the Iron Curtain, unable to escape, look to America as the one great protector of a Free way of life for the whole world!

The Greenwood Plan:
Ideas from the Man in the Street

Chauncery W. Lever, manager of the chamber of commerce in Greenwood, South Carolina, in 1950, conceived the idea of a contest conducted by chambers of commerce across the United States by "which the ideas of individual American citizens may be brought into the firing lines of the world in the battle for men's minds."[46] One of Lever's suggestions was, "collecting ideas from the man in the street on how to fight the cold war. All citizens with ideas that they think would work in piercing the Iron Curtain, with an idea that they think might bring renewed hope to some of the enslaved peoples of Europe and Asia, should send them to the Junior Chamber of Commerce."[47] The underlying premise was: "comb America's towns, cities and rural areas for suggestions on how best to spike Communist lies and promote world freedom and peace.[48]

Chambers of commerce in over 500 communities in the 48 states plus Hawaii and Alaska participated in the contest. The local chamber of commerce selected winning entries, sent them to the chamber of commerce in Greenwood, which collected, screened and forwarded them to the Crusade for Freedom headquarters in New York. Mrs. Alben Barkley (wife of Vice President Alben Barkley), General Lucius D. Clay, and Harold Stassen, 1951 campaign chairman, then acted as judges to select the final winning entries.

A "Greenwood Plan Information Kit" was provided to local chambers of commerce throughout the United States that included information on

- How to set up the Greenwood Plan-type Committee
- Suggested Committee Representation
- Subcommittees
- Prizes
- Procedures
- Program Committee
- Speakers Bureau
- Idea-soliciting Committee
- Study Groups

The kit also included other items: "The very latest and best material on Communism are made available along with all of the other supplies at no cost to the local community. The kit also contained Greenwood Plan brochures and posters.[49]

Elizabeth Porcherm, a librarian living in Greenwood, South Carolina, was given the first-place prize for her entry: "One way to fight ideas with ideas is to make fun of those ideas which lend themselves to jokes. Develop a cartoon strip ridiculing and poking subtle fun at all Communistic ideas and upholding and explaining the ideals of democracy and distribute by balloons and other methods."[50]

Michele A. Marraccini, Oakland, California, won second place with "Originate radio programs from social and festive gatherings in the United States of Americanized nationals from Iron Curtain countries so they can tell their countrymen what America means to them."

The third-place prize was awarded to William J. Schereck, Baraboo, Wisconsin, who called for the development of radio programs "emphasizing the history, science, literature and culture of the Iron Curtain countries to increase captive peoples realization that America is friendly."[51]

All three flew to Europe, visited Berlin, to see the Freedom Bell, and Munich, where their ideas were broadcast over Radio Free Europe.

Balloons, Statue of Liberty and Tablecloths

Seventeen balloons were lofted on October 2, 1951, at the base of the Statue of Liberty by Samuel Unger of the Crusade for Freedom, George Barasch, president of the Allied Trades Council, and a Romanian émigré identified as "Dinu." Six of the balloons were the same as those launched in Germany in August, the remainder were "toy" balloons. Reportedly, the balloons were sent aloft in an attempt to win over trade union support for the Crusade for Freedom.[52]

The October issue of *Popular Science* carried an article about the balloon launchings in Germany entitled "'Freedom' Leaps Iron Curtain." Two photographs were included in the article, including one showing the word "svoboda" on the balloons. The article pointed out that the balloons created "goodwill among housewives, who eagerly grab the balloons and use the plastic for wrapping food or as tablecloths."[53]

Balloons for Sale

As part of the 1951 fund-raising drive for Radio Free Europe and the Free Europe Press, newspaper readers in Madison, Wisconsin, found an advertisement that included,

> Now for the first time your *Crusade for Freedom* has been aide to intensify its tough idea war with Communist rulers with *written words — messages* carried in balloons blown by the "winds of freedom" deep into the captive countries. This new and dramatic means of piercing the Curtain is a significant step.

Contributors could fill out a coupon endorsed by forty "civic-minded business firms" that read:

> My contribution in any amount will be used to:
> (1) Help expand Radio Free Europe — broadcasting costs are $12 per minute — and begin similar truth broadcasts to Asia;
> (2) Buy a rubber Freedom Balloon for $2.50;
> (3) Buy a plastic "pillow" Freedom Balloon for $5.00.
> You may (may not) use my name on a freedom message to be sent by balloon through the Iron Curtain.

Readers were told that "Messages by freedom balloon bring to the Kremlin dominated lands written words of hope and friendship. With two means of communication — radio and balloons— your Crusade for Freedom will better able to encourage hope among the prisoner peoples of Poland, Rumania, Czechoslovakia, Bulgaria, Hungary and Albania. Your *Crusade* will continue its fight for Truth and Hope and Freedom — the ingredients of lasting peace."[54]

Other Local Balloon Activities

In Kalispell, Montana, a Crusade for Freedom float built by the members of the American Legion won first prize in the Northwest Montana Fair parade on September 13, 1951. "Operation Winds of Freedom" demonstration balloons were launched in Kalispell on September 20, 1951, when the Freedom Motorcade arrived. Crusade County Chairman Sykes said, "This is the third weapon in the struggle to help Truth fight Communism. The other two being the Freedom Bell and Free Europe Press." In Helena, Montana, balloons and leaflets were launched on September 15, 1951.[55] One balloon was found by deer hunter Marvin Johns a month later in the Spokane Hills. Another balloon was found stuck on a ranch fence 100 miles east of Lewistown, Montana, in October 1951.[56]

In South Carolina, one hundred balloons were launched during the Freedom Motorcade's travels around that state. In Pennsylvania, farmer Ralph H. Flood found one balloon with leaflets in his cornfield along the Tuscarora Mountains in Blair Mills. A yellow leaflet entitled "Operation Winds of Freedom" was in the balloon. This was described as a "significant new weapon to pierce the Iron Curtain in the war of Truth against Communism — supplementing the already hard-hitting Radio Free Europe broadcasts."[57]

As part of the state Crusade campaign in Idaho, balloons containing leaflets were launched in Boise. One balloon floated more than 600 miles (1,000 kilometers) to a half-mile east of Boulder, Colorado, where Mrs. John Boulter found it on September 27, 1951. In the balloon were copies of the "Winds of Freedom leaflet."[58]

The Freedom Motorcade was not successful everywhere. Motorcade No. 14 of the Crusade for Freedom "slipped through almost unnoticed" when it visited Alton, Illinois, on the morning of September 25, 1951. The newspaper headline read, "Freedom Truck Unnoticed as Fanfare Fails." The article went on, "Someone has 'snafued' the advance publicity and notices." The town's police chief was at home with a throat infection and the police sergeant was "working on a traffic case." The mayor was "discussing with a homeowner a matter of a garbage truck backing over a lawn." In a makeshift action, the local members of the Jaycee Crusade posed for a photograph and a balloon with leaflets was lofted. The town's newspaper reported, "It soared up, bounced off the power lines and disappeared in the grey sky. The crusade exhibit was not unpacked."[59]

1951 Campaign Results

At the January 18, 1952, NCFE Board of Directors' meeting, the "nature and scope" of the 1952 Crusade for Freedom was discussed. There was general agreement that the next Crusade "should be considerably reduced in scope, that the emphasis should be taken off publicity and placed on fund-raising with the promotional period being reduced from two months to two or three weeks." Lucius Clay announced that for personal reasons he would be "withdrawing" at National Chairman. Also, the Board accepted Abbott Washburn's resignation as Executive Vice Chairman.[60]

The 1951-1952 Crusade, which ran from April 1, 1951, to February 29, 1952, had expenses of $2,016,433. Contributions from the American public amounted to $1,930,134.57 (well under the stated goal of $3,500,000 for the 1951 Crusade).[61] From this amount, $1,806,552.66 was transferred to the National Committee for Free Europe. The balance of the contributions, amounting to $123,581.91, remained deposited in various banks around the United States as "cash on hand." "Contributions from other sources" (read Central Intelligence Agency) for the Crusade for Freedom Operating Fund came to $2,343,534.15. CIA support for NCFE and Radio Free Europe for Fiscal Year 1951 amounted to $8,681,715.50.[62]

CHAPTER FOUR

From Freedom-Grams to Flying Saucers

Boston Symphony Orchestra

The Boston Symphony Orchestra was scheduled to tour Europe for the first time in its history in the spring of 1952, including performing at the Paris cultural festival "Masterpieces of the Twentieth Century." The NCFE board of directors held a meeting on October 2, 1951. The directors were told that the costs of the tour were expensive and full financial support was not forthcoming for the planned budget of $200,000. The NCFE board of directors was told that the Congress for Cultural Freedom (another CIA covert project) pledged $30,000 of support, $40,000 was expected from the European Tour, and $100,000 would come from the United States tour. Thus $30,000 was lacking.[1]

C.D. Jackson, who was also on the board of directors of the Boston Symphony Orchestra, told the other NCFE directors that he "was very enthusiastic" about the participation of the Boston Symphony Orchestra in the Paris festival and "felt that the NCFE through Radio Free Europe could make a major contribution to its success," if "NCFE would give the necessary pledge of approximately $30,000, for which in turn, Radio Free Europe would receive the rights for broadcasting the entire festival program and the recording rights of the orchestra's European concert tour." The NCFE board of directors unanimously endorsed the support but would not approve the financial support without more information about the exact amount required and if NCFE had the funds to do so.[2]

At a special meeting held on January 16, 1952, the NCFE board of directors passed a resolution "that the sum of $30,000 is appropriated as a donation to the American Committee of Cultural Freedom, Inc, in return for which NCFE is secured the rights to broadcast and record the 'Masterpieces of the Twentieth Century Exposition' program in Europe, including all the performances of the Boston Symphony Orchestra during its tour of the American Committee for Cultural Freedom, Inc."[3]

On April 28, 1952, the "Masterpieces of the Twentieth Century" festival opened in Paris, with the Boston Symphony Orchestra playing Igor Stravinsky's ballet suite *The Rite of Spring.*

"Tail Wagging the Dog"

The perceived success of the Crusade for Freedom upset America's foreign policy bureaucracy in Washington, which saw the Crusade as a viable threat to the funding of the "official" Government international broadcasting service, the "Voice of America."

An extraordinary meeting of CIA and the U.S. State Department leadership took place in the private residence of State Department official Edward W. Barrett, Assistant Secretary of State for Public Affairs and an early member of the NCFE, on the evening of November 21, 1951. Representing the CIA were Messrs. Dulles, Wisner, Lloyd, Deputy Chief, Psychological Staff Division, and Braden, Chief, International Branch, Psychological Division, OPC. During the meeting, Edward Barrett said, "We ought to examine all RFE activities in the light of the following questions":

> 1. Is the activity one that is serving a useful enough purpose to justify the funds involved?
> 2. Can it be done better by this organization than by Government directly or by other existing organizations?
> 3. Is it jeopardizing the existence and success of other important activities?
> 4. How can it best be financed?

Allen Dulles, now Director of Central Intelligence, brought up the question about the future of the Crusade for Freedom in 1952. Barrett answered:

> The present type of campaign was harming the total United States effort and making people ask the question whether the Voice of America is really needed. He did not say that to his surprise no serious questions came up in the last Congress concerning the apparent duplication between Radio Free Europe and VOA. Mr. Barrett suggested that instead of the present type of Crusade for Freedom, a low-pressure program should be conducted. He said that something along the line of the tuberculosis seal campaign in magazines, with coupons, and so on, ought to be tried out.[4]

Committee for a Free Asia and Radio Free Asia

Attendees at the November meeting agreed that "Radio Free Asia would undergo no further expansion until the future course of the Committee for Free Asia had been settled in a manner satisfactory to both CIA and State." The CIA's Tom Braden said, "RFA is staying right there where it is until they are given further orders." CIA Director Dulles suggested "RFA be kept going on its present basis along with CFA for next few weeks until the new head of the organization is selected. He should then be brought in for a discussion of this whole operation."[5]

In December 1951, Radio Free Asia prepared a series of Christmas programs of popular Christmas carols that were recorded by the University of California Extension Choral. The programs were intended not only for China but also for Japan, to be broadcast over 118 radio stations of the Broadcasting Corporation of Japan.[6]

The Advertising Council put out another Crusade for Freedom fact sheet, in which Radio Free Asia was mentioned in some detail: "Although it is patterned generally after the National Committee for a Free Europe, there are substantial differences because of the more complex pattern of national viewpoints across the Pacific, and because of the different pattern of Red Aggression in Asia. For one thing, CFA is not only engaged in fighting Communism where it has already seized control, but is also waging a preventive battle to keep Kremlin doctrine from spreading to other Eastern nations." Three special programs of humor and satire were listed in the fact sheet: "Communist Bad Checks," "Big Mouth and the Professor," and "Answer Man."[7]

State Department Plausible Denial

On December 24, 1951, the U.S. State Department sent the following information to all American diplomatic and consular missions abroad:

> It is emphasized that Radio Free Europe is a private, non-governmental agency supported from contributions solicited in the United States by "The Crusade for Freedom." It concentrates its radio broadcasts on the captive countries behind the Iron Curtain.
>
> Radio Free Europe cannot be construed under any circumstances to be speaking for the United States Government. Any suggestion by other nations that the United States Government assumes responsibility and endeavors to control the output of Radio Free Europe has been rejected as contrary to democratic procedure and the principle of freedom of information.[8]

Follow-up Meeting

On January 17, 1952, there was a top-level meeting at the State Department office of Edward Barrett with the Central Intelligence Agency, including Allen Dulles and Frank Wisner. C.D. Jackson of the National Committee for Free Europe and Abbot Washburn, now Executive Committee Vice Chairman of the Crusade for Freedom, were present to discuss the Crusade's future. The State Department Memorandum of Conversation, which followed, included the following points:

Mr. Jackson said that he and his colleagues realize that they cannot repeat the 1951 type Crusade. He raised the question of whether there should be a Crusade at all and answered it by saying that he felt that some sort of Crusade had to continue. He said that a shorter Crusade pitched at a lower level would solve many of the problems that had occurred in the past year.

He said that one good idea that had been developed by local committees was to have a one-day civic organization doorbell ringing campaign. Some buildup of publicity would be necessary for a national doorbell ringing campaign but it would be nothing to compare with the extended Crusade of this year.

Mr. Jackson said that the direct mail approach had been tried this year with some success and could be expanded. He added that he felt the short campaign would have the additional advantage of removing the possibility of the public's making invidious comparisons between RFE and VOA. He said that with the short campaign there would not be time for the public to reflect on such issues.

Mr. Barrett reminded the group that NCFE had started as an organization to look after and make use of the various Eastern European refugee groups. He recalled that giving these groups a radio voice was something of a later development. He also recalled that the Crusade was established primarily as a cover for the governmental support of the enterprise. Mr. Barrett raised the question of whether or not the Crusade had grown to such proportions that it was now a case of the tail wagging the dog.

He also raised the question of whether the two or three million dollars that might be raised in the Crusade might be endangering the $85,000,000 involved in the appropriations for the USIE operations. He thought it was important to get back to the idea of just enough of a Crusade to give the minimum necessary cover to NCFE.

Mr. Jackson said that after the 1951 campaign it became clear to him that the Crusade had actually done an important selling job on the American public in the matter of psychological warfare and the importance of such an effort to our nation. He felt that this was a most important aspect of the Crusade and one that had been usually overlooked.

Mr. Washburn thought that the next Crusade need not have a specific goal and that such a change would help keep things in a low key.[9]

The meeting ended with full agreement that the 1952 Crusade for Freedom would be reduced in scope, with the details "worked out in close cooperation between NCFE, CIA and State."[10]

Reduction in Scope

General Clay was chairman of the Crusade for Freedom's board of directors meeting held on January 18, 1952. The board discussed the nature and scope of the upcoming 1952 campaign. They agreed that it would be "considerably reduced in scope, that the emphasis be taken off publicity and placed on fund raising with the promotional period being reduced from two months to two weeks or three weeks."[11]

DeWitt Poole Resigns

The resignation of DeWitt Poole as Vice-Chairman of the Board of Directors was announced and accepted with an effective date of March 31, 1953 — the third anniversary of DeWitt Poole joining the NCFE. C.D. Jackson was then approved as the next Vice-Chairman, effective April 1, 1952; he announced the receipt of the first contribution check of $500,000 to the NCFE from the contributions collected during the 1951 campaign.[12]

Fred Smith and Crusade Implosion

In February 1952, the public relations firm of Fred Smith & Company, New York, took over the public affairs and advertising activities of the 1952 Crusade for Freedom. Fred Smith himself replaced Abbott Washburn as Executive Vice Chairman of the Crusade campaign and reported only to the president and the Crusade's Board of Directors. Abbott Washburn remained in the position of a director for the Crusade for Freedom. C.D. Jackson wrote a letter to Fred Smith on February 15, 1952, giving him some details of what was expected from him. Jackson wrote, in part, "It is understood that the nature of CFF 1952 will be somewhat lower-keyed than in 1951. (The subsequently reduced budget for 1952 as compared with 1951 should take care of that.) The actual fund-raising campaign period in the fall will be shorter than formerly."[13]

Abbott Washburn wrote to Fred Smith on March 3, 1952, that one of his highest priorities was to find a replacement for General Clay as the National Chairman; the next priority was to find a 1952 Drive Chairman. Washburn included in this letter that the overall program and budget were to be submitted for approval to the Crusade's Executive Committee with the comment referring to the CIA, "Our friends in the South will also need to see this." According to the Washburn letter, one of the major problems that the 1951 Crusade faced was lack of 15 state chairmen.[14]

Fred Smith viewed his role as one to bring order and stability to a campaign and staff he saw as loose and informal under the leadership of Abbott Washburn. On April 28, 1952, he wrote to Crusade for Freedom president Admiral Harold Miller concerning the staff of the Crusade for Freedom:

> It must be borne in mind that the staff has not done anything constructive for a long period of time, and since it is made up of human beings, it doesn't relish the prospects of buckling down to a tight organization in which errors of omission can't talked out of existence or clouded beyond recognition.[15]

Smith continued to try to make fundamental changes to the structure and staff and wrote a strongly worded memorandum to the Crusade staff about the 1952 Plan:

This will require single-minded devotion to the project. It will require imagination, diligence and an absolutely irreducible minimum of freewheeling.

I realize that up until now, the Crusade has been a loose and informal operation. The type of campaigns, the ample budgets and the type of leadership in the past have all helped make that possible. We have a much more difficult campaign that the Crusade has ever faced. We have a budget that is only a fragment of previous budgets. The leadership of the Crusade is in differenthands; Abbot Washburn's talents make it possible for him to run a loose and informal organization. Mine don't.[16]

Crusade for Freedom Program for 1952

A summary plan for the Crusade campaign in 1952, presumably put together by Fred Smith or a member or his campaign team, identified its "handicaps," among which were:

- An almost fatally late start
- An all but disintegrated field organization
- A substantially reduced budget
- The loss of General Clay
- The absence of a dramatic new event in RFE picture, such as last year's opening of the 135 kW installation
- The continuing inherent handicap of trying to sell a largely intangible product.[17]

Opposed to these "handicaps," however, the plan listed some positive aspects:

- We still have an unassailable objective.
- We have a fairly solid reputation.
- The Crusade has a rather high acceptance among the media.
- The Crusade is associated with a respectable list of prominent figures at national, state, and city levels.

Fred Smith resigned as Executive Vice Chairman and was replaced by Richard B. Walsh, but the 1952 plans "were in disarray."[18]

The Crusade and Religion

In March 1952, Ralph Andrist, staff member of the Crusade for Freedom in New York, sent out a press release to almost 500 leading morning and evening newspapers with the title, "80,000,000 Christians and Jews in Fight Against Communism." The release began with "A movement, which will enlist the united spiritual strength of American Christians and Jews in establishing a bond of brotherhood with the victims of Communism ... will open with prayers by almost all communions and denominations on Saturday and Sunday, March 22 and 23, and will continue as a regular part of worship from that time on...."

The movement is entirely spiritual in nature, and will be tied in with no secular propaganda campaign."[19]

On March 10, 1952, Robert D. Jordan, Director of Church Promotion of the Crusade for Freedom staff, sent letters to the major religious groups in the United States: Catholic, Jewish, Anglican, Orthodox and Protestant, which, in part, read:

> In all, over 110,000 churches and synagogues are being asked to share in the commencement on March 23rd of a continuing program of prayer for those people in the captive countries of central Europe who have lost most of their freedoms and particularly their religious freedoms.
>
> The attached letter tells the simple story of the CRUSADE's objectives in this almost unprecedented request to the churches of America by a secular agency. We believe so very strongly that if we are ever to accomplish a world fellowship it must begin through a program such as this.[20]

The Million-Dollar Check

At the NCFE Board of Directors meeting on March 13, 1952, Admiral Miller announced that the Crusade for Freedom sent a check for its second contribution in the amount of $1,050,000 from the funds collected during the 1951 Crusade. At the same meeting, the Board agreed to appropriate $30,000 to the Committee for Cultural Freedom to be paid from the balance of funds remaining on hand in the Berlin Youth Movement special project fund account.

Clay Resigns

On April 19, 1952, Lucius D. Clay resigned as National Chairman of the Crusade for Freedom. The plan cited above the negative aspects of this for the Crusade: "His name has been of tremendous value; many chairmen and others have come aboard on the strength of Clay's participation.... It would be hard to find a name of such catholic power."[21] In his resignation letter to Admiral Miller, president of the National Committee for Free Europe who had joined the NCFE in April, Lucius Clay wrote, in part:

> I am grateful to have had the opportunity to serve in a cause devoted to the re-establishment of freedom in places where it has been lost.
>
> I am also grateful to have been associated with the hundreds of thousands American citizens who have joined the Crusade to indicate their desire to participate in this cause.
>
> However, I feel now that the Crusade can progress even more rapidly under new and fresh leadership. Thus, I would like to submit my resignation as Chairman to take effect immediately.[22]

On May 1, 1952, C.D. Jackson resigned as president of National Committee for a Free Europe but was elected Vice-Chairman of the NCFE Board of Directors to replace DeWitt Poole. Joseph Grew was elected President of NCFE.[23]

August 5 Special Meeting

Admiral Miller said at the August 5, 1952, special meeting of the Board of Directors, that the 1951 headquarters and field office expenditures amounted to $1,998,653 while the 1951 budget had been set at $1,173,000, or $825,652 over budget. The Board approved the expenditure to cover the difference. The 1952 budget was $44,454 per month for the 1952 fiscal year (March 1, 1952, to February 28, 1953), but the initial budget did not cover the months of January and February; thus the final budget approved by the Board was $533,448 — a dramatic decrease from 1951.[24]

Also at the August 5 meeting, Lucius Clay's resignation was reluctantly accepted by the board of directors, which then passed a resolution in gratitude of General Clay's leadership:

> WHEREAS, under his inspired leadership the Crusade for Freedom developed into a most important cause devoted to the re-establishment of freedom in places where it has been lost, and
> WHEREAS, millions of Americans have joined in the moral and financial support of the Crusade for Freedom to indicate their desire to participate in the re-establishment of freedom where it has been denied....
> BE IT RESOLVED: that the Board ... express to General Lucius D. Clay in behalf of millions of Americans as well as millions of enslaved peoples everywhere, their every sincere sentiment of gratitude and good wishes.

Henry Ford II and Other Business

During their August 5, 1952, meeting, the Board of Directors elected Henry Ford II to the offices of Director and Chairman of the Board of Directors of the Crusade for Freedom. C.D Jackson was elected to the Executive Committee.

The Board also approved $250,000 transfer to the Committee for Free Asia from the 1951 campaign in a ratio of 7:1. The original goal of the Crusade had been $3,500,000 with the intention of giving $500,000 to the Committee for Free Asia. Although that goal had not been reached, the Board decided to keep the 7:1 ratio, thus the Committee for Free Asia was given only $250,000.

Eleanor Roosevelt

Eleanor Roosevelt, in her syndicated column, *My Day*, on September 3, 1952, urged her readers to take urgent action to prevent war:

On Armistice Day this year the Advertising Council will begin its fund-raising drive and Crusade for Freedom drive.

One of the objectives of this group is to "step up the war of ideas against the Communists, especially behind the Iron Curtain, beat them in it."

If the Freedom Crusade people can do this they hope to reduce the chances of ruinous shooting war. They feel they must carry this fight into the Communist-dominated countries themselves.

Radio Free Europe and Radio Free Asia are increasingly proving effective weapons in this struggle, and the support of the American people in this crusade will mean that each one of us will have a chance to fight personally against Soviet aggression. Four million dollars is needed to help support this radio effort, so join the Crusade for Freedom when the drive opens on Armistice Day.

Freedom-Gram Centers

A test "Freedom-Gram Center" was set up at the Park Sheraton Hotel in New York, beginning on the weekend of September 21, 1952, for persons to tape-record a personal message that would later be broadcast over Radio Free Europe, Radio Free Asia, and the Voice of America.

Charles E. Wilson, former president of General Electric, was elected the Campaign Chairman. He opened a "Freedom-Gram Center" on Sunday and it would continue through the following Friday. Also on Sunday, Greek Orthodox, Jewish, Protestant, and Roman Catholic leaders recorded messages. In the hotel lobby, there was an electric sign that listed two of the "biggest" Communist lies broadcast by Radio Moscow and Radio Peiping. Visitors to the center could then tape-record responses to these lies.

Over the next days, broadcasts were reserved for specific exile group leaders to broadcast in their national language, e.g., Monday was set aside for the Baltic states, Tuesday for Albanian and Bulgarian, with Friday scheduled for "Far East" languages.[25]

The 1952 campaign, called "one of the free world's most successful weapons against Communism," was scheduled to run from Armistice Day, November 11, 1952, to December 15, 1952. The focus of the campaign was to be on Radio Free Europe and Radio Free Asia:

At stake will be the continued vigorous operation and expansion of Radio Free Europe and Radio Free Asia, both of them living proof that the average American citizen has a means of attacking Communism behind the Iron Curtain.[26]

Miller Letter to Newspapers

Retired Admiral Harold B. Miller, former Director of RFE, now President of the Crusade for Freedom, sent out an appeal letter to newspapers around the country on October 7, 1952. The letter read, in part,

The outcome of the psychological war may not only determine whether or not we are plunged into a global shooting war, but the kind of world our children and grandchildren may live in.

The best way to fight Communist aggression and oppression is to enlist the support of the American people. Then, and only then, will the Kremlin and its puppet regimes behind the Iron Curtain realize that America means business in the battle for men's hearts and minds.

Starting November 11, the Crusade for Freedom will conduct its Third Annual Campaign to gain the American people's moral and financial support in this fight against Communism. The Crusade needs $4,000,000 to continue and expand the activities of Radio Free Europe and Radio Free Asia. The Crusade will also ask Americans to sign millions of "Freedom-Grams" as their personal pledges of hope for a free world.

We hope, in addition to your support of other public service campaigns, you will — as you have for the past two years— publish this important Crusade message.[27]

Henry Fonda Film and Television Spots

By October 1952, the Advertising Council had produced for the upcoming Crusade two television spots, one for twenty seconds, the second one for one minute, plus a ten-minute motion picture narrated by famed actor Henry Fonda. The film was distributed to television station managers and sent to state and local chairmen for use in "men's clubs, women's groups, labor and fraternal organizations, and campaign meetings."[28]

Curtain-Raiser Meeting in Chicago

There was "Crusade for Freedom Campaigners" meeting for state, city, and regional chairmen in Chicago, Illinois, October 25–27, 1952, at the Hotel Knickerbocker. It was billed as a "curtain raiser," with the premise that "The Crusade will conduct a nationwide drive for funds, during which it will present a new idea in psychological warfare to back up and bolster its primary job, the operation of Radio Free Europe and Radio Free Asia." Chairman Henry Ford II gave the objectives of the campaign, which was to begin on November 11, 1952:

> In carrying the truth behind the Iron Curtain, we shall offer every American the opportunity to send messages of hope and friendship to captive peoples.... We must demonstrate not only to the captive peoples, but also to the whole world, that the objective of the American people is world peace, and in this campaign the broadcasting of truth over Radio Free Europe and Radio Free Asia is essential.[29]

President-Elect Eisenhower and Adlai Stevenson Open 1952 Crusade

Dwight D. Eisenhower was overwhelmingly elected President of the United States on November 5, 1952. Afterwards, he recorded a radio message in behalf of the third Crusade for Freedom campaign that was broadcast in a 15-minute program on November 11, 1952, carried by the four radio networks: CBS, ABC, NBC and Mutual Broadcast System. The next day, his message was quoted in newspapers throughout the United States. Crusade Chairman Henry Ford II, as program moderator, began the broadcast with these words:

> The words you are about to hear cannot be muffled or distorted or hidden away by the Communist suppressors of truth. Radio Free Europe and Radio Free Asia will carry the story and no force can stop it.

Eisenhower continued his Cold-War rhetoric in his radio address, when he said that the purpose of Radio Free Europe's broadcast "was actively to oppose communism — to fight the big lie with the big truth." He added,

> The Communists have isolated their people to keep them from ever hearing the truth — to create a vacuum in their minds which will absorb lies because there is nothing else for them to seize on.
> The only way to frustrate this evil manipulation of human minds and emotions is to supply the truth, which gives the oppressed people a measuring stick to lay against each lie that is told to them.
> People believe lies only when they have no opportunity to hear the truth.
> The Crusade for Freedom, through Radio Free Europe, is supplying the truth. Men and women who might otherwise have succumbed to the philosophy that it is good to be slaves still keep alive the sparks of freedom in their hearts.[30]

Eisenhower's opponent was Governor Adlai Stevenson of Illinois, who also recorded for his broadcast remarks about Radio Free Europe and the Crusade for Freedom. In part, Stevenson said:

> The programs have a spontaneity and freshness, which no official information agency can have. Freedom speaks most clearly between man and man, when its voice is neither muffled nor amplified by government intervention nor other official trappings.
> There are mounting indications of the effectiveness of free radio broadcasts.... One of the best tests is the shrill violence of the attacks upon them by Radio Moscow betraying the deep concern of the Communist rulers about these efforts.
> Freedom is shielded by other things than steel and gunpowder. Vigilance in freedom's defense is served by other than military means. The survival of freedom is best assured by the will to be free.
> It is the work of the crusade to tend the flame of the will to be free, to feed and fan it wherever possible, to keep it flickering in places where if may be burning low. The success of the crusade will mean firm friends and allies in places of critical need behind the enemy's walls erected to keep out the truth.

Henry Ford commented on Eisenhower and Stevenson's speeches: "The joint statement of the two political rivals showed this nation is strongly united in the cause of freedom."[31]

Advertising Council and the Freedom-Gram

The third Crusade for Freedom began nationwide on the local level on November 11, 1952. The objectives, as listed by the Advertising Council, were

> Obtain the moral support and signatures of millions of Americans who want a chance to participate personally in the fight against Soviet aggression by sending messages of freedom behind the Iron Curtain.
> Obtain the sum of $4,000,000 needed to support and expand the activities of Radio Free Europe and Radio Free Asia.[32]

The Advertising Council with Allan Brown, vice president of the Bakelite Company, acting as a "Volunteer Coordinator," sent out a kit early in October to newspapers around the Untied States. The editors were told that the proofs and scripts would be available by October 15, 1952. Brown wrote, "We appreciate the support of those who contributed time and space to this campaign in the past. And this year, the need for your help is even more urgent."[33]

The "Freedom-Gram," shown in Figure 9, replaced the Freedom Scroll and used a more personal religious theme than the one that was on the Freedom Scroll. The Freedom-Gram promoted citizen participation and individual communication with persons behind the Iron Curtain: "*Your* signature and those of millions of Americans are needed now on Freedom-Grams such as this." On the backside of the Freedom-Gram, this message was translated into Albanian, Czech, Slovak, Polish, Hungarian, Romanian and Bulgarian:

> Do you listen to Radio Free Europe? I hope you do, for I am one of millions of American citizens who has voluntarily contributed to build these stations, which bring Truth to you who are deprived of it.
> In America millions voluntarily pray for an understanding between our peoples. Please add your prayers to ours. Surely our common faith in God is the place where hope for freedom begins.
>
>   I am a (occupation) _____
>   Name _____
>   Address _____
>
> Note to Contributors: Replies to this Freedom-Gram may be received in a foreign language. If you should be unable to translate them, free translations may be obtained by forwarding the letters to Crusade for Freedom c/o your local Postmaster.

Six million Americans signed Freedom-Grams, which were then sent to Germany for inclusion in the balloons provided by the Free European Press and sent over the Iron Curtain in the months that followed.

Figure 9. Freedom-Gram and cover of information pamphlet, including mention of Radio Free Asia, used in 1952 Crusade campaign.

"Flying Saucers"

The Advertising Council sent out the following advertisements in October 1952 for the Crusade campaign with information about the Free Europe Press balloon operations and Radio Free Asia:

This "Flying Saucer" carries Truth!
The word "SVOBODA" on the balloon in this picture is the Czech word for "Freedom." Supplementing Radio Free Europe in 1951, thousands of these "Flying Saucer" balloons were released by Crusade for Freedom along the borders of the Iron Curtain countries. They contained messages of hope and courage from millions of Americans who joined in the 1951 Crusade for Freedom.

LOOK WHAT YOU DID
In the last two years the contributions of Americans to the Crusade for Freedom have amounted to $3,500,000. This money helped make possible Radio Free Europe's thirteen transmitters in Germany and Portugal. It also helped establish Radio Free Asia, which broadcasts to China in four different languages. These facilities are used daily to spike Communist lies and satisfy the hunger of millions for truth.

MORE HELP NEEDED!
In 1952, at least $4,000,000 and the signatures of millions more Americans on

leaflets ("Freedom-Grams") are needed — not only to carry on this operation but also to expand it on an even bigger scale.

Give us this day ... Our daily truth

This is the whispered prayer of millions behind the Iron Curtain. This prayer, this plea is addressed to you — to every American whose contributions have made Radio Free Europe possible.[34]

Pavel Tigrid and Religious Leaders

In December 1952, Pavel (Paul) Tigrid, Program Director of RFE's Voice of Free Czechoslovakia, who had spoken at the inaugural radio broadcasts of Radio Free Europe in Munich, traveled around the United States in support of the Crusade campaign by speaking before local civic groups. For example, after leaving Milwaukee, Wisconsin, he visited four cities in Montana in early December: Billings, Helena, Great Falls, and Missoula. On December 15, 1952, the local newspaper of Austin, Minnesota, used a UPI report for one of its articles, which said that Tigrid gave a "tingling" report of the successes of RFE. Tigrid was quoted as saying, "The violent reactions our broadcasts have brought from the Communists are evidence of their success.... The programs go through. The letters we get and the refugees who slip through the Iron Curtain tell us daily of the program's success."[35]

As part of the notice announcing Tigrid's visits, three religious leaders appeared in an advertisement "A Plea to All Americans of All Faiths." Short statements from each accompanied their photographs and the Freedom-Gram:

The Reverend Blahoslav Hruby, Union of Czechoslovak Protestants in USA and Canada:
And ye shall know the truth and the truth shall make you free! — These words of Jesus are a great source of hope and inspiration to captive churches and nations. Radio Free Europe is keeping alive the spirit of freedom among the victims of the Communist imperialism. It is not only a privilege but it is a duty for all of us— Protestants, Catholics, Orthodox and Jews— to support wholeheartedly the cause of liberty and democracy in captive countries which is being espoused by the 1952 Crusade for Freedom.

Monsignor Bela Varga:
Having lived and fought against the Godless terror of the Communists behind the Iron Curtain, I know how they use the weapons of hate and lies and torture to gain control of the hearts and minds of men. Over Radio Free Europe, on which I am privileged to broadcast to my imprisoned countrymen, the spirit of hope and freedom is kept alive. Through the Crusade for Freedom all Americans can support the campaign of Truth against Communism.

Rabbi Simon G. Kramer, President of the Synagogue Council of America:
We, together with our fellow Americans of all faiths and races, are deeply grateful to the Almighty for the greatest measure of freedom we enjoy here in America. We join all liberty-loving men and women throughout the world in a prayer for

a new dawn when freedom will be granted to those people of all faiths now imprisoned by the Communists behind the Iron Curtain. The Crusade for Freedom is fighting for this new day and I heartily urge all Americana to support its goals.

In Colorado, the editorial in the *Greeley Tribune* newspaper on December 5, 1952, not only encouraged Greeley residents to support the Crusade with donations and Freedom-Gram signatures but also cited the Crusade for Freedom as four proofs of the effectiveness of Radio Free Europe:

- Thousands of letters from behind the Iron Curtain attest to the fact that Radio Free Europe and Radio Free Asia are listened to avidly and are doing an effective, hard-hitting job.
- The Soviets threatened all the station's Germany personnel with execution by hanging when Russia "liberates" Western Europe.
- The Czech Communist government issued an official note of protest to our Government demanding that Radio Free Europe be taken off the air. (The United States replied by reminding the Red rulers that Freedom of Speech is a fundamental of our American democracy.)
- Escapees from behind the Iron Curtain report a tremendous interest in the broadcasts.

Harold B. Miller visited Ogden, Utah, in the first week of December and demonstrated the balloon launchings and spoke to employees of the Clearfield Naval Supply Depot. In his remarks, Miller said, "There's no such thing as Communism, but only a murderous Stalinism bent on enslaving the world to the Russians." He was further quoted as saying, "the prospect of Stalinism sweeping the world is most frightful and this country must buoy up people behind the Iron Curtain with the assurance that there are better days ahead."[36]

Advertising Council Threats to Pull Plug

The Advertising Council campaign review committee meeting on December 17, 1952, noted that newspaper mat orders were 11,000 in 1950, 8,000 in 1951, but only 4,000 in 1952. This was "due in very large part to the fact that Crusade for Freedom local committees were almost nonexistent." While the Advertising Council was apparently pleased that the advertising for the previous three years of the Crusade had been excellent, and the results were due mostly to the Crusade's own administration and organization, there would be no further support from the Advertising Council for another year unless "convincing evidence is presented that defects in the Crusade for Freedom have been remedied and that there are sufficient numbers of active, local committees to take advantage of national advertising."[37] Such evidence was evidently produced as the Advertising Council continued with its massive public relations and advertising campaigns in support of the Crusade for Freedom.

Doubts about Radio Free Asia

The Advertising Council leadership was doubtful about continuing an advertising campaign for the Committee for a Free Asia and Radio Free Asia:

Consideration must be given to our relationship, if any in 1952 to Committee for Free Asia. In 1951, when CFA got organized (with funds supplied by NCFE), as recited in CFA's prospectus, Crusade raised its stated goal from $3 to $3½ million to get Radio Free Asia started. This was done largely in deference to the attitude on the West Coast, which tends still to be oriented more toward Asia than toward Europe. This association with RFA doubtless was advantageous to Crusade on the Coast, even though we could speak of RFA in only the vaguest terms (it did not begin its broadcasts until September and when it did do so the explosion was inaudible).

The advantage to the Crusade of having RFA on its team to round out the feeling of a world fight against Communism presumably remains the same. Over against this is the possible danger of the Crusade being associated in the public mind with an organization with which it has no close association. There is no discoverable body of opinion in CFF/RFE/NCFE which holds that RFA or it corporate parent, CFA, knows what it's doing or is going about it wisely or adeptly.

The problem of Communism (and combating it) in Asia is considerably different from that in Europe, strategically and philosophically (as anyone reading Charles Malik's recent LIFE article is likely to be persuaded)—let alone tactically. It solves no problem to recite this fact to our West Coast friends as a reason why "we" (RFE) don't add a transmitter aimed at China. Committee for Free Asia is an established fact. It has prestige on the Coast by reason of its membership. But so far no word of its doings has come to our attention which spells large accomplishment.[38]

Civil Air Patrol

On Saturday December 13, 1952, the Civil Air Patrol, at the request of North Carolina state chairman Gordon Gray, dropped Freedom-Grams over towns and cities in North Carolina. Twenty-three squadrons, each with four planes, of the CAP were used. Newspapers advised readers: "You can help truth fight communism by Joining the Crusade for Freedom and contributing to this important fight. When you receive your 'Freedom-Gram' as they are dropped from Civil Air Patrol planes, fill in the bottom with your occupation, name and address, and return it with your contribution to Gastonia Junior Chamber of Commerce."[39]

Freedom Girl and Santa Claus

On December 3, 1952, the *Pittsburgh Press* newspaper carried a small article and photograph with the caption: "Pittsburgh 'Red Invader' Surrenders—'Russian Soldier' Stephen Radkoff, really a Pittsburgh actor, remains grim to the end as he surrenders to Freedom Girl Miyal Harvey and Howard G. Burr, center, chairman of Western Pennsylvania Crusade for Freedom." The article described how local Crusade chairman Burr had arranged for Radkoff to walk around the streets of Pittsburgh in a Russian soldier's uniform on December 2, 1952, hoping to get some sort of reaction from passersby. But, the newspaper reported that the "Red Invader" had gathered little attention from the citizens of Pittsburgh.

Chairman Burr also arranged for a "take-over" of a Pittsburgh television broadcast at 11 P.M. by three men pretending to be "Red Agents." For a few minutes, they turned the television station into a "Communist propaganda outlet," according to the newspaper account. Burr told the newspaper, "These were stunts, but we think that they are necessary to bring home to all of us just what is going on behind the Iron Curtain."

Chairman Burr was also seen in a local newspaper photograph, with the caption "A Christmas Message of Hope," with Santa Claus and three young girls, two of whom were holding a Crusade for Freedom poster. Burr was quoted as saying,

> Christmas isn't a happy day behind the Iron Curtain, but neither is any other day. We have to let those people, who are on our side in this struggle, know that we here in the United States have not forgotten them. Everyone must know what the Crusade is doing, and join in its work, either though contributions or by signing Freedom-Grams—the messages of hope which the Crusade transmits behind the Iron Curtain.[40]

On December 19, 1952, in cooperation with the Crusade for Freedom and Radio Free Europe, ABC's nation-wide radio network broadcast the program "Caroling Through the Iron Curtain."

Nevada Campaign

In some states, the local Crusade got off to a rather late start. In Nevada, for example, the state Crusade was announced in December 1952, but the associated activities began on January 18, 1953, because of a conflict with the local March of Dimes campaign. The goal was 50,000 signatures on the Freedom-Grams and contributions of $10,000. In some cities in Nevada, the campaign would last only a week and there was heavy emphasis on local school children to take home the Freedom-Grams for their parents' signatures. Perhaps because of the late start, the Nevada Crusade did not have enough Freedom-Grams and more had to be ordered. One example of this was this "heart-warming" story:

> With the campaign only a day old in Humboldt County the chairman there, Howard W. Lindsay, had to request additional supplies of Freedom-grams for signing, having nearly reached his goal in a day's time. On top of that 20 children of the Clover Valley School at Red House, near Getchell Mine, wrote to the Crusade headquarters asking for a supply of Freedom-grams. The letter was signed by 20

students, some just able to scrawl their names, and it advised the Crusade headquarters that not only were the students anxious to sign the Freedom-gram but had also been saving their pennies and dimes to make a school contribution toward the expansion of the radio transmitter facilities of Radio Free Europe and Radio Free Asia.[41]

In the Nevada 1952 campaign, a local version of Freedom-Gram was used. This one included space to write in 50 words, or less, the message the reader wanted to send behind the Iron Curtain:

> Join the Crusade for Freedom!
> Perhaps your message to the peoples of the Communist Satellites will win one of three Nevada prizes to be awarded by the Slate Committee for the Third Annual Crusade for Freedom.
> This Announcement in the Interest of Truth Against Communism Sponsored by SIERRA PACIFIC POWER COMPANY.[42]

James S. Brennan, a University of Nevada student, won a $25 U.S. savings bond for his Freedom-Gram entry that won the first prize:

> To all the enslaved people in the nightmare of Communist administrations: The free peoples of the world have not forgotten you. Through the United Nations and all possible means, we are tirelessly working for your freedom. Keep up your courage. We have not forgotten you.[43]

Whitney Shepardson

On April 10, 1953, the new President of the National Committee for a Free Europe, Whitney Shepardson, sent a complimentary copy of the NCFE's President's Report 1952 to CIA Director Allen Dulles. In his cover letter, he praised his predecessor Admiral Miller and then wrote: "As his successor, I assure you that our officers and staff will continue to improve the effectiveness and quality of this vital undertaking." The President's Report concluded with:

> Accomplishments such as those described in this report can be brought about only through the inspired efforts of dedicated people. Space does not permit naming even a small fraction of those whose work has made this organization possible. In closing, I would like to record personal and official thanks to the following groups and individuals:
> • To every man, woman and child among the 25 million who have given moral or financial support to the Crusade for Freedom; to those who signed the Freedom Scrolls or Freedom-Grams.
> • To every volunteer worker for the Crusade for Freedom throughout the length and breadth of the United States of America.
> • To every church, every school, every labor union, every service organization or club, whose members have given us backing, official and unofficial.
> • To all of those in the great profession of communicating ideas— the columnists, the feature writers, the cartoonists, the editors, the owners of newspapers; to the great radio chains and the men operating small stations; to the commen-

MR. AND MRS. MURDERER!

Radio Free Europe is telling all of Romania about this bloodthirsty couple and their secret torture chamber!

UNTIL 10 A.M., December 27th, they were simply Mr. and Mrs. Margineanu, distinguished citizens of Blaj, respected and admired by the entire community. And then ...

"This is Radio Free Europe. People of Romania, listen to this information we have received from the underground at Blaj. Among the foremost aides of the Chief of the Security Police are a young married couple named Margineanu. Together with other members of the governmental gang, they patronize blood orgies nightly. Those freedom-loving Romanians not in sympathy with the Communist regime are dragged before them and beaten to death. While the torture goes on, the wine bottle is passed around—and there is much toasting and singing.

The names of other regular participants are as follows ..."

The crimes against the captive nation are revealed each day by Radio Free Europe. Traitors, informers and "quislings" are named. Lives of anti-communist patriots are saved. Truth is piercing the Iron Curtain and spreading fear and confusion among Communist overlords and their collaborators.

Support the Crusade For Freedom!

Slowly but surely the true face of Communism is being exposed and the cold war is being won. But Radio Free Europe urgently needs more help from its sponsor—You!

The Crusade for Freedom needs at least

$4,000,000 this year to support and expand the operations of Radio Free Europe and Radio Free Asia.

This Crusade cannot succeed without your help. Radio Free Europe and Radio Free Asia need your contributions to help fight red lies with truth and to win the cold war.

Get behind this truth campaign now! Help bring to millions the promise of future freedom. Send your contribution to Crusade for Freedom, c/o your local Postmaster.

Help Truth Fight Communism.
Give To CRUSADE FOR FREEDOM

 Contributed in the public interest by **SPONSOR'S NAME**

Figure 10. Mr. and Mrs. Murderer. Illustrated advertisement seen in newspapers in 1952-1953 Campaign (courtesy Advertising Council).

tators, the announcers, and those who write or produce radio and television shows; to the great public figures and bit actors, the property men and others in radio and television who are responsible for the immense backing given to the Crusade for Freedom.

• To those foundations and corporations which have generously given funds to support the work of this Committee. Particular mention should be made of those who have donated, with the help of the Advertising Council, radio time or newspaper space dedicated to the Crusade for Freedom.[44]

Federal Campaign and CIA

Edward F. Bartelt, Fiscal Assistant Secretary of the Treasury since 1945, was the National Chairman for Federal Employees for the 1952 Crusade for Freedom. James E. Chaney, United States Attorney General, wrote to Bartelt on October 23, 1952, on the subject of the RFE, RFA and the Crusade for Freedom:

> In these troubled times there is no more important cause than the fight against Communism. Truth is the most devastating weapon against Communism. To broadcast the truth is the high objective of the distinguished Americans sparking this noble mission — the mission to destroy the Iron Curtain that deprives hundreds of millions of enslaved persons from learning the real facts about this vicious ideology and its tyrannical leaders.
>
> To win through peaceful methods and education, Radio Free Europe and Radio Free Asia greatly need more facilities to combat the evil forces so that truth will ultimately prevail. The success of the Crusade for Freedom spells peace and happiness for mankind everywhere.[45]

On October 27, 1952, Edward F. Bartelt wrote to Walter Bedell Smith, Director of the Central Intelligence Agency, in a surprising effort to get that agency to support and endorse the Crusade for Freedom and Radio Free Europe through individual contributions:

> My dear General Smith,
>
> On November 11, the Crusade for Freedom will open its third annual drive to get the popular support of the American people in order to help Truth fight Communism.
>
> I am enclosing for your information a 10-page Fact Sheet that tells the story of Radio Free Europe; its aims; how it operates and its effectiveness. Beginning at page 6 of this Fact Sheet are set forth the operations of the CRUSADE FOR FREEDOM against Communism in Asia.
>
> The purpose of this letter is to solicit the support of your department in the 1952 CRUSADE FOR FREEDOM, both in Washington and in the field. One of the ways in which your department could contribute to the success of the 1952 CRUSADE would be to arrange for as many group meetings of employees as possible, particularly among the supervisory staffs who would be in a position to convey the message to the employees under their respective jurisdiction. Also, it would be helpful if the CRUSADE FOR FREEDOM might have your endorsement and if the head of each bureau and office would address an appropriate letter to all field offices calling attention to the CRUSADE and requesting their cooperation.

On 18 November, 1952, an unidentified person at the Central Intelligence Agency telephoned Bartelt's office and said that, "CIA as a matter of policy does not participate in campaigns, and apologizes for his not having been earlier informed."[46]

Drew Pearson Exposes Source of Funds

Drew Pearson exposed the true source of RFE's funding when he wrote in his syndicated column on March 13, 1953:

> To get around this fact and the further fact that official U.S. propaganda must be far more cautious than unofficial propaganda, Radio Free Europe and Radio Free Asia were set up. However, it's now pretty well known in Europe, including Russia, that these two organizations are actually subsidized by the United States. That's why Radio Free Europe has lost part of its effectiveness. And if congressional investigators ever started probing Radio Free Asia they would find about $6,000,000 spent with little accomplished.
>
> Radio Free Europe was a live-wire influential organization when C.D. Jackson, able chief of Ike's psychological warfare board, was in charge. But it's gone downhill since.
>
> General "Beetle" Smith, the astute undersecretary of state who is now ruling on the Voice of America, happens to be in a paradoxical position regarding propaganda. As former head of Central Intelligence, Smith poured several millions into Radio Free Europe, which was partly competing with the Voice of America. Many State Department officials deeply resented that competition and the publicity buildup given it in the United States.[47]

Final Numbers

The 1952 Crusade for Freedom was a financial disappointment as it took in contributions of only $861,340.92 against expenses of $922,130.45. This was the lowest amount of money raised in the Crusade's history.[48]

CHAPTER FIVE

Help Stop World War III
Before It Starts:
With Truth Dollars!

Clay and Washburn Resign from Crusade for Freedom

On January 28, 1953, Lucius Clay resigned from his positions as a member of the Board of Directors and as a corporate member: "While I have been honored to serve as a member of the Board of Directors and a Corporate member of the Crusade for Freedom, I have found that in the past year it has been increasingly difficult for me to give the time to this cause which it deserves. I therefore tender my resignation."[1]

Abbott Washburn was appointed by President Eisenhower to the Committee on International Information Activities and resigned from the Crusade's Board of Directors and as a director on February 5, 1953, effective January 20, 1953: "I do so regretfully and with every good wish for continued success in this very important undertaking."[2]

Dwight Eisenhower also resigned from the Crusade for Freedom, but his letter, seen by Henry Ford II, was lost between the Ford Motor Company and the Crusade for Freedom office in New York.[3]

American Heritage Foundation

Due to the rather disappointing results of the 1952 Crusade campaign in terms of contributions and performance of the staff, Arthur Page of the National Committee for a Free Europe (NCFE) had preliminary discussions with Thomas D'Arcy Brophy, president of the American Heritage Foundation (AHF), with the view that the latter take over the fundraising campaign for the 1954 Crusade. At the NCFE director's meeting on March 17, 1953, Page reported that he and Brophy had agreed, in principle, that

1. The Crusade for Freedom should finish its current campaign and conclude its money-raising activities not later than June 30, 1953, and should thereafter cease all activity, it being understood that whatever steps possible would be taken to preserve the name "Crusade for Freedom" in view of its established value and widespread acceptance.

2. The Heritage Foundation would take over full responsibility for the next year's money-raising campaign for NCFE, assuming the same position vis-à-vis NCFE as the Crusade for Freedom has heretofore occupied, the sole NCFE responsibility being to check the Heritage Foundation publicity to be sure it accurately reflected the facts.

3. The Heritage Foundation may use the "Crusade for Freedom" name during its fund-raising campaign but that right, title and interest in the name "Crusade for Freedom," to the extent possible, would remain in the National Committee for a Free Europe.[4]

On March 31, 1953, Admiral Harold Miller, president of the Crusade for Freedom, wrote to the Trustees of the American Heritage Foundation with a formal request that full responsibility for operating the "Crusade for Freedom" be taken over by the American Heritage Foundation "because it believes that this important citizen's movement can best be carried on" by that organization. He concluded his letter with, "Should you decide that this job can be undertaken by the American Heritage Foundation, the Crusade for Freedom, Inc., is prepared to underwrite your basic expenses."[5]

At the April 3, 1953, Harold Miller at the annual meeting of the board of directors, asked Arthur Page, chairman of the Executive Committee, on how best to achieve the planned relationship between the Crusade and the American Heritage Foundation. Page suggested the following:

1. Dissolve the Crusade for Freedom
2. Consolidation
3. Leave the corporation intact

The Crusade's board decided to "preserve the corporate entity of the Crusade" and that the American Heritage Foundation would conduct the next campaign under a contractual agreement.[6] On April 6, 1953, the president of the American Heritage Foundation, Thomas D'A. Brophy, replied,

Our Trustees gave careful consideration to your proposal at a meeting held on March 31, 1953. After discussion, it was the unanimous decision of the meeting that the American Heritage Foundation accept responsibility and undertake the program. This commitment is subject to reconsideration by us after a period of one year.[7]

At the April 21, 1953, monthly meeting of the NCFE, Arthur Page reported on developments of the next Crusade for Freedom campaign to be conducted by the American Heritage Foundation. He added that the Crusade for Freedom had not been dissolved and its name could continue to be used in the future. Harold Miller said, "Crusade, for all practical purposes, was sub-contracting the Crusade for Freedom campaign to the Foundation for a year and that appropriate notices would be sent out by the Crusade." On May 15, 1953, Henry Ford II was elected chairman of the board of trustees of the American Heritage Foundation.[8] Harold Miller and Thomas D'Arcy Brophy signed a "Memorandum of Understanding between Crusade for Freedom and American Heritage Foundation" on July 1, 1953.[9]

The budget for the National Committee for a Free Europe for 1953-1954 was approved at $18,336,206, the bulk of which went for Radio Free Europe's operating costs of $11,173,748, and capital expenses of $1,559,275.[10]

The budget transferred to the American Heritage Foundation for the 1953-1954 Crusade for Freedom, for the twelve months from July 1, 1953, to June 30, 1954, was $900,000.[11]

Radio Free Asia Ceases Broadcasting

On March 31, 1953, Harold Miller, president of the Crusade for Freedom sent a letter to the American Heritage Foundation which included information about Radio Free Asia. In particular, "The Committee for Free Asia is a different kind of operation. It works with and for Asia groups and individuals in *free countries*. Because of the delicate nature of any Western relations with Asian groups and individuals, particularly in those countries which have only recently become independent, CFA's operations must necessarily be less militantly anti–Communist."[12] Apparently unbeknownst to the Crusade, in March 1953, the Central Intelligence Agency reviewed Radio Free Asia's broadcasting operation and decided to stop broadcasting. The CIA then sent its findings in a report dated April 1, 1953, to W.H. Jackson, chairman of the President's Committee on International Information Activities. C.D. Jackson was on the Committee. The findings were summarized in the committee's report to President Eisenhower on June 30, 1953.

1954 Crusade Outline Plan

In July 1953, the John Price Jones Company completed a "Preliminary Outline Plan for the Crusade for Freedom sponsored by the American Heritage Foundation." There were two optimistic objectives:

1. To raise at least $5,000,000 for the work of the National Committee for a Free Europe and Radio Free Europe.
2. To enlist the participation and support of at least 25,000,000 American citizens, as a demonstration of the broad interest in restoring freedom to the enslaved nations and as evidence of an awareness of the danger to this nation by communist aggression.[13]

There was to be a fundamental shift in the method of conducting the campaign:

1. An intensive campaign for advance special gifts from corporations, foundations and wealthy individuals. This effort will be carried on as in-family effort without attendant publicity.
2. A nation-wide popular campaign for gifts of money and for pledges of participation and support for the cause.[14]

The fund-raising goal of the July 1953 plan was $5,000,000, with "the hope that $3,500,000 to $4,000,000 of this might be raised in a very selective special gifts effort." That was a fundamental shift from the emphasis on individual American contributions to that of large corporate contributions.

Continuing Cover

The question of "cover" of CIA involvement with Radio Free Europe became central to the 1953 Jackson Committee report to President Eisenhower on United States International Information Activities:

Certain specific problems arise in connection with NCFE activities, particularly RFE. There is first the question of cover. It has been suggested that, because the present cover has worn thin, RFE's official connections be freely admitted. Such a course, however, would vitiate the principal reason for the existence of RFE as a separate organization. So long as its government connections are not officially admitted it can broadcast programs and take positions for which the United States would not desire to accept responsibility. The Committee believes that the present cover is adequate for this purpose.[15]

Operation Prospero

PROSPERO was the code name for the balloon program in the summer 1953, when over four days, 6,500 balloons with over 12,000,000 Free Europe Press leaflets were launched into Czechoslovakia.[16] The balloon launching started approximately at midnight July 13, 1953, in the Bavarian town of Tirschenreuth. This was the first time balloons were launched in conjunction with specific Radio Free Europe programs. RFE attacked the regime's new currency reforms and dropped a leaflet in the form of a banknote and an aluminum replica of a newly introduced Czechoslovak coin bearing the Freedom Bell and the inscription, "All Czechs and Slovaks for Freedom — all the Free World for Czechs and Slovaks."

At the July 14, 1953, NCFE Meeting, Spencer Phenix showed the other directors samples of the leaflets and read translations of the message texts. Reportedly, the NCFE "expressed great interest in the operation and pleasure at the dynamic content of the printed message."[17]

There was coverage of the balloon launchings throughout the United States. For example, on July 22, 1953, the Reno *Evening Gazette* newspaper published a photograph of a balloon launching with this caption:

> ON THE WINDS OF FREEDOM—A German student prepares to launch a huge balloon filled with messages to residents of Soviet controlled Czechoslovakia from a secluded farm close to the Czech border in project sponsored by Radio Free Europe and known as "Winds of Freedom." Man in foreground is using counting device to tally the balloon, one of 8000, which were released carrying news of the June 17 riots in East Berlin and the ouster of Laventy P. Berla.

The Czechoslovak government protested this balloon action on July 20, 1953. The U.S. State Department rejected the protest on July 29, 1953, "on the grounds that the operation was carried out by the Crusade for Freedom, a private U.S. organization."[18]

"Freedom Tank"

After two years of secret planning and preparation, on July 25, 1953, Vaclav Uhlik crashed an armor-plated vehicle through the Iron Curtain near the Bavarian town of Wald-Muenchen, along the Czechoslovak-German border. With Uhlik were seven other passengers, including his wife and two children. One historian has described them as being "plucky."[19] They were taken by German police and handed over to American military authorities for processing as refugees and eventual asylum in the United States.

The German-made World War II vehicle was carefully modified to resemble that of a Czechoslovak army vehicle. The August 3, 1953, issue of *Time* magazine carried an article entitled "The Wonderful Machine" that described the escape:

> Czech border guards stood by, mouths agape, as the machine snorted through the wire and crossed into West Germany. None fired, or even raised a Tommy gun. The car rumbled westward for several miles before West German police caught up with it.

Carl Koch of Radio Free Europe negotiated the purchase of the vehicle and it was driven to Radio Free Europe headquarters in Munich, which broadcast the story to Czechoslovakia.[20] The vehicle was sent to the United States in September 1953 and put on display with a sign that read "Czech Freedom Tank Escaped from Iron Curtain." The term "Freedom Tank" was thereafter used in describing the vehicle.

The Uhlik family, Walter Hora, Vaclav Krejcirik and Josef Pisarik, arrived in the United States in December 1953, when they were presented as "heroes" to the American media and public. The Uhlik family appeared on Ed Sullivan's popular Sunday night television program and a photograph of Ed Sullivan and Uhlik family on the "Freedom Tank" was used in the Crusade campaign.

A Paramount Pictures newsreel released on December 12, 1953, was narrated by Bill Watson, who said:

> Arriving in New York from Frankfurt, Germany, seven Czechoslovak refugees are ready to participate in the fund raising campaign for Radio Free Europe, whose broadcasts sustained their hope and courage. They crashed through the iron curtain last summer in a fake armored car in a daring escape plan.[21]

The newly arrived refugees were settled in Springfield, Massachusetts, with the assistance of the American Heritage Foundation, which financially supported the families. They were able to supplement their income through television appearances and newspaper and magazine interviews. During the Crusade campaign, Vaclav Uhlik was quoted in Advertising Council newspaper advertisements saying, "People believe RFE broadcasts like the Bible."

Vaclav Uhlik, his family, and the other passengers arrived in December with some publicity: a Paramount Pictures newsreel showing their arrival was narrated by Bill Watson, who said: "Arriving in New York from Frankfurt, Germany, seven Czechoslovak refugees are ready to participate in the fund raising campaign for Radio Free Europe, whose broadcasts sustained their hope and courage. They crashed through the iron curtain last summer in a fake armored car in a daring escape plan."

The newly arrived refugees were settled in Springfield, Massachusetts, with the assistance of the American Heritage Foundation, which financially supported the families. They were able to supplement their income through television appearances and newspaper and magazine interviews. During the Crusade campaign, Vaclav Uhlik was quoted in newspaper advertisements, "People believe RFE broadcasts like the Bible."

During a Crusade parade in New York, on January 21, 1954, the tank broke down during the planned 15-mile drive from the Bronx to the City Hall in Manhattan. The first problem was a radiator leak which Vaclav Uhlik and fellow Czech Walter Hora fixed. There were other problems and finally the motor just stopped running and had to be towed to Times Square but by then it was too late for the final leg of the trip to the City Hall.[24] One newspaper carried the story with the headline, "Home-Made Czech Tank Meets Waterloo in Bronx."[25]

For the remainder of the nation-wide tour, the Freedom Tank was placed on a flatbed truck with a large empty telephone cable reel for transportation to numerous cities in the Crusade fund-raising campaign. The cable reel was used as a "short snorter" to tape, glue, or somehow connect the Freedom Scrolls together and roll them around it.[26] For example, on February 22, 1954, in New Castle, Pennsylvania, the Freedom Tank was on display for a few hours. American Legion officers pasted together and attached 80 Freedom Scrolls with 6000 signatures (75 on each scroll) to scrolls from other cities that already were wrapped around the cable reel.[27]

The story of the Freedom Tank was broadcast as a radio drama "The Tank That Jan Built" for the 1956 Crusade campaign with spot announcements by film starts.[28]

Eisenhower and the 1953-1954 Campaign

President Dwight D. Eisenhower began the first of his dinners for fifteen influential corporate executives on behalf of the Crusade for Freedom on September 23, 1953. The letter sent from the White House on August 15, 1953, to the executives was explicit that this would be an effort to raise money for the NCFE and RFE:

> I am asking a group of people who are interested in the activities of the National Committee for a Free Europe and Radio Free Europe, and it is expected that there will be a thorough briefing on the work of these two organizations.
>
> As you probably know, the fund raising activities of the organizations are this year being carried on by the American Heritage Foundation. Quite frankly, I believe you will be asked to take the leadership, within your industry, in support of this campaign.[29]

The fifteen guests at the White House dinner in behalf of the NCFE and Radio Free Europe included

- Henry Ford II, American Heritage Foundation
- Arthur Page, Crusade for Freedom
- Morse Dial, President, Union Carbide and Carbon Corporation, representing Chemicals
- Frank Abrams, Chairman, Standard Oil of New Jersey, representing Petroleum
- Benjamin F. Fairless, Chairman, United States Steel Corporation, representing Steel
- Harlow Curtis, President, General Motors Corporation, representing Automobiles
- F.G. Gurley, Chairman, Atchison, Topeka, and Santa Fe Railway Systems, representing Railroads
- Barney Balaban, President, Paramount Pictures Corporation, representing Motion Pictures

5 Percent Tax Deduction for Crusade for Freedom?

Harold R. Harris, president of Northwest Airlines, had concerns about corporate gifts to the Crusade and wrote to President Eisenhower on September 15, 1953, without mentioning the Crusade for Freedom. In part, he wrote:

> The pressure on corporations becomes constantly greater to support the great number and variety of voluntary non-profit enterprises, which mean so much to our way of life.
>
> Many of us who as officers and directors of corporations have a trusteeship rela-

tionship to stockholders' money are confused as to what should be the national habit in corporate giving.[30]

President Eisenhower's response on September 22, 1953, with a little pressure on corporate America intended, read in part:

> America is unique among all nations of the world in the variety, scope, and size of its non–Governmental support of worthwhile non-profit enterprises.
>
> The Congress granted corporations the 5% tax-exempt deduction from income, and I am unaware of any language in the law, which explicitly or implicitly restricts such contributions to "local" activities or enterprises. The nationally endorsed campaigns such as the Red Cross, the U.S.O., and the Crusade for Freedom, and many others ... can and should properly be considered eligible for such assistance.
>
> As you doubtless know, the national statistics show that corporate giving is around one-fifth of what it might be.
>
> Countless private American citizens are doing their utmost. By joining in the effort, it seems to me that American corporations will properly and legally be assisting in the propagation of our American faith.[31]

Pentagon Conference

On October 20–21, 1953, 291 persons met at the Pentagon and the Mayflower Hotel, Washington, DC, for the 1953-1954 Crusade for Freedom conference, presided over by Henry Ford II. One hundred eighty-four individuals representing 149 national organizations (including 29 labor) and 207 individuals representing 142 industrial corporations attended. Also attending were twenty-nine Crusade state chairmen. The meeting at the Pentagon on October 20, 1953 (Figure 11), was for heads of national organizations; the one on October 21 was for corporate executives. There was a dinner for all attendees at the Mayflower Hotel on the 21st, at which three purposes of the upcoming public Crusade, scheduled for February 1954, were announced:

1. Enlist the participation of large number of Americans
2. Secure millions of signatures
3. Create a favorable climate for the fund raising drive.

The fund-raising goal of the 1953-1954 campaign was announced as $10,000,000. As a "kick-off" conference for the upcoming Crusade, workshops were held for Crusade state chairmen and other organizational leaders to "better prepare themselves for making known to the American public the threat of international communism, and what is being done to combat it." Henry Ford II announced to the conference:

> You will hear in detail about the Crusade and the effort it is having through Radio Free Europe on the captive peoples under Communism behind the Iron Curtain.... You will hear from top people in the Government that this Crusade is indispensible to the security of the United States at a time when the threat to our way of life is real, ominous and growing.

CRUSADE for FREEDOM CONFERENCE
Washington, D. C.
October 20 and 21, 1953

Figure 11. Cover of information package given to delegates at the American Heritage Foundation meeting at the Pentagon, Alexandria, Virginia, October 20–21, 1953.

The Freedom Tank was delivered to the Washington meeting. A Paramount Pictures newsreel, released October 23, 1951, covered the events of the meeting and at one point showed some of those who attended the meeting looking intently at the Freedom Tank. Audiences in movie theaters heard Jackson Beck, the film's narrator, solemnly proclaim:

> This symbol of resistance to Kremlin tyranny was constructed by Vaclav Uhlik, a Czech mechanic. For three years, Mr. Uhlik listened to Radio Free Europe broadcasts and from them took courage and hope while he worked patiently and in secret to build this vehicle in which he and seven others dashed across the frontier to freedom. Behind the iron curtain are seventy million Vaclav Uhliks to whom this crusade for freedom is the messenger of the Lord.

One of the "top people in the Government" to whom Ford referred was Allen Dulles, Director of the Central Intelligence Agency, after President Eisen-

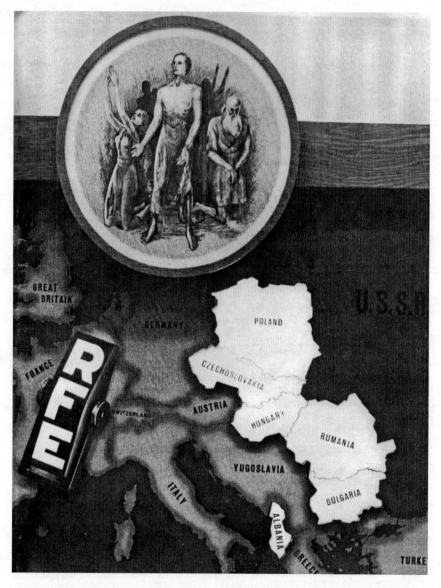

Figure 12. Illustration used in information package to delegates at the American Heritage Foundation meeting October 20–21, 1953.

hower had appointed him to the directorship. Prior to the October meetings, DCI Allen Dulles wrote a confidential memorandum to the Secretary of Defense, Charles Wilson, on October 16, 1953, and gave a full background report of the NCFE and Radio Free Europe, including

> The National Committee for a Free Europe is a private citizens' organization which employs the skills of exiles in this country and abroad to lend hope and

encouragement, and in some instances actual physical assistance, to their fellow countrymen behind the Iron Curtain.

We here consider Radio Free Europe to be about the hardest hitting and most effective weapon we have for reaching people in the satellite areas [Figure 12] directly. Most defectors agree with us.[32]

Dulles told Wilson that he was "asked by D'Arcy Brophy to relay to you his suggestion that you stress in your preliminary remarks the importance of private citizen participation in the present struggle against the totalitarian system." As a postscript to the letter, he told Wilson that

CIA's interest in the Crusade and Radio Free Europe is entirely *covert* and should not be mentioned. My appearance at the two briefings is solely as Director of Central Intelligence to give a factual picture of conditions behind the Iron Curtain.[33]

Dulles told the assembled group:

It must be one of the objectives of the free world to find a peaceful way of bringing the Soviet Union back to its historic boundaries. I think that one of the important ways of doing it is showing the Soviet Union that it can never tame and can never subdue the millions of people in this area (the Iron Curtain countries)....
What we must try to do is to find every means of showing the Soviet Union that that will growingly be more of a liability to the Soviet Union than an asset.

We estimate that Radio Free Europe is a powerful weapon, one of the most powerful in keeping the hope of freedom alive. We believe that it is powerful in very large measure because it is viewed in those countries not as an instrument of government propaganda, but as something supported by millions of American people, with whom the contacts with those people have always been close.

We consider it one of our strongest and most important weapons we have in peacefully winning the cold war.[34]

The final speaker at the first day's conference was Thomas D'Arcy Brophy. After giving the reasons why the Heritage Foundation decided to take on the Crusade for Freedom, he concluded his remarks by thanking the Advertising Council for being "the most important partner" of the American Heritage Foundation. Brophy looked forward to "publicity support unparalleled in the history of such activities in this country." Brophy finished his remarks by quoting President Eisenhower, "I urge every American to support this independent American enterprise dedicated to strengthening the will to Freedom."[35]

The Advertising Campaign

On October 21, 1953, a letter from the Crusade for Freedom, A Project of the American Heritage Foundation, was released over the name of Thomas D'Arcy Brophy to Fellow Americans asking for support of the Crusade for Freedom. The stated goal was the enlistment of 25,000,000 Americans in "a campaign to carry the truth behind the Iron Curtain." The letter went on to appeal to the public:

Radio Free Europe is a private undertaking—not a government activity. It has been and must continue to be supported by us independent Americans. For the success of this enterprise depends on free people working together for their own ultimate interests. Employed immediately and unstintingly, truth and money can help end World War III before it starts.

Make up your mind to give. Make up your mind to inspire your family, your friends and your associates to give with you.[36]

The Advertising Council sent out an advanced master campaign kit to local Crusade supporters about Radio Free Europe and the Crusade for Freedom, as a public service campaign, that started with "Another War? Best way to stop it before it starts—at the lowest possible cost." On the cover was a graphic of a microphone with RFE, Radio Free Europe and Truth. President Eisenhower's September 21, 1953, letter was included. The theme of the campaign was "Help End World War III before It Starts."

The advance kit included "supplementary material for your local campaign" that could be ordered through the American Heritage Foundation. Included in the 17 items was a "Program Kit for Churches: Specially designed for use on Freedom Sabbath, February 13th and 14th. Kit includes background information for pastors, notes for church bulletins, etc." There was a supplementary "Monthly Radio Packet: Contains spot announcements of various lengths. Regularly distributed by the American Heritage Foundation to over 3,000 radio stations." For use in local newspapers, a series of advertisements were made available for order that would "carry hard-hitting, factual messages about the work of Radio Free Europe."

A sheet of questions and answers on RFE and the Crusade for Freedom also was included in the advance kit. One question about RFE was, "What sort of programs does it broadcast?" The answer was: "Good shows—shows that out pull in popularity the Communist's own programs. Worldwide and local news, advice, music, religion—better and more complete than they get from Radio Prague or Radio Moscow. And HOT TRUTH through it all. And *hope*."[37]

One variation of the question and answer sheet that was used in the 1954 campaign in magazines and newspapers was entitled, "General Clay answers the questions everybody is asking about Radio Free Europe." A photograph of General Clay was included. One question was, "How much is needed now?" The answer was, "At least 10,000,000, but as important as the money, the WIDEST POSSIBLE PARTICIPATION—to communicate the truest possible feelings of FRIENDSHIP FROM MILLIONS OF AMERICANS."[38]

November American Heritage Foundation Meeting

On November 18, 1953, the Trustees of the American Heritage Foundation (including Lucius Clay) attended a meeting at the University Club in New York

Figure 13. Television personality Ed Sullivan, a long-time supporter of the Crusade for Freedom, seen in the Radio Free Europe master control room in Munich (courtesy RFE/RL).

City. The budget for the 1953-1954 campaign was approved at a revised figure of $705,000.

Thomas D'Arcy Brophy told the gathering that because of the expected "great volume of work connected with the Crusade," he asked for and received a two-month release from his parent advertising company, Kenyon and Eckhardt, while remaining on the company's payroll. He was not optimistic of reaching the $5,000,000 goal, but hoped for only $1,500,000. He added that if the Post Office would allow the letter carriers to do house-to-house canvassing, perhaps an additional $1,000,000 could be raised. Also, if movie theaters could be used for fund-raising, perhaps another $1,500,000 to $2,000,000 could be raised. He also announced that entertainment stars Bing Crosby, Art Linkletter, Arthur Godfrey, Ed Sullivan (Figure 13) and Edward R. Murrow, among others, had agreed to make short films for the television campaign.

As for corporate "advance gifts" from large corporations, they had been pledged $1,000,000, with perhaps another $500,000 due. The two single largest "advance gifts" were from Ford Motor Company, which had pledged $250,000, and the same amount from Standard Oil of New Jersey. Brophy added that it was "essential to get contributions in from the large corporations before December 31 when the excess profit tax expires."[39]

General Clay Criticism

Lucius Clay said, "The Crusade apparently had gotten to be big business." To Clay, the Crusade for Freedom was getting away from its original objective. Large funds from corporations might be hard to explain to people behind the Iron Curtain since the impression given so far was that individual Americans were the ones assisting Radio Free Europe. He wanted no publicity on the contributions from large corporations for that reason. This was basically turned down by other board members, as there was no control of publicity from large corporations who were contributing to the Crusade or keep the contributions secret from stockholders.[40]

Important Luncheon

On January 15, 1954, at 1 P.M. Crusade chairman D'Arcy Brophy, CIA Director Allen Dulles, at least one other CIA officer, and Walter Bedell Smith, now Undersecretary of State, met for lunch at the Metropolitan Club, Washington, DC, concerning an unknown but "important matter relating to the Freedom Crusade requiring a discussion."[41]

Reader's Digest

The February 1954 edition of *Reader's Digest* contained the article by Pulitzer Prize winner Leland Stowe, "They Hit Communists Where It Hurts Most." Stowe wrote, "Radio Free Europe is a bold innovation in the East-West battle for men's minds. It is unique because it is nongovernmental...." Among the personal stories of escapes through or over the Iron Curtain which Stowe wrote about was the one about the Freedom Tank: how within two hours RFE was broadcasting the story to Czechoslovakia, "It was an inspiration to every Communist-hating Czechoslovakian. To the Reds it was a sting of humiliation." The article ended with an appeal to contribute to the Crusade for Freedom, "If you wish to join those Americans who make Radio Free Europe's work increasingly effective."

"Truth-Dollars" and General Clay

One of the major themes by the Advertising Council was prevention of World War III with slogans such as "Truth Can Stop H-Bombs. The best way $1.00 from you can help stop World War III before it starts," "Atomic War? The best way $1.00 from you can help end it before it starts," and "World War III, How $1.00 from you can help end it *before it starts.*" One advertisement even went so far as to state, "Dollars may be the salvation of us all. Send yours today — the Big Dollar to fight the Big Lie."[42]

On these full-page advertisements was a clearly marked space the size of a dollar bill in which the reader could lay one dollar bill over a "lie" from a Communist source: "The American cannibals want to exterminate whole human races, particularly those belonging to the Far East or South East Asian Peoples." The source was the Hungarian daily newspaper. The newspaper advertisement told the reader, "Take a $1 bill out of your pocket right now and see how neatly it covers the lie. Then tuck it into an envelope with your name and address and send it to "Crusade for Freedom c/o your local Postmaster."

Grass-Roots Activities

Philadelphia Liberty Bell Tapping

On Lincoln's birthday, February 12, 1954, seven women dressed in native costumes of the "captive" East Europe nations sent a "freedom message" by lightly tapping the Liberty Bell in Philadelphia, Pennsylvania, seven times with a rubber mallet. The women were identified as ex-refugees who declined to give their names "on fears of reprisals on relatives still living behind the Iron Curtain in Europe." The seven strokes stood for Poland, Czechoslovakia, Hungary, Bulgaria, Romania, Albania and the Baltic States.[43]

Dancing in Bismarck

On Thursday, February 4, 1954, there was a "Crusade for Freedom Dance" at St. Mary's Central High School in Bismarck, North Dakota, sponsored by the Moose Lodge, with music provided by the T. Texas Tyler Western Dance and Recording Band. Admission for adults was $1.50 and for children, 75 cents. The admission price included one hour of a "professional stage show" starting at 8:30 P.M., followed by three hours of dancing. Proceeds that night went to the Crusade for Freedom. A helicopter from Chicago was flown to Bismarck to help promote the Crusade campaign.[44]

Two weeks later, on Thursday, February 18, 1954, in the Moose Lodge Hall of Bismarck, North Dakota, there was an "Old Fashioned Basket Social." The evening began at 8 P.M. with a film about the Crusade for Freedom, followed by the Basket Social and dancing at 9 P.M. Proceedings of the evening were sent to the Crusade for Freedom.[45]

For the last night of the Bismarck activities, February 22, 1954, all citizens of Bismarck were invited to the American Legion Hall for a "March to the Mike" evening. Bismarck's Crusade coordinator John Z. Miller acted as the moderator for the event. Miller quoted from Radio Moscow propaganda and those assembled were given the opportunity to go before the microphone to answer the propaganda in their own words. These answers were tape-recorded and sent to the Crusade's national headquarters in New York for collection, editing, and eventual shipment to Munich for broadcasting over Radio Free Europe. Bismarck Radio station KFYR loaned the recording equipment for the event.[46]

Foodmarket Freedom

In Lima, Ohio, Prangles Foodmarket combined sponsorship of a Crusade for Freedom advertisement with one for its store in the February 19, 1954, local newspaper edition:

TRUTH vs. LIES

Freedom Scroll

In the belief that *freedom* is the most precious of human rights, I gladly sign my name to this Freedom Scroll as evidence of my participation as a free citizen In the Crusade for Freedom, supporting the National Committee for a Free Europe and its striking arm, Radio Free Europe. In so doing, I join hands with millions of other Americans in bringing *truth* and *hope* to the courageous freedom-hungry people behind the Iron Curtain.

Have every number of your family sign the Freedom Scroll.

Pin a "truth dollar" to it and mall to CRUSADE FOR FREEDOM, in care of your local Postmaster.

Your dollar will pay for 100 words of truth broadcast through the Iron Curtain

Low Prices Prevail Every Day

Open 8:30 A.M. to 10:30 P.M., Daily, Sunday 8:30 A.M. to 1:30 P.M.[47]

Eagles' Flight for Freedom

The Fraternal Organization of Eagles (F.O.E) sponsored a nation-wide balloon campaign called "Eagles Flight for Freedom" in cities and towns throughout the United States during Freedom Week in 1954. Four hundred thirty-seven Eagle Aeries launched 4,164 helium gas-filled balloons, similar to the ones launched by the Free Europe Press in Germany, that contained messages from local Eagle leaders, with identification cards and envelopes asking for Truth Dollar contributions from the finder as well as the place and date of the finding. In Cedar Rapids, Iowa, the person who brought in the identification of a balloon that had traveled farthest before February 22, 1954, would receive a $25 bond.[48] The February 1954 cover of the Eagles magazine showed balloons being launched with leaflets.

Free Europe Committee, Inc.

At a "special meeting of members" on March 4, 1954, the National Committee for a Free Europe Certificate of Incorporation was amended to show a change of the corporate name to the "Free Europe Committee, Inc."[49]

1954 Crusade Preliminary Report

At the April 16, 1954, meeting of the Board of Trustees of the American Heritage Foundation, a preliminary report of the Crusade for Freedom was submitted, stating that approximately 10 million pieces of educational literature were distributed through national organizations, labor unions, service clubs, fraternal, patriotic and youth organizations, schools, retail groups, federal government departments, volunteer state and county committees and military establishments. The breakdown included

- 625 thousand Freedom Scrolls
- 6 million contribution envelopes
- 2 million Crusade for Freedom booklets
- 25 thousand *Reader's Digest* reprints
- 30 thousand posters
- 18 thousand radio kits

Most of the top television and radio shows mentioned or featured the Crusade, including appearances by Vice President Nixon and Henry Ford II on the Ed Sullivan Show, *Toast of the Town*. TV kits were sent to 300 television stations, in addition to the four networks. The 15-minute film on the Crusade for Freedom narrated by Lowell Thomas was shown on many local stations. There were 26 million homes with televisions in the United States. The estimated number of "home impressions" from network spots of the Crusade for Freedom was 3 billion.[50] In addition, there were 18,500 spot announcements on local television stations. Radio kits were sent to 2,700 local radio stations that resulted in an estimated 700,000 announcements.

One hundred fifty copies of a film that was produced from "materials borrowed from the military services, Radio Free Europe and various film libraries" were distributed to state and local committees, national organizations, and federal and military establishments. The Outdoor Advertising Industry put up 8,200 billboard size posters resulting in an estimated 1.5 billion "advertising impressions."[51]

Advertising Council Letter Blitz

On March 16, 1954, Whitney Shepardson, president of the Free Europe Committee, wrote to Thomas D'Arcy Brophy of the Advertising Council and president of the American Heritage Foundation:

> Apart from the financial support which has been forthcoming, and apart from the moral support given by many millions of people who have signed the Freedom Scrolls, there is no doubt that there now exists all over the United States a broader, deeper understanding of the work we are doing and a better grasp of the struggle in which we and the rest of the Free World are engaged against Communist aggression and Soviet Imperialism.
>
> Credit for this rapid growth of awareness and understanding belongs, in great part, to American Heritage Foundation. The Foundation, in turn, must share our feelings of gratitude to the Advertising Council for its experienced and masterly contribution to the cause — all given with great enthusiasm and great generosity.[52]

Brophy began a letter campaign in April 1954 to various corporations asking not only for contributions but also for support within specific industries, which were not coming in as fast as or in the amounts of what was hoped. One such example was his letter of April 9, 1954, to Paul Hahn, president of the American Tobacco Company:

> The American Tobacco Company has generously contributed $5,000 for which we are most grateful, but we have had poor success from others in the industry. With the exception of a $5,000 gift from the R.J. Reynolds Tobacco Company, we have had no other contributions.
>
> The purpose of this letter is to ask if you will help us to obtain support from other important factors in the tobacco industry.[53]

Another letter was sent to Lee H. Bristol, president of the pharmaceuticals giant Bristol-Myers Company, on April 21, 1954:

> If Radio Free Europe is to continue to be effective as it has been, it must be supported by private contributions. Unlike the Voice of America, which is recognized as a Government operation, Radio Free Europe is privately operated and therein lies its strength.... A contribution from the Bristol-Myers Company would be a great stimulus to others.[54]

Another example of a request for not only a financial contribution but for help in getting similar corporations to contribute was the pressure in the less-than-truthful letter Brophy sent to Texas oil magnate Clint W. Murchison also on April 21, 1954:

> The cost of operating and maintaining Radio Free Europe is approximately $10,000,000. This year for the first time, business and industry have participated in an important way in supporting this essential undertaking, and while the full amount required has not as yet been subscribed, the response has been encouraging.
>
> It would be most helpful if a few contributions in the $50,000 to $100,000 range could be obtained in Texas.

If you wish to participate, checks may be sent to me or to Henry Ford II, national chairman, Crusade for Freedom....[55]

CIA Reduces Budget

On April 21, 1954, Tom Braden of the Central Intelligence Agency wrote to Arthur Page of NCFE not only to give the CIA's views on the success of the Crusade for 1953-1954 but also to show that agency's concern about the future Crusade and its fund raising philosophy. From this letter it is clear that the CIA did not control or direct the Crusade for Freedom but did maintain the oversight of the budget and the overall direction of fund-raising:

> I understand that Henry Ford has appointed a committee of the directors of the American Heritage Foundation to consider whether the Foundation should undertake the Crusade for Freedom again next year and, if so, how it should be done.
>
> Do you mind my saying I hope very much that the Committee will decide affirmatively on this question? Since I have watched the Crusade in progress, I have not seen a better job done. You have had more experience with it than I have but I would bet that you feel pretty pleased also with the way it turned out this year.
>
> We here are thinking of underwriting a budget for next year of $800,000 to $900,000. This would be a reduction of $100,000 to $200,000 over the Foundation's 1954 budget. You know this is the big era of reductions and I'd like to be able to say to Allen that with the excellent ground work that was laid in 1954 we can make some cuts and still carry on a successful campaign. As you know, we have to submit budget figures for 1955 by June. If the cut I suggest is not in line with your thinking, I hope you will let me have your comments right away or as soon as possible.
>
> Another thing we have considered here is the importance of continuing, within the limits of funds at hand, to encourage small contributions by large numbers of Americans. You will remember that our first objective in the Crusade is broad financial support and that while we consider the amount of funds raised to be important, we think "amount" is secondary to "breadth." I am not by any means suggesting that there is any disagreement here between ourselves and you, Mr. Brophy, and others on the Heritage Foundation, but simply mention it as a point, which we here have very much in mind.[56]

Operation VETO: Balloons to Czechoslovakia

In April 1954, the Free Europe Committee and the Free Europe Press started Operation VETO as an integrated balloon and broadcast campaign over the Voice of Free Czechoslovakia aimed at achieving eventual "liberation from Communism" in Czechoslovakia.[57]

RFE developed a strategic plan of integrating of the radio programming with the balloon-leaflet campaign. Radio Free Europe's objectives were to build up the moral strength and action potential of an internal force that would lead to the liberation of Czechoslovakia. This would occur only when both external and international political developments would demonstrate to the Soviet Union that it would be more costly to intervene in domestic political affairs than not to intervene.

Radio Free Europe increased its broadcast times to Czechoslovakia and spoke directly to the people of Czechoslovakia and told of the existence of an intangible People's Opposition movement. According to RFE, this was not a formal underground political organization: there was no headquarters or material basis. Every Czech and Slovak citizen who was opposed to Soviet domination belonged to this "spiritual movement."

Radio Free Europe had spent months piecing together a picture of complaints collected from refugee statements and intensive review of the Czechoslovak media. The leaflets, for example, listed a nonviolent political program of Ten Demands including "Housing for Families, not the State" and "Better Pay — Less Talk." Small decals were included that could be concealed in a closed hand and contained only the number 10. Later they were pasted on Communist Party posters as a symbol of opposition.

Czechoslovakia Protests

On May 5, 1954, the Czechoslovak government protested, to no avail: the American Embassy delivered a note on May 24, 1954, to the Czechoslovak government rejecting the protest:

> The U.S. Government is informed that the Crusade for Freedom Committee has sent messages to the people of Czechoslovakia by the vehicle of balloons. The Crusade for Freedom, an organization of private citizens, is supported by millions of Americans and expresses the aspirations of the American people for the freedom of all peoples.... The operation was undertaken by this private corporation and neither the U.S. Government nor the U.S. authorities in Germany were involved.[58]

Sam Walker, director of the balloon operation, said the protest "demonstrates the sensitivity of the Prague-Communist regime to any effort on the part of free peoples to communicate with their brothers behind the Iron Curtain."[59]

From May to August 1954, over 41,000,000 leaflets were sent into Czechoslovakia via balloons during Operation VETO.[60]

Results of Crusade

The Freedom Scrolls were put on microfilm and sent to the Radio Free Europe in Munich for placement in the cornerstone of the building. The 1953-1954 Crusade ended on June 30, 1954, with the highest contributions of all Crusades: $3,139,376 against the Crusade for Freedom's final expenses of $876,667.[61]

CHAPTER SIX

How YOU Can Help Fight Communism!

Leaping Lena

A German racing pigeon was to fly from Munich back to her home base of Katzenbach, near Nuremberg, not far from the Czechoslovakia border. She got lost and landed in Pilsen, Czechoslovakia. Someone in that city then attached a message for Radio Free Europe to her leg and let her go. Two days late, she flew back to Katzenbach. Her owner found the message and notified RFE. The pigeon and message were given to RFE. Leaping Lena (Figure 14) became her nickname.[1] The message she reportedly carried from behind the Iron Curtain was this:

> We plead with you not to slow down in the fight against communism because communism must be destroyed. We beg for a speedy liberation from the power of the Kremlin and the establishment of a United States of Europe. We listen to your broadcasts. They present a completely true picture of life behind the Iron Curtain. We would like you to tell us how we can combat "bolshevism" and the tyrannical dictatorship existing here. We are taking every opportunity to work against the regime and do everything in our power to sabotage it.
> Unbowed Pilsen

Leaping Lena was brought to the United States in August 1954, where four World War II hero pigeons from Fort Monmouth, New Jersey, and 15 news photographers greeted her. One thousand American pigeons released in her honor carried a copy of the message to President Dwight Eisenhower and Henry Ford II, President of the Crusade for Freedom. After three weeks of quarantine at the U.S. Department of Agriculture, she then went on a press tour, helping to raise funds for Radio Free Europe in the 1954-1955 Crusade campaign.

Jozef Swiatlo and the Crusade for Freedom

In December 1953, Jozef Swiatlo, a colonel in the Polish secret police, "defected" in Berlin. Whether he was a double agent already under control of

Figure 14. "Leaping Lena," the racing pigeon who flew over the Iron Curtain with a message for Radio Free Europe. She was afterwards sent to the United States in a publicity campaign to help the Crusade for Freedom (courtesy RFE/RL).

the CIA or a genuine defector is a matter of historical debate. For example, according to one report, Swiatlo had been sent to the West with the purpose of killing Mrs. Wanda Bronska, a former Communist Party member and effective RFE Polish Service broadcaster.[2] After this defection in West Berlin, the Americans sent him to a CIA Defector Reception Center in Frankfurt, Germany.

There he was "debriefed" by CIA official Ted Shackley, who established his bona fides as a "defector" and reported his findings to CIA headquarters. He and Swiatlo then flew to the United States in April 1954.[3]

The CIA then gave Radio Free Europe access to Swiatlo. One RFE staffer interviewed Swiatlo and wrote the program's scripts, which were then recorded by Swiatlo. Broadcasts of his "revelations" over RFE's Voice of Free Poland started on September 28, 1954. Through December 31, 1954. Swiatlo was a constant figure on RFE's Voice of Free Poland broadcasts: over one hundred taped programs and 150 news items.[4]

Swiatlo's name is translated as "light" and, since listening to RFE was considered a crime, listeners referred to his programs by asking "will there be any light at your house tonight?" For the next months, RFE's other language services as well as the RFE's sister station Radio Liberation used his "revelations." The radio programs were described as "a brilliant tactical decision that brought unforeseeable strategic gains," and "one of the most successful pieces of radio propaganda ever."[5]

Based on experiences in the previous balloon programs, and to continue with the propaganda barrage, on February 12, 1955, the Free Europe Press started sending copies of a forty-page summary of his testimony, "The Inside Story of the Bezpieka (Security Apparatus) and the Party," to Poland. This balloon campaign was called Operation SPOTLIGHT, which "was designed as a means of bringing to the Polish people the revelations of corruption and immorality in the hierarchy of the Polish Communist regime."[6]

The purpose of the Free Europe Press was "to weaken the Communist control apparatus, and through, detailed exposure of Communist techniques, to enable the Polish people better to defend themselves against the Communists."[7] The Free Europe Press engaged in more cold war rhetoric in the pamphlet's foreword:

> Swiatlo is a man who has drunk from many a filthy well. Does he regret it today? Has he resolved to improve his ways in the innermost recesses of his heart? Does he treat his story of his experiences as an act of contrition or does he regard it as an act of vengeance of his former Party comrades? We have no first hand information on this matter. We only know that he is to be believed. This booklet is like a hand-grenade. It may become dangerous should you try to keep it in your possession. It may also be dangerous to repeat the text of this booklet to your neighbor. On the other hand, no harm will be caused to the public good should this pamphlet reach the hands of representatives of the regime.[8]

Swiatlo's revelations broadcast over Radio Free Europe reportedly caused a major chain reaction in Poland with the dismissal, transfer, and worse, of thousands of Communist Party members and government officials. Perhaps as many as 150,000 party members, according to one estimate, were affected by RFE's programming.[9]

As late as February 1956, Swiatlo's testimony was used by the Crusade for Freedom with this newspaper appeal:

SHAKE-UP

MUNICH— A series of broadcasts by Radio Free Europe have caused great upheaval and embarrassment in Poland.

They were based on highly inflammatory information about corrupt Polish police operations obtained from Josef Swiatlo, Polish Security Ministry official who had defected to the West. As a result of the broadcasts, the Reds were forced to dismiss four of Swiatlo's former chiefs and reorganize the ministry.

This is just a single example of the influence of Radio Free Europe's words of truth. Up to 20 hours of truth a day are broadcast to five key satellite countries— Poland, Czechoslovakia, Romania, Bulgaria and Hungary. *And the truth is getting through,* despite costly Red jamming attempts.

Millions take the risk daily to listen. Millions more hear the truth from Radio Free Europe as it is passed cautiously from mouth to mouth.

Truth builds hope and continued resistance. Each dollar sponsors a minute of truth. Send your truth dollars to: CRUSADE FOR FREEDOM, c.o. Local Postmaster.[10]

By the 1960s, Jozef Swiatlo, once called "the most successful Western agent in the history of the Cold War," effectively had become a nonperson. Former CIA Director Allen Dulles' book *The Craft of Intelligence,* published in 1963, contained only a two-sentence and incorrect reference to Jozef Swiatlo saying that he had defected in Berlin in 1954, not 1953. Ted Shackley, the CIA officer who debriefed Swiatlo in Frankfurt, wrote:

> Once he had fulfilled his obligations to the U.S. government, he sank quietly into private life as a legal resident of the United States. According to what little I have heard about him, he moved to New York — whether City or State I don't know — and opened a small business. The absence of any news to the contrary gives me confidence that his resettlement was a success.[11]

On 24 November 1982, the Polish Intelligence service decided to "close" the examination of his case because of "the lack of information where he lived, where he is, and what he did."[12]

Operation FOCUS

Operation FOCUS was the name of the Radio Free Europe Press balloon and printed message (leaflet) campaign for Hungary that started on October 1, 1954. FOCUS was timed to coincide with local November elections in Hungary and was meant to "focus" the attention of Hungarian citizens on attainable goals. The budget had been approved for $321,000 at the Free Europe Committee Directors Meeting on July 19, 1953.[13]

The FOCUS leaflets were copies of a "Manifesto and Twelve Demands (similar to the Ten Demands of VETO) of the National Opposition Movement." As with the VETO operations, small decals with the number 12 were included in the balloon operation and were later found on Communist Party posters. The balloons were launched in the southeast part of Germany close to the Austrian border. Thus in effect, the balloons had to travel over a neutral country to land in Hungary. With the launching of the balloons, RFE first began using its transmitter in Lisbon, Portugal, with 20 hours of programming each day on the Voice of Free Hungary as the RFE Hungarian language service was then called.

From the first broadcast in Hungarian in October 1951 to just before the FOCUS campaign in 1954, the Hungarian regime and other East European ignored RFE's Hungarian language broadcasts. In the three years preceding FOCUS, RFE noted only 19 media attacks against the Voice of Free Hungary. In the first week after FOCUS started, 20 media attacks were noted in Hungary and other East European countries against FOCUS. By the time FOCUS stopped in early 1955, over 16,000,000 leaflets had been sent to Hungary.[14]

The Crusade for Freedom and the Advertising Council used Operation FOCUS in its nation-wide 1955 and 1956 newspaper campaigns in the search for public support and contributions for Radio Free Europe:

OPERATION FOCUS
Hits Red regimes
Truth Dollars back it
MUNICH — Capitalizing on the insecurity and softness of the Hungarian Communist Party, Radio Free Europe and Free Europe Press have struck behind the Iron Curtain with the powerful Operation "Focus." It concentrates on 12 basic demands for the "National Opposition Movement."
Balloon-borne leaflets and round-the-clock radio announcements poured into Hungary. Within hours the 12 demands were known everywhere.
The Communists began agitated protests. But the campaign continues with telling effect. *You can help it spread:*
The Reds fear this truth. It builds hope and continued resistance.[15]

On December 20, 1954, the U.S. State Department released a statement to the press in response to the Hungarian protest of October 15, 1954. Similar to the rationale of the rejection of protest note sent to Czechoslovakia concerning Operation Veto, this response to Hungary read, in part, "The Legation is instructed by the United States Government to state that the activity in question was undertaken by the Crusade for Freedom and Radio Free Europe on their own initiative and responsibility. These are private organizations established and supported by private American citizens."[16]

At the December 20, 1954, monthly meeting of the Free Europe Committee, president Shepardson told the other directors that Hungary had on October 15, 1954, "violently" protested Operation Focus to the U.S. Government. The State Department reviewed the leaflets and "could see no basis of concern and accordingly rejected the complaint. This action of the State Department was very gratifying since it constituted complete State approval of the FEP balloon-leaflet program."[17]

Another enthusiastic response from a director of the Free Europe Committee to the State Department response to Hungary and the Swiatlo revelations came from Lewis Galantiere, FEC Counselor. In his letter to Free Europe Directors, he wrote that 1954 ended "with a bang and not a whimper," adding, "I don't imagine that ever before has the United States Government taken the words of a private propaganda organization and made them its own, handing them back to that organization, as it were, in the guise of a statement of public policy."[18]

Eisenhower's Letter to the People

The White House released to the press a letter from President Eisenhower addressed to the American public on the subject of the Crusade for Freedom and Radio Free Europe on November 4, 1954. This letter would effectively be used in the 1954-1955 campaign.

> Every American who joins this Crusade for the support of Radio Free Europe can be sure in his heart of these things:
> 1. He is supporting the cause of peace throughout the world.
> 2. He is helping arm the spirits of captive people with hope, and courage.
> 3. He is helping to keep Central and Eastern Europeans strong hearted, nationally proud, determined to win their own way back to freedom.
> I urge every American to support this independent American enterprise dedicated to strengthening the will-to-freedom overseas.[19]

Changes at the Top of the American Heritage Foundation

Also on November 4, 1954, the Crusade for Freedom/American Heritage Foundation in the name of Henry Ford II issued a press release announcing the retirement of D'Arcy Brophy as president of the AHF, a post he had held since the establishment of the AHF in 1947. He would remain a trustee of the AHF. General Walter Bedell Smith, former Director of Central Intelligence and Undersecretary of State, succeeded Brophy as president of the American Heritage Foundation. William (Bill) Aldreich Greene was elected a member of the Board of Trustees of the AHF and appointed National Chairman of the 1955 Crusade for Freedom. The AHF also announced that the Crusade for Freedom was the only project of the American Heritage Foundation for 1954-1955.[20]

The Crusade for Freedom 1954-55 budget had been set by the AHF at $850,000 but on December 3, 1954, Robert L. Smith of the AHF wrote to the Crusade's president William Greene to advise him that this budget did not include such items under consideration as closed circuit television programs (est. $50,000), newspaper boy solicitations ($100,000), and a press trip to Munich ($20,000). Smith added that he hoped that the money would be found or they would have to reduce some other items should the considered items become reality.[21]

One of the Advertising Council's newspaper sheets featured General Bedell Smith. The advertising sheet identified him as "Former Under Secretary of State and former American Ambassador to Moscow." Conspicuously absent was mention of his tenure at the Central Intelligence Agency.

Bedell Smith "answered" nine "vital" questions including "What is the difference between Radio Free Europe and the Voice of America?" The answer was "The Voice of America speaks as the official information agency of the United States Government.... Private citizens, on the other hand, operate Radio Free Europe. It is not restricted by diplomatic relations, and it can hit the Communists hardest behind the Iron Curtain where it hurts them the most."[22]

The Grim Memento

As Brophy was leaving his position as president of the American Heritage Foundation, on November 5, 1954, he sent to Dulles a strand of barbed wire from the Iron Curtain that was encased in Lucite and had this inscription: "This authentic barded wire from The Iron Curtain is awarded in recognition of distinguished service to Crusade For Freedom." His note to Dulles read:

> Upon leaving the presidency of the American Heritage Foundation I would like to present to you as our great and good friend a memento of barbed wire taken from the Iron Curtain, encased in Lucite.
>
> These mementos were prepared as awards to individuals and organizations in recognition of outstanding assistance to the Crusade for Freedom this year. A few were left over so I am sending them to friends of the Foundation.
>
> The Dinner in the White House last week was a fine occasion. Your remarks were most effective, and I am confident that the 1955 Crusade for Freedom will meet with great success.
>
> With appreciation of your friendship and with warmest personal regards....[23]

Dulles responded with:

> Many thanks for your letter of November 5. I have received the grim memento from the Iron Curtain.
>
> I appreciate your kind statement about my remarks of the other evening. It seems to me that, thanks to you, the dinner was a real success. I remain deeply appreciative of all of the work you have done during the past months and look forward to your continued cooperation in the future.[24]

Radio Free Europe's 1955 Budget

At the Board of Directors of the Free Europe Committee meeting on November 15, 1954, the 1954-1955 total budget of $14,755,621 was approved, including $9,277,353 operating costs for Radio Free Europe. RFE's capital expenses were approximately $125,000 for new projects (reduced from the $325,000 new project budget approved in October 1954) and over one million dollars for "incomplete items and commitments" from the 1953-54 budget.[25]

In 1951, the NCFE board had resolved that "all donated funds donated to the Crusade for Freedom for the benefit of Radio Free Europe would be used for defraying capital costs (costs and maintenance of land, buildings, and equipment)." For the 1954-1955 budget, the board of the Free Europe Committee resolved that Crusade for Freedom funds would also be used for Radio Free Europe's operating expenses. Accordingly, the board resolution changed the Free Europe Committee's charter:

> It is the policy of the Free Europe Committee, Inc. to regard all funds on hand as on June 30, 1954 received from donations to previous Crusade for Freedom Campaigns and all funds to be received by it from future donations to the Crusade for Freedom Campaigns as earmarked for the overall benefit of its Radio Free Europe Division and to apply such funds toward defraying the capital and operating costs of the Division in transmitting messages of truth, encouragement and hope to the millions of enslaved people behind the Iron Curtain.[26]

The Free Europe Press 1954-1955 budget was approved at $1,379,163. Almost half of that was used to finance the first three months of the balloon-leaflet Operations VETO, FOCUS, and SPOTLIGHT, which totaled $633,250.[27] An additional $390,000 was held in reserve to cover the expenses if Operations VETO and FOCUS went beyond December 31, 1954.[28]

Corporate Gifts

As of January 12, 1955, corporations with the largest gifts to the Crusade were

Fort Motor Company	$250,000
Standard Oil of New Jersey	$250,000
Goodyear Tire & Rubber	$100,000
Firestone Tire & Rubber	$100,000
General Motors	$100,000
B.F. Goodrich	$75,000[29]

Gwilym A. Price, president of Westinghouse Electric Corporation, asked Arthur Page, Executive Committee of the Crusade for Freedom, for a recommendation of a gift from that corporation. Page answered on February 10, 1955: $50,000.[30] In March 1955, the Trustees of the Westinghouse Electric Fund approved a contribution to the Crusade for Freedom and Gwilym A. Price sent Arthur Page a check for $37,500, which he passed on to the American Heritage Foundation.[31]

Study Trip to Europe

Starting in October 1954, and for the next seven years, prominent Americans were flown to Europe to visit Radio Free Europe (RFE) locations in Germany and Portugal, the Czech-German border, and the cities of Berlin and Paris. This was in conjunction with the domestic fund raising activities of the Crusade for Freedom in support of RFE. Those who participated in these "study tours" were given the nickname "Trippers" and were expected to brief their respective state and local Crusade chapters and national organizations on "Radio Free Europe's role in the fight against Communist propaganda.

The first trip was October 20–29, 1954, when seventy-two "Trippers" (Figure 15) made a whirlwind trip to Europe. The group included Crusade for Freedom state chairmen and national organizations representatives, including the National Council for Catholic Women, Disabled American Veterans, National Association for the Advancement of Colored People (NAACP), Camp Fire Girls and the Veterans of Foreign Wars (VFW).

The American Heritage Foundation, with Henry Ford II as chairman, was

Figure 15. Campaign volunteers known as the "Trippers" leaving on their Study Tour of Radio Free Europe in Europe on October 20, 1954 (courtesy RFE/RL).

the sponsor of the 1954-1955 Crusade for Freedom. Thomas D'Arcy Brophy, president of the American Heritage Foundation, sent a letter, to each "Tripper," in which he wrote,

> We are confident that Radio Free Europe will inspire you, as it did us, and that you will feel impelled, as we did, to communicate your enthusiasm with others ... When you return, I think you will agree that supporting this vital undertaking will

Figure 16. "Tripper" being interviewed by Radio Free Europe journalist in front of the Iron Curtain at the German-Czechoslovakia border (courtesy of RFE/RL).

Figure 17. "Trippers" launching balloons containing leaflets destined for Czechoslovakia (courtesy RFE/RL).

help better the chances for peace, prosperity and well being for all America and the Free World.

Prior to their departure, they were hosted at a buffet dinner in the Keystone Room of the Hotel Statler in New York City, with Thomas D'A. Brophy as the featured speaker. C.D. Jackson, Joseph C. Grew, and Whitney Sheapardson sat at the speaker's table.

The flight time from New York to Munich was 19 hours on a chartered Pan American DC 6B airplane—the *Yankee Clipper*. The first night in Munich included a two-hour buffet reception at the American Consulate. The next morning the Trippers went on a two-hour tour of Radio Free Europe's headquarters building. In the afternoon, they were individually photographed sitting in front of a microphone marked RFE and making a short statement for broadcasting to RFE's target countries. On Saturday afternoon, they visited the RFE transmitting site outside Munich at Holzkirchen and later that day they went to the large RFE monitoring station at Schleissheim, north of Munich.

Sunday was an all-day tour by car to the German-Czechoslovak border for a personal look at the Iron Curtain (Figure 16), followed by a visit to

Figure 18. "Trippers" at the Schoeneberg Town Hall, Berlin, looking at the Freedom Bell (courtesy RFE/RL).

one of the Free Europe Press balloon launching sites, where they individually launched a helium filled balloon containing leaflets, as in Figure 17.

On Monday they finished the tape recording of broadcast messages, signed the Freedom Scrolls and flew to Berlin, where the "Trippers" were greeted by the mayor of Berlin, Ernst Reuther, and saw the Freedom Bell in the Schoenberg City Hall (Figure 18).

On Tuesday, they were briefed by the Commanding General at the headquarters of the U.S. High Commissioner as well as a staff member of the Eastern Section of Radio in the American Sector (RIAS). In the afternoon, they went on a bus tour of the Soviet Sector of Berlin. Wednesday they flew to Paris, where General Alfred Gruenther and other officers at Supreme Headquarters Allied Powers in Europe (SHAPE) briefed them. After a sight-seeing trip of Paris, they flew back to New York to begin the domestic phase of their support for Radio Free Europe by making public appearances and giving media interviews about their experience in Europe. A 14½ minute film about the trip, "How Your Truth Dollars Fight for Freedom," was made for television distribution and was distributed to over 200 television stations in the United States.

A striking example of post–study trip activity is that of Edwin (Ed) L. Haislet, who was Minnesota co-state chairman of the Crusade for Freedom and executive secretary of the University of Minnesota Alumni Association. The February 1955 issue of *Minnesota Alumni Voice* on "Freedom and Democracy" was dedicated to the Crusade for Freedom. The feature article was "I Pierced the Iron Curtain" by Ed Haislet, in which he detailed his experiences in Europe. The article including a photograph of him standing under the Freedom Bell in Berlin, at the Czech-German border as well as his sending of a balloon over the Iron Curtain. Haislet wrote,

> The people of the United States, by supporting Radio Free Europe, are fulfilling their own obligation to decency, proving to their own belief in the essential dignity of the individual human being, the fundamental equality of all men and their inalienable rights to freedom justice and a fair opportunity.

Eisenhower Communicates Directly with Crusaders

On February 8, 1955, President Eisenhower, former Undersecretary of State Bedell Smith, and Henry Ford II appeared in a closed-circuit television program that was sent from the White House broadcasting room to nation-wide Crusade "kick-off" meetings of corporate leaders in 35 cities. The broadcast was intended to be the "basis of corporate fund raising" meetings. Eisenhower told the assembled guests:

> I am happy to be with you tonight for I strongly believe that Radio Free Europe and the Crusade for Freedom are vital to success in the battle for men's minds.
> Many of us learned during the war that the most potent force is spiritual; that the appeal to men's minds produces a dedication, which surmounts every trial and test until victory is won.
> I have long given the Crusade for Freedom my strong endorsement. I did that because I am familiar with its purposes, its operations, the people who run it, and perhaps, more important — its hard hitting effectiveness as an independent American enterprise.[32]

Arthur Page wrote a revealing letter to Allen Dulles on February 9, 1955, in which he seemingly expressed doubt about the cover for Radio Free Europe and the dependency on corporations for most of the contributions to the Crusade for Freedom,

> We can't run a half-hearted campaign.
> If we get $5,000,000 or anything like it from corporations, we must get $5,000,000 or something like it from the general public.
> Public support is essential to our general picture. Moreover, we get some two million dollars worth of advertising space and radio time from the Advertising Council. The Council will not do its part for a half-hearted campaign.
> If we get $10,000,000 or anything near it in 1955 or 1956, we can honestly say that we are the main support of the "operations" of Radio Free Europe.
> Moreover, $10,000,000 is not a large campaign in this country. That is the

smallest sum that would justify a National campaign or support the education of the American public in the continuing necessity of a continuing campaign for liberty—for men's minds in the President's words.[33]

CIA and Other Federal Campaigns

The Crusade for Freedom fund raising campaign in the Central Intelligence Agency ran from February 14 to March 31, 1955. The amount collected is not known.

General Smith

General Walter Bedell Smith, as president of the American Heritage Foundation, was active in behalf of the Crusade for Freedom: on January 5, 1955, he spoke at a luncheon of 25 invited communications leaders, and on January 9, 1955, he invited 45 press and broadcasting personnel to the State Department, asking for their assistance in support of the Crusade by developing public awareness. A full-page advertisement with his photograph appeared in newspapers in February 1955 with the headline "Walter Bedell Smith answers nine questions about the anti-communist network RADIO FREE EUROPE." To the question, "Why is Radio Free Europe important to all of us?" he answered

> Because this is one really personal way in which all of us can fight Communism. We can help keep the Kremlin off balance and deter aggression by supplying truth to the Soviet's enslaved populations. There is no more effective or more efficient weapon in the cold war.[34]

"How YOU Can Fight Communism"

Allan Brown, vice president of the Bakelite Company, was the advertising coordinator for the American Heritage Foundation and the 1955-1956 Crusade for Freedom. The theme of the campaign was "How YOU Can Fight Communism."

The Bismarck Tribune newspaper issue of February 19, 1955, contained a full-page advertisement with the question: "CAN WE— the people of Bismarck FIGHT COMMUNISM?" The answer was, "Yes with Truth Dollars you can hit Communism in its own backyard — behind the Iron Curtain."

One either side of the question and answer were drawings of a hand holding dollar bills with the slogan: "Fight Communism with 'Truth Dollars.'" Just above the list of local persons and businesses that contributed to the advertisement in the public interest was the comment: "Crusade for Freedom — Sunday,

Feb. 20 Attend the Church of your choice — learn how Communism has affected your religion."

College Crusade for Freedom

Twenty-five universities adopted a combined education and fund-raising campaign in support of the Crusade for Freedom. For example, Barbara Gibbs, president of the student government at Ohio State University, said, "This is just the kind of program that will capture the interest of the university student. To know you are helping to alleviate the world crisis is a gratifying thing." J.W. Ashton, vice president of Indiana University, remarked, "It is most appropriate that as a part of their experience in the world of scholarship students should be given the opportunity to participate in so significant an activity."[35]

Senator-to-Be Frank Church

Frank F. Church, Idaho state chairman of the Crusade, announced on February 5, 1955, that Cantril (Flash) Nielsen, Bannock county commissioner, was appointed county chairman of the Crusade for Freedom. Commenting on Nielsen's acceptance of the county chairmanship, Church said:

> The Crusade for Freedom gives every citizen of Idaho a chance to fight Communism right in the Russian front yard. By supporting Radio Free Europe with "truth dollars," we can keep alive the spirit of resistance in the satellite countries.
> Radio Free Europe gives these people hope and strength by keeping alive their religion, their national culture, and other blessings of freedom denied them. Radio Free Europe is also helping to keep the satellite governments off balance, and thus contributes in practical way toward lessening the chances of a third world war.

Church pointed out that a single dollar would finance the broadcast of 100 words of truth behind the Iron Curtain.[36] Frank Church was elected to the U.S. Senate in November 1956 at age 32 and later became an outspoken critic of CIA covert activities.

Balloon Launchings

The January 1955 issue of Reader's Digest contained an article about the Free Europe Press balloon programs, which was described as "evidence of support in the magazine area."[37] Domestically, the Fraternal Order of the Eagles repeated their successful 1953-1954 campaign of launching balloons filled with leaflet messages from Eagle leaders urging support of the Crusade for Freedom. 5,000 balloons, in over 500 nation-wide launchings, carried a request that the finder send the enclosed postcard showing the date and place of the find, an envelope for a "Truth Dollar" contribution, and 12 envelopes to be distributed to other potential contributors.[38] Martin Mol, Michigan Grand Worthy of the Fraternal Order of Eagles and national Freedom Committee chairman, was a participant of the October 1954 Study Trip to Europe. Mol later went on speaking engagements around the United States, spoke about his trip and showed a film at F.O.E. lodges of the Free Europe Press balloon launchings.

The largest launching took place in downtown Springfield, Illinois, home of Abraham Lincoln, when 2,000 balloons, with the stamped words "Crusade for Freedom" in large letters, were lofted with a message from Robert W. Hansen, national president of the Eagles. The February 22, 1954, issue of *Life* magazine carried a photo essay, "Fund Raising Takes to Air," on the Springfield launching including one showing the balloons, inflated by Girl and Boy Scouts, being carried in a massive parade through the center of the city to the launching site in Lincoln Square. The second photograph showed the balloons being lifted into the air in a northeast direction.

In Bismarck, North Dakota, local Eagles Fraternal Order from the steps of the post office launched twenty-one balloons on February 12, 1995. Freedom Scrolls, contribution envelopes, and a letter offering $5 prizes were in the balloons. The Bismarck Eagles offered one prize was for the first reporting back of a balloon and the other for the reporting farthest from Bismarck. All persons who reported on the balloon received $2. The balloon launching was in support of the "Valentines for Freedom" theme that originated from 15-year-old Patty Collins of Bismarck, who had suggested that the balloons launched over the Iron Curtain contain valentines from American children. Balloons were found in both North and South Dakota as far as 153 miles away in South Dakota.[39]

General Alfred M. Gruenther, Supreme Commander of Allied Forces in Europe, visited Bismarck, North Dakota, on February 22, 1955, and was honored at a dinner at the Apple Creek Country Club. General Gruenther had flown directly from Paris to speak before the North Dakota State legislature. Invited North Dakota Crusade directors and officers, sponsored by Crusade for Freedom state chairman Floyd Boutrous, attended the dinner; Marilyn Wentz and Deloris Paulsen, two former "Miss North Dakota" winners, were among those who provided the evening's entertainment. Paramount News filmed the events surrounding Gruenther's visit for a newsreel.[40]

Balloons and leaflets were also launched from Fargo, North Dakota, on February 7, 1955. One balloon was found in June 1955 in Decorah, Iowa, by Mrs. Levi Quandrahl and Mrs. Walter Quandrahl, who found it while they were "out picking berries" on the Quandrahl farm.[41]

During Freedom Week, Free Europe Press balloons were lofted from the launching site at Freyung, Germany, with leaflet messages from Fraternal Order of Eagles leaders as a show of solidarity with the Eagle launchings in the United

States: "To keep up the morale of the Communist-ruled peoples, and express the kinship of the free nations, with the captive peoples."[42] The launching site at Freyung had a plaque on display for visitors that read: "Permitting the addition of the written word to Radio Free Europe's spoken communication with the peoples behind the Iron Curtain. This facility is made possible by the contributions of American citizens to the CRUSADE FOR FREEDOM."

Freedom Sky Drop

The Civil Air Patrol and the American Legion on Washington's Birthday sponsored the Freedom Sky Drop project jointly, February 22, 1955. One thousand small airplanes flew over 200 American cities and dropped

- Replicas of the Freedom Bell medallions sent to countries behind the Iron Curtain
- Freedom scrolls for the signatures of 41 persons
- Envelopes in which "Truth Dollar" contributions to the Crusade could be mailed
- Leaflet on Questions and Answers about Radio Free Europe
- Booklet entitled *Your Crusade*
- Reprints of the January 1955 *Reader's Digest* article "Balloons Over the Iron Curtain"

Not all cities approved of the Freedom Drop. For example, New Hampshire's plans to scatter 150,000 leaflets from airplanes were canceled in Manchester, Concord, Nashua, and Portsmouth when police chiefs objected that fluttering paper would be a menace to motorists.[43]

Scholarly Study of Freedom Sky Drop

The Freedom Sky Drop became a subject of communications research at the University of Colorado, *Message Diffusion Under Uncontrolled Conditions*, after the dropping of 9,000 leaflet packages over Boulder, Colorado.

The researchers placed an advertisement in the Boulder newspaper with the headline "You can contribute to National Defense.... We are trying to help the Crusade for Freedom by evaluating the effectiveness of this leaflet drop. YOU CAN HELP by filing out this questionnaire and mailing it to us. PLEASE DO THIS IMMEDIATELY." Four hundred twenty-eight persons in Boulder were interviewed after the airdrop. Of this number, only 24 actually had a leaflet in their possession at the time of the interviews, and only 5 persons interviewed had previously contributed to the Crusade for Freedom after a Freedom Sky Drop.[44]

Local Doorbell Ringers

In the January 17, 1955, interim report of the Crusade for Freedom, after a review of everything that had been done to that point in preparation of the upcoming campaign, it was written, "One ingredient still missing from the campaign is the door-bell ringer who is a pre-requisite to the usual mass collection of funds.... Much more grass-roots activity organized at the local level is needed." Boy Scout and newspaper organizational charters prevented direct solicitation of funds but did allow for the passing out of campaign materials. The contribution envelopes the recipients themselves addressed to the Crusade for Freedom c/o Postmaster were apparently the accepted method to use by the "door-bell ringers."

The Advertising Council distributed advertisements prior to Freedom Week to newspapers that showed a newspaper boy riding his bicycle and contained this message:

Saturday morning, Feb. 26, 1955, I am going to bring you a contribution envelope. I am doing this so that you and members of your family, if you so desire, can contribute to this great movement to bring truth and eventual freedom to 70 million people who are forced to live in intellectual darkness under Communist masters. If you like our kind of freedom ... if you think that all people should be free as we are ... then your contribution, regardless of amount, will help show the enslaved people behind the Iron Curtain that we have not forgotten them.

If you wish to make a contribution to the Crusade for Freedom, I will have with me a special envelope in which you can seal your contribution. Any contribution you may wish to make will be sincerely appreciated. The money will go to the Free Europe Committee, which operates Radio Free Europe and the Free Europe Press ... which by means of balloons sends millions of printed leaflets and miniature newspapers across the Iron Curtain so the people there may read the truth about what is going on in their own countries and throughout the world.... In this way they get the real facts.[45]

In April 1955, President Eisenhower, who was himself a former newspaperboy, told a gathering of newspaper journalists at the White House: "Certainly, I am inspired by the knowledge that boys of this nation will freely give of their time and energy — and their hearts— to help bring information of today's world to those whose masters provide propaganda." Over 20,000 newspaperboys from 23 newspapers collected $90,000 for the Crusade for Freedom in 1955.[46]

Four newspaperboys were selected based on their collections for travel to New York, where they visited Radio Free Europe and broadcast messages "of hope to youngsters behind the Iron Curtain."[47]

Radio Tea Party

In April 1955, newspapers in the United States carried a photograph of two RFE "actresses" representing Polish Women on the "Radio Tea Party" program — identified as "one of the most popular RFE programs." The "Radio Tea Party" program consisted of "political satire, songs and witty dialogue panning the Polish regime." The caption of the photograph added, "Some of the people who have come over to the West say they made the decision after listening to Broadcasts." Another photograph showed balloons being launched with the word "svoboda" clearly visible with the caption, "Across the border, the balloons drop leaflets. They are launched by the Crusade for Freedom, a privately supported organization which supplements the U.S. government's efforts to win the propaganda war."[48]

Results of 1954-1955 Crusade

Contributions for the 1954-55 Crusade campaign reached $3,019,580, against expenses of $922,130.[49]

CHAPTER SEVEN

Newspaper Boys and Balloons Against Communists

The Crusade Returns to the Crusade for Freedom

After two years of leadership by the American Heritage Foundation, the running of the Crusade campaign returned to an independent status under the Crusade for Freedom, Inc. Henry Ford II stepped down as the national chairman after three years at the helm but remained on the Crusade's board of directors.

Planning for the 1956 Campaign

A Crusade for Freedom board of directors meeting on April 21, 1955, which included planning for the 1956 campaign, took place in the Ford Motor Company offices on Madison Avenue, New York.[1] One of the Crusade's objectives was to raise $10,000,000 by "substantially broadening the base of contributions from corporations, the public and national organizations" and "increase mass public understanding of the Crusade for Freedom by a year-round educational campaign with the assistance of the Advertising Council, the national organizations and all public information media." The budget for the 1955-1956 Crusade campaign was set at $1,298,000. Among the problems identified at the meeting were:

A. The American people are generally NOT aware that:
   1. The ultimate victory over global Communism must come through the winning of men's minds.
   2. RFE and FEP relentlessly exploit the weaknesses of the Communists and their puppet regimes—in the main Soviet base of operations—in the satellite countries behind the Iron Curtain.
   3. Consequently, one of the most effective instruments for keeping the peace by neutralizing and undermining the Communist empire in its own backyard is to support the work of RFE and FEP through the Crusade for Freedom.
B. Further, the American people generally have not identified themselves with the need for personal participation in the Crusade for Freedom and the work of RFE.

135

Strategy Meeting July 1955

On July 28, 1955, there was an important strategy meeting that included William A. Greene, president of the Crusade for Freedom; Whitney H. Shepardson, president of Free Europe Committee; Theodore S. Repplier, president of the Advertising Council; and representatives of the J. Walter Thompson Company, which was going to coordinate the advertising campaign, starting in February 1956.

Theodore (Ted) Repplier had just returned from a six-month fact-finding tour of United States information programs as requested by President Eisenhower. At the July 28 Crusade meeting, he said he was "dissatisfied with the Crusade's performance up to now." In his opinion, "The average American did not know we were working for the liberation of the Satellite peoples." Repplier added that the advertising "had been pitched too low" and the "Truth Dollar" program was insufficient. He wanted a renewal of the Crusade campaign to include full-page advertisements to convince Americans "of the extreme urgency and importance of continuing RFE's effort."[2]

Second Study Trip

The second "Trippers" travel to Europe started on October 14, 1955, and ended on October 24, 1955. Thirty state Crusade chairmen and fifteen representatives of national organizations took part, including Dr. Nancy Woolridge, vice president of the National Council of Negro Women. A publicity photograph showed her at a special ceremony at Radio Free Europe's headquarters, during which microfilmed copies of signatures of millions of Americans were encased behind a bronze plaque that read:

> Behind this plaque are the signatures of ten million Americans of all walks of life who wholeheartedly support the Crusade for Freedom and the work of Radio Free Europe and Free Europe Press, which brings enlightenment and truth to the peoples behind the Iron Curtain — so that their desire to gain freedom will be strengthened and realized.
> Dedicated This 17th Day of October 1955

Vice Presidential Dinner

President Eisenhower suffered a heart attack while vacationing in Colorado on September 24, 1955. He was hospitalized in Denver for six weeks and then recovered at his farm in Gettysburg, Pennsylvania, for another six weeks. On October 22, 1955, Vice President Nixon sent out an invitation to selected persons to attend a dinner at the Anderson House in Washington, DC, on November 29, 1955. He explained that President Eisenhower could not hold his annual corporate dinner and had delegated the responsibility to Nixon: "You know of the President's interest in the Crusade for Freedom and Radio Free Europe. Since he cannot pursue his plan to invite you to the White House for a briefing on the work of the Crusade and its beneficiaries, he asked me to hold this dinner for that purpose in his stead." As with the Eisenhower dinner invitation, Nixon's letter ended with, "You will undoubtedly be asked to help enlist the support of other leaders in the country for this year's campaign."[3]

Prior to the dinner, President Eisenhower sent a letter to Nixon, which Nixon then read at the dinner. Eisenhower's letter included his personal view of the Crusade for Freedom:

> As you know, the Crusade for Freedom is the only fund raising cause which I felt it appropriate and desirable to support personally through an occasion such as this. I hope it is obvious to everyone that I would not have done this if I did not feel keenly the Government's interest in seeing this vital work of the Free Europe Committee — notably Radio Free Europe — continue unabated. I know that you, and Herbert, and Allen, and Bedell, and the others will make clear once again why this work is necessary and why it is essential to its effectiveness that it have private direction and as much private support as possible.[4]

At the dinner on November 29, 1955, Nixon made a few opening remarks, including

> Those of us who are in constant touch with what is still very much a cold war being fought between the ideologies of freedom and slavery, fully recognize the absolute necessity of maintaining, and if possible, increasing the output of Radio Free Europe and Free Europe Press.[5]

Former Undersecretary of State and CIA Director Bedell Smith gave a five-minute overview of Radio Free Europe and the Free Europe Press, followed by CIA Director Allen Dulles, who gave a situation report on the Soviet Union, which also included references to Free Europe Committee (FEC):

> This brief review of current Soviet strategy and tactics will, I hope, serve to reinforce what the Undersecretary of State has said regarding the indispensible role of FEC as the major instrumentality of keeping the alive the hope and possibility of reducing and eventually removing effective Soviet power from a crucially strategic area.[6]

Nixon's closing remarks included,

> I think you will all agree that the support you and other industry leaders give to the Crusade for Freedom should not be considered in the same category as ordinary philanthropy, but more as a long-range investment in world peace and our own future.[7]

Real Source of Funding?

J.R. Wiggins, Executive Editor, *Washington Post* and *Times Herald*, wrote a letter dated January 4, 1956, to Eugene Holman, Chairman of the Board, Crusade for Freedom. Wiggins was concerned about the true source of funding for the Crusade:

> Some time when you are in Washington I would like very much to talk to you about the Crusade. It has troubled me somewhat that all of us are selling this activity as a private endeavor. I think we are being somewhat less than candid about the sources of its funds.... However it is done there should be no deceit about the matter, and I am a little afraid there has been some deceit in this connection.
>
> Some day when you have the time I would like to discuss with you the possibility of putting the campaign on a sounder philosophical footing.[8]

Earl Newsom, Crusade for Freedom director, drafted a letter for Holman's reply to Wiggins, which Arthur Page sent to Cord Meyer of the CIA "from which you can depart to more appropriate and effective language."[9] Holman responded with a letter dated January 16, 1956, in which, in part, he wrote:

> It is helpful to have your comment on what is certainly a basic problem we face in each year's Crusade for Freedom. As you can imagine, it is a most complex one, and those who have been close to the whole operation since its inception have not found a satisfactory way for resolving it without creating much larger problems.[10]

Holman went on to suggest that Wiggins and Arthur Page meet the next time that Page was in Washington, DC. There is no record that such a meeting took place. In any event, there was no public disclosure in the *Washington Post* about the true funding of Radio Free Europe until March 1967, when *Ramparts* magazine revealed the Radio Free Europe and Radio Liberty connection to the Central Intelligence Agency, and the disclosure was picked up by the American media.

Freedom Week

The official Crusade public campaign (Figure 19) was scheduled to run from February 12, 1956,

Figure 19. This poster was used in the 1956 Crusade Campaign between Lincoln's birthday and Washington's birthday.

Lincoln's birthday, to February 22, 1956, Washington's birthday, but some states began campaigns before and afterwards. For example, in St. Paul, Minnesota, Sharon Kay Ritchie, Miss America 1956, struck a replica of the Liberty Bell that had been placed in the capitol rotunda and made a silver five-dollar contribution to the Crusade on February 7, 1956. Her actions began the Minnesota Crusade campaign. The bell then continually pealed while Governor Orville Freeman, state officials, the American Legion, labor, agriculture, industry and religious representatives made contributions.[11]

President Eisenhower's endorsement was again used in newspaper advertisements:

> The Crusade is an effective and practical expression of American citizens' firm conviction that peoples who historically have been independent and who have been unjustly deprived of their right to self-government must be restored to freedom, once again proud in their individual heritage, strong in their independence.
> Radio Free Europe is giving these people moral strength and purpose. It is especially effective because it is a private *effort.*
> For these reasons the Crusade for Freedom has my wholehearted support.

Fraternal Order of Eagles

On January 27, 1956, Robert W. Hansen, National Program Chairman of the Fraternal Order of Eagles, sent out an information package to local Eagle Aeries announcing continuing support of the Crusade campaign. The information package included a poster with the word GIVE in bold red letters next to a clenched fist holding a microphone with rays of light and the words RFE and Crusade for Freedom and a graphic display of balloons carrying leaflets being launched. Hansen's letter read:

> On Blesdoe's Island in New York Harbor ... where incoming and outgoing ships pass near it ... stands a great symbol of America, holding the Torch of Liberty three hundred feet above the waters of the bay.
> Her torch is a steadfast reminder of freedom.
> Crusade for Freedom Week starts on Lincoln's Birthday, February 12.
> The Fraternal Order of the Eagles is one of the American organizations supporting the Crusade for Freedom. If your Aerie would like to join in the observance of Freedom Week, it can present a FREEDOM AWARD to any individual, group, local paper, radio or TV station in recognition of efforts to preserve freedom and combat communism ... initiate a Freedom Class ... exhibit the Freedom poster ... quote in the Aerie bulletin from the enclosed booklet, "Why?"

The Eagles' press release included a quote that local Aerie presidents could use, "These broadcasts, and the balloon launchings in Europe, will carry the messages of hope to the captive populations ... have proved exceedingly effective as evident by the fact that the Communists shoot them down whenever possible, and impose jail penalties for anyone who transmits the printed material."

Montana Campaign

Montana was a very active state in the 1956 Crusade campaign. The state chairman was John E. Corette, president and general manager of the Montana Power Co. He had been one of those on the October 1955 study trip to Germany and was shown in a newspaper photograph sitting behind the RFE microphone broadcasting a message to East Europe.[12] The Helena newspaper *The Independent Record* devoted a full page on February 12, 1956, with photographs, map of Europe, a graphic illustration of "Winds of Freedom," and detailed photographs of how the Free Europe Press balloon operations worked, including one of FEP workers measuring the dry ice used as one balloon technique. Another photograph showed workers packing miniature newspapers in cartons carried by the balloons. Former Crusade state chairman Arthur Wong, Cascade County chairman in 1956, was shown in one photograph sending a balloon aloft, when he and 71 other Crusade supporters were on an inspection trip to Germany to review Radio Free Europe and Free Europe Press operations in October 1955.[13] The newspaper section two headline was: "Montanans Join Crusade for Freedom this month." Sub headlines included,

Dissemination of Truth to People Behind Iron Curtain
Carried On By Free Europe Press, Radio

Effectiveness of Crusade for Freedom's Operations Is Shown by Communist
Efforts to Jam U.S. Broadcasts and Shoot Down "Truth Balloons"

"Truth Dollars" Are Featured in '56 Crusade

Captive Peoples Seek News of Own Countries

Crusade Chairman Holman was quoted as saying, "The battle for men's minds is a critical issue of modern times. We in America believe that truth will prevail if freedom-loving peoples everywhere can have day-in, day-out objective reporting to offset dictatorial attempts to confine them to the slanted distortions of Communist propaganda. "The first county in the United States to exceed its 1956 quota was Prairie County, Montana with 2,400 residents, which collected $63.00 — 50 percent above its quota. Chairman Holman sent a congratulatory telegram to the county chairman, Alfred F. Brubaker, telling him that he hoped "Montanans will follow as the first state to complete its quota."[14]

Colleges Crusade

Twenty-five colleges with a student population of over 300,000 accepted the invitation to be part of the 1956 campaign on a national basis, with the purpose of "making the student aware of the international crisis facing his generation and what he can do help."[15] The Advertising Council sent a publicity kit to college newspapers and a promotional package was sent to different student groups.

In April 1956, college fraternities and sororities around the United States celebrated "Greek Week" by holding dances, parties, dinners, stage presentations, and other social events. At the University of Iowa, "the Greek letter groups planned activities to make the campus and community aware of the efforts of Radio Free Europe and the Crusade for Freedom." Included was the musical show *Damn Yankees* prepared by the Phi Kappa fraternity and Kappa Kappa Gamma sorority, with the proceeds going to the Crusade for Freedom. William T. Rafael, program director of RFE, was the principal speaker at the "Greek Week" campus convention. The Cedar Rapids Gazette also carried photographs of the university students dressed in "Balkan" costumes.[16]

The University of Minnesota had been chosen by the Crusade for Freedom as a "combined educational and fund-raising campaign" for the 1954-1955 "on an experimental basis." In February 1955, the 12th Annual Greek Week organizers at the University of Minnesota also used Radio Free Europe and the Crusade for Freedom as its theme. Proceeds of its variety show were contributed to the Crusade campaign. The February 1955 edition of the Minnesota Alumni magazine was dedicated to the Crusade for Freedom and featured a photograph of the Minnesota Alumni Association Executive Secretary Ed Haislet standing under the Freedom Bell in Berlin, with a rhetorical caption, "Today its penetrating reverberations tingle the spines of freedom lovers behind the Iron Curtain with hope and chill the spines of evil-doers and informers with ominous warning."[17]

Newspaperboy Crusade

Seventy-five daily newspapers sponsored the 1956 Newspaper Boy Crusade — this was an increase from the 1955 campaign, when 25 newspapers raised $90,000 in contributions through the efforts of 20,000 newspaper carriers. The 1956 estimation was 100,000 newspaperboys representing newspapers with 13,000,000 readers. One 1956 advertisement showed a smiling newspaper boy carrying the Freedom Bell card with the words "GIVE Crusade for Freedom" that would be used for identification by the newspaperboy. The advertisement, which explained that the Freedom Bell "symbolizes Radio Free Europe and Free Europe Press, carried this message:

He's collecting for the newspapers that go behind the Iron Curtain.
That is not part of his job.
But today your newspaperboy is giving freely of his time and enthusiasm to help millions of people he'll probably never even see.
The funds which he and 100,000 other newspaperboys have volunteered to collect will go to the support of Free Europe Press— the important sister service of Radio Free Europe.
Free Europe Press prints the truth ... and delivers it regularly to the Iron Curtain countries by long-range Freedom Balloons. Truth is a rare commodity there.

Even Communist fighter planes and anti-aircraft have been fired in a vain attempt to stop the balloons.

A letter over the signature of Crusade chairman Eugene Holman was sent to newspapers around the country with an "Award for Exceptional Service" in recognition of the efforts of both the newspapers and carriers. Newspapers accordingly printed the text of the letter, which read:

> To salute those citizens and organizations whose efforts in behalf of the Crusade for Freedom have achieved outstanding results, the Board of Directors has established an Award for Exceptional Service. Recipients of the Award are elected by the Board and receive a certificate of recognition and appreciation.
> It is my pleasure to inform you that your newspaperboys have been elected to receive the Crusade's Award for Exceptional Service.
> We hope this certificate may always serve as a reminder that they have helped hold high the torch of liberty. We do know that captive millions have felts its rays, sometimes fleetingly, sometimes boldly, but always hopefully.
> Please accept our gratitude and our congratulations.

Another example of positive feedback from the National Crusade headquarters was the letter David Agnew, assistant to the president of the Crusade, sent to the editor of *The Daily Inter Lake* newspaper in Kalispell, Montana:

> We are all delighted to learn that your newspaperboys have collected a total of $100.12. This certainly is a very important contribution to the Crusade for Freedom not only in money collected, but also in the impact it will produce when news of it is sent behind the Iron Curtain. Your newspaperboys can be very proud of their fine effort.
> So far we have reports in from over 100 newspapers, indicating that the overallcampaign will be very successful this year. As soon as we have a summary of the Newspaperboy Crusade in other parts of the country, I will send it to you.
> Thanks again for the fine support the Inter Lake has given Crusade for Freedom.[18]

A total of $147,000 was collected nationally. The following are but three examples of the widespread activity of the newspaperboy campaign at the local level:

> 1. The highest per capita collection was in Ames, Iowa, where $600 was collected. The Ames per-capita contribution was 13.4 cents against the national figure of 3.4 cents. The carrier who collected the most money in Ames, Iowa, was Andy Williams, who was selected to fly to New York, where he visited the Crusade for Freedom headquarters, resulting in favorable publicity in his home town.[19]
> 2. The *Morning Herald*, Hagerstown, Maryland, carried a photograph of two newspaperboys receiving a Crusade award with a note from Crusade President, William A. Greene: "I think the Herald and the Mail newspaperboys did a splendid job in collecting $129.19 for the Crusade for Freedom."[20]
> 3. Newspaperboys in Waco, Texas collected $1,000 and received the Crusade's "Award for Excellence." Featured in a newspaper photographs and story were two boys who collected the most money: 14-year-old Tommy Kittlitz and 13-year-old Bobby McCauley, who collected $46.00 and $27.00 respectively.[21]

Domestic Balloon Activity

By September 1955, the Free Europe Press balloon launchings in Germany had reached 200 million leaflets and newspapers, weighing more than 400 tons. Balloons played a major role in the 1956 Crusade campaign: Operation Focus balloon launchings to Hungary were printed in newspaper advertisements throughout the United States, such as "Operation Focus Hits Red Regimes; Truth Dollars Back It." Another Advertising Council advertisement printed in newspapers nationwide began with "Capitalizing on the insecurity and softness of the Hungarian Communist Party, Radio Free Europe has struck behind the Iron Curtain with the powerful Operation 'Focus.'" Hostile and negative reactions to Operation Focus by the Communist regimes in Czechoslovakia and Hungary were also printed in various United States newspapers as evidence of successful FEP balloon operations.

Photographs of balloons, launching stations in Germany, and the various balloon techniques received widespread newspaper coverage. The Fraternal Order of the Eagles (FOE) for the 1956 Crusade repeated its support with local launchings of symbolic balloons and contribution leaflets. For example, on Saturday, February 11, 1956, 12 balloons carrying the contribution-reply card were lofted from city hall plaza in Cumberland, Maryland. FOE Aerie President Robert E. Danner, who participated, said "The ceremony will symbolize the balloon barrages that carry truth-telling leaflets by the millions over Europe's Iron Curtain to the freedom-hungry people of the satellite nations."[22]

Balloons Against the Communists *and Other Films*

At the January 13, 1956, Crusade for Freedom Executive Committee meeting at the Recess Club in New York, Eugen Holman reviewed the public information program under the guidance of the Advertising Council and J. Walter Thompson Agency. Crusade President William A. Greene announced that a 12½ minute film "The Big Lie" was being distributed to television stations and Crusade field and state offices. Illinois state chairman Ron McCloud, for example, presented the film during a Men's Club dinner at the Atonement Evangelical Church in Chicago.[23]

A four-minute film that also was used in the 1956 television broadcasting campaign, in support of Radio Free Europe and the balloon programs of the Free Europe Press, was entitled *Balloons Against the Communists.* On February 27, 1956, Fred Thomson, Director of Information for the Crusade for Freedom, sent the film and a letter to television stations describing the film as one that "revolves around everything in the headlines." He also expressed urgency for its showing, when he wrote, "The film is Free. Our only concern — and hope — is that you use it as soon as possible. Timeliness is of the essence."[24]

Another film for television, featuring chairman Eugene Holman, began airing in March 1956. The film showed Holman sitting at a desk, saying: "The Crusade for Freedom was started so that the American people — all of us — could take a hand in halting the spread of Communism throughout the world. The Crusade hits where it hurts the most — behind the Iron Curtain." On March 9, 1956, E.K. Meade of Newsom & Company wrote an enthusiastic memorandum about the television film to Earl Newsom, then a director of the Crusade for Freedom:

> You will be delighted to know that the Holman TV film is going great great guns all over the country. Stations are returning their reply cards with comments such as these: excellent film, timely, well done, congratulations, will use as often as possible until recalled.... It is being used between bouts of televised boxing matches, on morning programs and before and after evening entertainment programs. In short, we've got a success.[25]

Figure 20. Television personality Art Linkletter, a long-time supporter of the Crusade for Freedom (courtesy of RFE/RL).

The Tank That Jan Built

Based on the true story of the Czech refugees who crashed through the Iron Curtain in a homemade tank, the Advertising Council produced a two-recording set for radio stations: one was a 15-minute radio "dramatic playlet" for the 1956 campaign entitled "The tank that Jan built." Actor Vincent Price narrated the radio show. The second recording was that of personal appeals from motion picture stars Walter Brennan, Bing Crosby, Alan Ladd, Pat O'Brien, Jimmy Stewart, Robert Stack, Barbara Stanwyck, and Dick Powell, plus television stars Art Linkletter (Figure 20), Dinah Shore, and Jack Webb, for the Crusade for Freedom in support of Radio Free Europe.[26]

Eisenhower Letter

At a White House ceremony, Mrs. Eisenhower handed a letter from President Eisenhower to William A. Greene, president of the Crusade for Freedom, March 23, 1956. The letter in support of the Crusade and RFE omitted Hungary and included the Baltic States and Albania, to which Radio Free Europe did not broadcast.

The captive European peoples behind the Iron Curtain — Poles, Czechoslovaks, Bulgarians, Rumanians, Albanians, and residents of the Baltic States— are constantly bombarded by Communist propaganda designed to break their will to resist and destroy their hope for a better future.

In the continuing work of combating such propaganda, Radio Free Europe, the radio arm of the Crusade for Freedom, plays a major and effective role. Day in and day out its broadcasts extend the hand of friendship and hope to the people behind the Curtain, assuring them that their plight has not been forgotten by the free world and fortifying their devotion to liberty.

To the National Committee for a Free Europe, I extend congratulations on this and the other valuable activities of the organization, with my best wishes for success in enlisting, through the Crusade for Freedom, the support of the American people. I am confident they will respond generously and thus forward this vital work for the cause of freedom and peace.[27]

Crusade and Labor

At the January 13 Executive Committee meeting President Greene said that exploratory contacts had been made with labor groups in the United States. William Weiss, a former public relations expert for the Steelworkers Union in Pittsburgh, was hired by the Crusade for Freedom to work out of the Washington office. Through Weiss' efforts, the Steelworkers Union contributed $5,000 to the Crusade fund and the president of the Steelworkers Union sent out a letter to almost 3,000 steelworkers, along with a brochure on the Crusade and its work. Greene also said that Weiss was now concentrating his efforts on the autoworkers, teamsters, and postal workers.[28]

Disappointing Results

At the next Executive Committee meeting held in the New York offices of the Standard Oil Company (New Jersey) on January 17, 1956, Tuthill said that corporate contributions were being received "at a rate somewhat below that of the previous year." He pointed out that the Nixon dinner was relatively late, which impacted the mail solicitation program. Tuthill requested assistance from others in working with a list of companies he had put together according to industry classifications for which chairmen were needed.[29] One example of how this worked was that on January 27, 1956, Arthur Page wrote to Juan Trippe, president of Pan American Airways, telling him that "Pan American could properly give $25,000." Page then wrote that he hoped Trippe would sign letters to be sent to other airlines asking for contributions to the Crusade.[30]

Contributions from federal employees and military staff started trickling in by January 1956. The largest single contribution of almost $20,000 came from the combined military and federal campaign in Japan and Okinawa. Contributions from the U.S. Army Air Corps and U.S. Air Force in Europe came in at approximately $17,000 and $10,000 respectively.

Within the Crusade for Freedom, there was criticism of Owens Corning Fiberglas Corporation, which contributed $500. The Crusade's corporate gifts division was disappointed with the amount and believed that the contribution should have been $5,000, which would have been expected of comparable size corporations. Earl Newsom contacted Ben Wright of Owens Corning and told him "It was ridiculous for his group to contribute only $500 and he had hoped that the corporation would contribute $25,000 instead. Ben Wright told Newsom he would look into the matter.[31]

Greene Resigns as Crusade President

At the May 31, 1956, meeting of the Crusade's Executive Committee, president William Greene announced his resignation as "a dollar a year president" effective November 1956. The Committee accepted his resignation and took up a discussion as to his successor to work with Greene before the date of resignation. The Committee also accepted the appointment of John M. Patterson as Executive Vice President, with an annual salary of $20,000. The Committee also decided to close the Washington, DC, office as a cost-cutting measure and move the New York office closer to the Free Europe Committee office to "improve liaison" with the FEC.

Freedom Crusaders

A new project planned by the Earl Newsom Company in March 1956 was a school citizenship project called "Freedom Crusader" and directed at American school children. Earl Newsom wrote that "it offers great promise of helping us to expand the base of the Crusade for Freedom over the years ahead." The project was based on the idea that students would participate themselves while informing others. Photographic, printed, and other materials would be sent to schools for "specific age groups and grades, which are most appropriate for the subject matter." There were three aspects of the project:

 • Inform American school children of totalitarian practices behind the Iron Curtain that they may have a better practical understanding of the differences between democratic and undemocratic systems.
 • Demonstrate to American youth the effectiveness of truth in the battle for men's minds.
 • Assist schools in their important work of building in young people a deeper appreciation and understanding of American democracy.[32]

Dr. W.H. Griffen, Teacher's College of Columbia University Citizenship Education Project (CEP), expressed interest in the project at the planning stage and asked to participate. Arthur Page thought it was too early for the CEP participation and wanted to solicit "Washington's" reaction first before committing the Crusade to the project.[33] The continued covert CIA sponsorship of the Crusade for Freedom bothered both Arthur Page and Earl Newsom; the next month, Newsom expressed his concern to Arthur Page about going beyond any planning; "It will apparent to you that we should be careful about proceeding with it beyond this point until we're straightened out on Candor.[34] I have serious doubts about inviting the participation of the American school system in an enterprise of this kind under present circumstances."[35]

On June 1, 1956, Earl Newsom wrote a "personal" letter to Allen Dulles, Director of Central Intelligence, giving a short summary of the project. He explained,

 Several of us have given a great deal of time and study in the past six months to the problem of how the 25,000,000 school children in the United States might properly be brought in to the Crusade for Freedom's program.
 Arthur and I have been in the thick of the developing and sharpening of this whole concept, and it seems to us most important that we carry it through. To do so, however, will necessitate having the Crusade use about $200,000 of its collections for this purpose.[36]

The project did not go beyond the planning stage.[37]

Contributions Fall Short

The contributions goal of the 1956 Crusade for Freedom was $10,000,000. The campaign received $2.9 million in contributions against $1,000,000 expenses.[38]

CHAPTER EIGHT

The One Thing the Iron Curtain Can't Keep Out — TRUTH

The 1956 Hungarian Revolution

The tragic 1956 Hungarian Revolution was a focal point for the 1957 Crusade for Freedom campaign. One of the ever-lasting controversies that has remained alive for over half a century is the role that Radio Free Europe (RFE) played in its broadcasts to Hungary leading up to and during the 1956 Revolution.[1]

The new installed Communist government needed a bogeyman to blame for the Revolution, rather than publicly admit to any shortcomings of the political system. Radio Free Europe as a recognized symbol in Hungary was the ideal candidate. The post–Revolution Hungarian government issued a "White Paper" on the events of the Revolution and directly blamed Radio Free Europe as one of the agitators guilty for not only inciting the revolution but also allowing it to continue longer than necessary — a charge that continues to have believers today. The Hungarian White Paper included the following charges:

> The subversive broadcasts of Radio Free Europe — backed by dollars, directed from America, and functioning on the territory of West Germany — played an essential role:
> • In the ideological preparation and practical direction of the counter-revolution,
> • In provoking the armed struggle,
> • In the non-observance of the cease fire, and
> • In arousing the mass hysteria, which led to the lynching of innocent men and women loyal to their people and their country.[2]

Both the United Nations and the West German government investigated these and other allegations against Radio Free Europe and concluded differently. The West German government found that

> This investigation has shown that the assertions, which appeared in the press, that Radio Free Europe promised the Hungarians assistance by the West — armed

148

assistance by the West — are not consistent with the facts. However, remarks were also made which were liable to cause misinterpretations. But a discussion, an exchange of views, took place, which also resulted in personnel changes and I believe that the matter can be considered settled for the time being.[3]

The United Nations report concluded:

It would appear that certain broadcasts by Radio Free Europe helped to create an impression that support might be forth coming for the Hungarians. The Committee feels that in such circumstances the greatest restraint and circumspection are called for in international broadcasting.[4]

George Urban, former Director of the Radio Free Europe Division, wrote in his memoirs: "The Radio was young and inexperienced. After barely five years of broadcasting, its management was still testing the instruments and boundary lines of the Cold War and was simply not up to the task of responding with clarity or finesse to its first great challenge. Hungary, its baptism by fire cost it dear."[5]

"Trippers" and Hungarian Revolution

C.D. Jackson, Eugene Holman and Arthur W. Page briefed sixty "Trippers" at a luncheon in their honor on October 18, 1956, prior to their departure to Europe.

The "Trippers" were being sent to Europe as part of the now annual "study tour" of Radio Free Europe facilities, including a tour of the headquarters building in Munich, where they heard a musical program sung by the Hungarian Radio Choir, including "God Bless America." The "Trippers" were in Munich when the Hungarian Revolution began on October 23, 1956. On that day they visited a Free Europe Press balloon-launching site, where they individually launched balloons with miniature newspapers.

On October 24, 1956, the group visited the RFE monitoring station outside Munich at Schleissheim, where they listened first-hand to the local rebel stations broadcasting in Hungary. They then flew on to Berlin, where Dr. Otto Suhr, West Berlin mayor, gave them each a small replica of the Freedom Bell. The "Trippers" then flew to Paris for the annual briefing by General Gruenther "on the role of NATO and psychological warfare in Western defense efforts."

Some members of the group were newspaper persons and published accounts of their activities and experiences after their return to the United States. For example, after she had returned, Mrs. R.I.C. Prout, president of the General Federation of Women's Clubs, was interviewed on the NBC television shows *Home* and *Today*, wherein she detailed what she personally had seen and heard in Europe.

Negative Impact of Hungarian Revolution

On November 2, 1956, Cord Meyer of the CIA wrote to Arthur Page, advising him that a letter or note from President Eisenhower to the Crusade for Freedom "would not be what we wish. Particularly in view of the news just received of the Soviet intervention in Hungary."[6] The annual White House luncheon meeting of corporate executives supporting the Crusade had to be temporarily postponed "because of the international situation."[7]

Green Candles

Drew Pearson wrote in his syndicated column that appeared in newspapers on November 8, 1956, about a meeting he had with a Hungarian émigré named Dr. Fabian who told him about

> The Green candles in the windows. Green is the color of the peasants' party. It has become the symbol of freedom, the symbol of protest, or revolt. All over Hungary you will see green candles in the windows. The Soviets can't stop them.
>   You will also see the green paint on the walls—slaps of green paint. It's a symbol. Your Crusade for Freedom has helped this. Your balloons have helped. They have carried messages, which keep the spirit of freedom alive. They have spread green all over Hungary.[8]

Flight #367 from Budapest

The NBC television network series *Armstrong Circle Theater* aired a drama on November 13, 1956, that was "an actual drama of how a small group of Hungarians escaped to West Germany." The television show was "based on research material supplied by the Crusade for Freedom in support of Radio Free Europe and Free Europe Press." The host of the program was newsman John Cameron Swayze and one of those who appeared in the program, presumably as a commercial for the Crusade for Freedom, was Bela Varga.[9]

Advertising Council

In November 1956, Arthur W. Page became President of the Crusade for Freedom and John M. Patterson was elected executive vice-president. Eugene Holman continued his role as Chairman of the Board of the Crusade for Freedom. Page wrote to the staff and volunteers of the Crusade, "I am well satisfied that this year's organizational planning will result in more contributions than ever for the vital work being carried on by the Crusade through Radio Free Europe. Page added, "We are again fortunate in having the backing of the Advertising Council, the services of Robert P. Kelm as account executive for the Crusade, and the advice and counsel of Allan Brown, vice president of the Bakelite Co., who has served for three years as volunteer coordinator of our advertising campaign."

The Public Policy Committee of the Advertising Council met at the Plaza Hotel in New York City on November 28, 1956, with Paul G. Hoffman as the chairman. Among the topics discussed were the upcoming Crusade for Freedom campaign, Radio Free Europe, and the Hungarian Revolution. George Nauman Shuster, whom the *New York Times* once called "one of the most distinguished Roman Catholic laymen of the 20th Century,"[10] was a member of the Ad Council Public Policy Committee and of the Free Europe Committee, and President of Hunter College. Dr. Shuster pointed out that "one must look at the work of RFE from two sides. It is necessary to keep people behind the Iron Curtain informed by the free world and provide some measure of correction for what is drummed into them by the Communists day in and day out." He added that "Radio Free Europe does not incite the satellite countries to rebellion." Dr. Shuster stated "that nine-tenths of the anti–Radio-Free-Europe propaganda came from disaffected, extreme, militant minorities, and if the Council discontinued the campaign at this time it would be a great shock to the people behind the Iron Curtain."[11]

The Committee voted to reaffirm its support of the Crusade for Freedom campaign. They also agreed that Shuster "should confidentially report the hope that Radio Free Europe would maintain, as in the past, constant investigation and re-examination of their operations." The Advertising Council, and J. Walter Thompson Co., the Crusade's volunteer advertising agency, agreed to provide the equivalent of $5 million worth of material, air time on radio and television as well as newspaper and magazine advertising space for the 1957 campaign. The campaign would focus on,

- Fund-raising by voluntary national organizations, e.g., the American Legion Auxiliary
- Newspaperboy solicitations in an estimated 200 cities and towns
- Federal Service Overseas Fund Campaign and the Federal Services Joint Crusade
- Corporate Gifts.

Religious Themes

One 1957 Crusade poster developed by the Advertising Council and published with co-operation of the Newspaper Advertising Executive Association showed a broken strand of barbed wire on the Iron Curtain with the slogan, "The one thing the Iron Curtain can't keep out — TRUTH" (Figure 21). Adver-

Figure 21. Entertainer Bob Hope and actress Barbara Lawsen holding 1957 Crusade for Freedom poster (courtesy of RFE/RL).

tisements carried religious themes for the 1957 campaign; one with a broken strand of barbed wire quoted the Bible, "The Truth shall make you free, St. John viii. 32." Another advertisement with barbed wire and a religious theme was: "...above all things TRUTH beareth away the victory — Apocrypha: 1 Esdras, iii. 10." Yet another one was, "...great is TRUTH and shall prevail — Thomas Brooks, The Crown and Glory of Christianity."

Crusade for Freedom Newsletter

The December 1956 Crusade for Freedom Newsletter sent out to supporters focused on the events in Hungary. There were photographs and first-person accounts of the events in Hungary. The newsletter editorial was "RFE must continue to bridge the Iron Curtain" and began with

> The Soviet Empire is in upheaval. Long years of oppression and brutality are reaping their harvest.... The smiling faces of the Russian overlords have been ripped from their faces.... One of the major instruments keeping the truth alive behind the Iron Curtain through these dark years was Radio Free Europe, supported by the American people through the Crusade for Freedom. And today, more than ever before, Radio Free Europe is needed by the people behind the Iron Curtain.[12]

In a press release, published in full in the December newsletter, Joseph C. Grew, Chairman of the Board of Directors of Free Europe Committee, not only denied in detail that Radio Free Europe incited the Hungarian Revolution; he added, "Radio Free Europe and Free Europe Press have performed the functions of a free press for the people behind the Iron Curtain. It is vital that they continue this work until freedom is regained. It has never been the policy or practice of Radio Free Europe to incite rebellion; instead it has been the policy to keep the hope of ultimate freedom alive and to encourage the captive peoples to seek expanding freedom by peaceful means."[13]

Eisenhower Morale Boost

On January 8, 1957, President Dwight D. Eisenhower sent a letter to Crusade Chairman Holman that demonstrated his continuing interest in and support of the Crusade campaigns:

> Since the Crusade for Freedom began six years ago, I have wholeheartedly endorsed its concept and its activities. More than ever before, contributing to the Crusade is an effective way for every American to reassert his belief in the indivisibility of human freedom, and in the right of peoples, wherever they may live, to have governments of their own choosing.
>
> Events of the past several months are dramatic evidence of the profound depths of the spirit of freedom, which motivates the peoples of captive Europe. Soviet military intervention and repression in Hungary, designed to crush the spirit of freedom so bravely shown by the Hungarian people, make it more vital than ever that Radio Free Europe continue to provide all the subjugated peoples with unbiased truth about events in their own lands and in the Free World. These peoples must remain assured that their courageous demonstration of mankind's everlasting love of freedom is not passing unnoticed.[14]

Arthur Page as president of the Crusade for Freedom sent out a letter to Crusade leaders on January 15, 1957, quoting from the Eisenhower letter and adding,

> We of the Crusade more than ever must rise to the increased responsibilities which 1957 is placing on us. We know now—because of the way in which the American people responded to the Hungarian situation—that Americans will expect much of the Crusade. We must more than fulfill their expectations.[15]

1957 White House Luncheon

The fall 1956 meeting of Crusade leaders, which had been postponed because of events in Hungary, became a small White House luncheon on February 5, 1957, for 54 top industrial and business leaders. The invitation sent out in President Eisenhower's name on January 16, 1957, gave the rationale for the meeting:

> I am asking a group of people having a special interest in Crusade for Freedom and the operation of Radio Free Europe. There will be some exchanges of ideas concerning these subjects, and you will undoubtedly be asked to enlist the support of other leaders in the country for the 1957 campaign.[16]

President Eisenhower spoke for a few minutes and was followed by Secretary of State John Foster Dulles, who spoke on conditions of countries behind the Iron Curtain. CIA Director Allan Dulles spoke for about ten minutes and Gene Holman spoke for a few minutes on the Crusade for Freedom.[17]

Twenty-five executives who attended the luncheon were then named as "industry chairmen" of the Crusade for Freedom. They were expected to actively recruit other corporate executives to contribute to the Crusade. Chairman Holman wrote to Richard C. Doane of the International Paper Company on February 14, 1957, asking for a $5,000 contribution and his support by again serving as the "Paper Industry Chairman." Holman wrote that the luncheon "marked the beginning of national corporations' participation in the campaign. Doane was tasked with writing to "a selected list of major producers, converters or container manufacturers."[18] Another "industry chairman" was long-time Crusade supporter Frank Stanton of CBS, who was asked to write to "broadcasters, record companies, booking agencies, rating services, etc."

Corporate Gifts

Most large corporations repeated their 1956 Crusade contributions, which were defined as gifts, and two corporations increased their 1956 contributions: Sears, Roebuck & Company from $15,000 to $25,000 and Columbia Broadcasting System from $5,000 to $10,000. The breakdown of highest corporate gifts for the 1957 Crusade was:

Standard Oil Company (New Jersey)	$250,000
Ford Motor Company	$250,000
General Motors Corporation	$100,000
American Telephone & Tel. Company	$75,000
Republic Steel Corporation	$60,000
Chrysler Corporation	$50,000
Standard Oil Company of California	$50,000

| Socony-Mobile Oil Company | $50,000 |
| The Texas Company | $50,000[19] |

Television, Radio and Film

The Crusade's Radio and TV department prepared a 15-minute documentary on Radio Free Europe that was narrated by actor Ralph Bellamy and broadcast on approximately 300 radio stations. The reverse side of the radio transcript included appeals for funds from entertainers Debbie Reynolds, Eddie Fisher, Basil Rathbone, Linda Darnell, Sammy Davis, Jr., Steve Allen, Arthur Godfrey, Ray Bolger, Dinah Shore, and heavy weight champion boxer Rocky Marciano.

The 1957 Crusade film *Lifeline to Freedom* premiered on the NBC national television show on January 30, 1957. By March 1957, the film had been shown on more than 50 television stations.

Radio Free Europe broadcast pre-written scripts, using phonetics, read by famous jazz musicians Duke Ellington, Gene Krupa, Woody Herman, Oscar Peterson, Earl Hines, and Stan Kenton. The programs were then made available

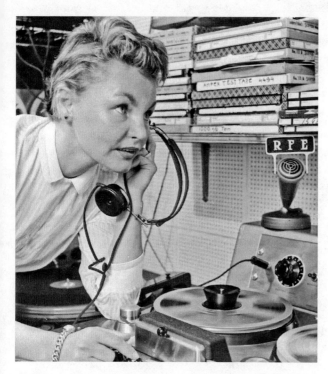

to U.S. audiences through the Crusade for Freedom. The Czech disc jockey, described as a "lovely and vivacious refugee," lived in New York and taped her programs at the New York RFE office. Her program was called "Date with Eva." She traveled throughout the United States giving interviews over domestic radio stations and played dubbed excerpts from her broadcasts and interviews with jazz greats.

Radio Free Europe's popular Czech disk jockey Eva Stankova ("Date with Eva") at work at RFE's broadcast studios in New York (courtesy RFE/RL).

Federal Services Joint Crusade

Starting on January 1, 1957, fund raising became a joint project with the humanitarian organization CARE and with members of the military and civilian government service. CARE (Cooperative for American Remittance to Europe) was founded in 1945 to send millions of emergency relief packages of food to Europe. The first joint Crusade was directed by Under Secretary of Commerce Walter Williams and was based on a White House directive that provided "an opportunity for every member of the federal and military establishment to make an individual, private contribution to CARE and/or Crusade for Freedom."[20]

Grass-Roots Activities

Freedom Week took place February 12–22, 1957, and 71 national organizations agreed to participate in the 1957 Crusade campaign, which exceeded the number of organizations in the previous years. The Crusade for Freedom's Director of Field Operations, A.F. Rhoads, declared in February, "Well organized and underway in every section of the country.... And because of wonderful cooperation from the American Legion Auxiliary, we can truthfully say that this organization has undertaken a nation-wide fund-raising campaign for the Crusade — this gives us far more extensive 'grass roots' coverage than ever before."[21]

In Times Square, New York City, the D'Arcy Brophy Advertising Company made possible a running electric sign on the Budweiser beer advertisement, which for two months read, "You can fight Communism by supporting the Crusade for Freedom." In Philadelphia, Pennsylvania, a large ad with the words "Crusade for Freedom" was placed over the archway of the City Hall.

One newspaper advertisement of the Advertising Council and the Newspaper Advertising Executive Association showed a stretch of land somewhere behind a visible fence of barbed wire. The text was "Target for the Truth: the barbed wire and armed guards mark the edge of the Iron Curtain.... The Reds fear the truth. But it's the one thing the Iron Curtain can't shut out. Keep in coming with Truth Dollars."[22]

On February 17, 1957, the first page of Section Two of the newspaper the *Independent Record* in Helena, Montana, was a full page devoted to the Crusade for Freedom with local, national, and international stories, illustrations, and photographs of the October 1956 balloon launching in Germany. The page headline was "Montanans Joining in Supporting Crusade for Freedom." One read that "Truth Dollars are Being Subscribed to Provide Barrage of Information," "Oppression of People, Not Charges of Outside Aid, Chief Cause of Revolution," "Struggle Is Not Over There," and "Crusade Given Endorsement of U.S. Labor."

American Legion Auxiliary

At the Annual Convention of the American Legion Auxiliary in Los Angeles in September 3–6, 1956, the Auxiliary made the 1957 Crusade for Freedom a special fund-raising project under the mantle "national security." During Freedom Week in 1957, the Legion Auxiliary set up manning booths and tables in banks and grocery stores nationwide to hand out Crusade literature and for collections. In some cases, the Auxiliary made door-to-door solicitations for contributions.

In Chicago, James C. Worthy, the Illinois state chairman, arranged for 200 collection locations for the Auxiliary.[23] In south Chicago, where the third district Auxiliary set up local collection centers with Crusade for Freedom posters and literature, Mrs. Caroline Cullen, district director, said, "Funds are being collected to help inform the suppressed peoples throughout the world" and "the drive to finance the spreading of truth will be a very appropriate way to celebrate the birthdays of Lincoln and Washington."[24]

Another example was in Newport, Rhode Island, where the local Legion Auxiliary not only distributed collection boxes but also had a radio program on station WADK with themes "Freedom Week" and "Americanism." On the evening of February 19, the Newport Auxiliary had an open house, which included the showing of the film *Lifeline to Freedom* on the Crusade, followed by an "Americanism" program and refreshments.[25] At the parent-teachers association (PTA) meeting in Helena, Montana, on February 18, 1957, the Legion Auxiliary also showed the *Lifeline to Freedom* film.

In Ogden, Utah, the Auxiliary sponsored a "sweetheart dance" on Saturday night, February 16, 1957. Donations were accepted as admission to the dance. Hamburgers and coffee were served and the proceeds went to the Crusade.[26]

The Legion Auxiliary operated at a "micro" level, too. For example, in Three Oaks, Michigan, on February 19, 1957, the local Auxiliary voted to contribute $5 to the Crusade for Freedom.[27] Thirteen members of the Kasson-Mantorville, Minnesota, American Legion Auxiliary met on February 12, 1957, and collected $40.43, which was sent to Crusade organizers.[28]

College Campaign

The 1957 campaign targeted over 250,000 students in 45 colleges and universities. Students at Brigham Young University wrote scripts and made tape recordings for local radio stations, made a half-hour program for broadcast over the local television station in Salt Lake City, and covered the Crusade in the campus newspaper. There was a leaflet drop at the University of Minnesota, which also witnessed an "Iron Curtain" dinner and forums "Are We Gaining in our Fight for Eastern Europe" and "How True Is Our Propaganda."[29]

In March 1957, Evansville College, Drake University, and Emory University had College Crusade programs. At the University of Illinois, during the annual Greek Week, the Crusade program included a jazz concert and variety show, with the proceeds going to the Crusade for Freedom. In Toledo, Ohio, students washed cars, manned gasoline pumps, and changed tires in support of the Crusade. At Ohio State University, 80 sororities and fraternities combined their effort during "Greek Week" for group discussions, dinners, a Stunt Night, and a variety show. $2,300 was collected.

Twenty-five schools participated in a contest sponsored by the Crusade for Freedom and Radio Free Europe for the most outstanding College Crusade. From the winning college or university, one student was selected for a summer intern job with Radio Free Europe in Munich.

Eagles and Balloons

The Fraternal Order of the Eagles (FOE), for the fourth consecutive year, made the Crusade for Freedom a national project with the lofting of balloons filled with literature about the Crusade and postcards to be returned with contributions and landing information.

In Petersburg, Virginia, for example, FOE Aerie No. 822 launched 10 helium-filled balloons on Saturday, February 6, 1957, at 11 A.M. from the courtyard lawn. February 6, 1957, was the 59th anniversary of the founding of the Fraternal Order of Eagles in Seattle, Washington. Aerie No. 822 president E. I. Zuskin said, "We are inviting all citizens of Petersburg to join in this important event. In this period when the forces wanting freedom in Eastern Europe are making themselves feel more strongly than ever, it is important that Radio Free Europe receive the support it needs to continue broadcasting its message of hope and inspiration."[30]

Another example was the launching of 20 helium-filled balloons with leaflets from the capital building in Helena, Montana, on February 9, 1957. FOE Aerie 16 members and Montana state officials and legislators launched the balloons after a short ceremony with music. The Eagles drill team filled the balloons with helium. Gerald L. Crowley, local Eagles President, said, "The Eagles lodge strongly urges everyone to support the Crusade for Freedom." He added that two balloons were presented to the state of Montana to be displayed in the House and Senate Chambers respectively to "remind the legislators of the importance of the Crusade."[31]

In South Chicago, Illinois, 40 balloons were lofted on February 17, 1957, at 1 P.M., in front of the Eagles hall on S. Houston Avenue. Ray Lamberth of the Eagles said, "Disturbances in Poland, Hungary, other satellites and reported disturbances in Russia prove that people are still willing and ready to fight for liberty despite the torture and brutality of the Kremlin leaders."[32] Outside

Chicago, in Burnside, Illinois, Friday night, February 22, 1957, FOE Aerie lodge No. 1968 lofted Freedom Balloons with leaflet requests for contributions to the Crusade. A special program in the lodge hall included an address by the Rev. Arpad George of the Hungarian Reformed and Evangelic church. An appearance of refugees from Hungary was also included in the program.[33]

Person-to-Person Link

The editor of a March 1957 newspaper editorial entitled "Crusade for Freedom is Person-to-Person Link," asked:

What keeps the Crusade for Freedom going?
It's in its seventh year and that is rather surprising, in a way. Seven years is a long time on a completely voluntary effort to continue when no earth-shaking results can be chalked up for the time and money invested.... Nobody in any government sets the pattern of policy, or tells what Crusade for Freedom must do. Its real power comes from the men and women along Main Street and on the side streets who think truthful news is an ingredient of civilized living and who therefore want to share it with people who can't get truthful news in their own countries.... Crusade for Freedom links the spirit of men and women across the barbed wire boundaries. It keeps alive the flame that one day will dissolve the barbed wire. It if takes seventy times seven years, it is still worth supporting.[34]

The 1957 Crusade for Freedom activities took place between Lincoln and Washington birthdays in February. Newspaper advertisements contained slogans such as

• "Great is TRUTH and Shall Prevail,"
• "Underground by Air,"
• "Above all things TRUTH beareth away the Victory."

The events of Hungary in October and November 1956 played an important role in the local campaigns: in the materials given to the 1957 Crusade participants there was a letter from RFE's President General Willis D. Crittenberger: "You may be assured that no broadcast by Radio Free Europe has been designed to incite to rebellion the captive peoples behind the Iron Curtain. Nor has Radio Free Europe ever offered promises of American military intervention."[35]

His letter continued,

It is a multimillion-dollar operation supported by funds from the United States. RFE and the U.S. government insist all the money comes from private donations, but the suspicion persists in many places that some of its funds come from the U.S. government. RFE says 10 million dollars a year are raised in a campaign drive by the Crusade for Freedom, which sponsors RFE. It will not say where the rest comes from or how much is involved.[36]

Crusade chairman Holman answered on December 14, 1956, with a letter to Crittenberger, in which he said, "I fully agree that the captive people behind the Iron Curtain have never needed Radio Free Europe more.... I assure you that the Crusade will strongly increase its efforts further to enlist the support of the American people, whose generosity has made Radio Free Europe possible."[37]

Newspaperboys Crusade for Freedom

Thousands of newspaperboys around the country again volunteered to support the Crusade for Freedom. "They're out to rip the propaganda of Communism wide apart," began one newspaper advertisement in support of the 1957 newspaperboy campaign. Four boys were seen carrying newspapers who carried donation envelopes and wore or presented a "Freedom Bell Badge," with a graphic display of the Freedom Bell with the face of a boy. The text continued,

> These boys are newspapermen who know the *value* of truth — the basic principle by which the news is written in a free nation. And they believe in the *power* of Truth. It is the backbone of our newspapers and our way of life. Truth is the backbone of freedom, too— it is spread to Europe's captive people by *Free Europe Press* and its sister service, *Radio Free Europe*. People living in the Satellite countries are subject to the confusion of Communist propaganda. They must rely on the Truth reporting of *Free Europe Press* and *Radio Free Europe* as a scale for measuring true values.[38]

Highlights included the collection of 1,171 pounds of coins worth $12,700 in Dallas, Texas, by the newspaperboys of the newspaper *Times-Herald*. In Philadelphia, 6,000 carriers of the *Philadelphia Bulletin* collected almost $36,000 in two days— to pay for "25 solid days of broadcasting over Radio Free Europe."[39] The Crusade active campaign ended effectively on February 28, 1957: by that date newspaperboys from 150 daily newspapers had raised $150,000 for the Crusade for Freedom. President Eisenhower congratulated the boys "for the fine record you made in gathering Truth Dollars in the Crusade for Freedom."[40]

Results of Fund Raising

The 1956-1957 Crusade campaign received $3,027,960 from public and corporate contributions against expenses of $997,381.[41]

CHAPTER NINE

Freedom Is Not Free!

April 1957 Crusade for Freedom Meeting

The Executive Committee of the Crusade for Freedom met at the boardroom of the Standard Oil Company (New Jersey) office, Rockefeller Plaza, New York City, on April 15, 1957. Among the agenda items discussed was the planning for the 1958 Crusade, the budget of which was set at $1,000,000: $263,870 for the Executive Department; $271,370 for Public Information; and $464,760 for Public Drives. The national goal in contributions was set at $10 million.[1]

The John Price Jones Company would handle the corporate solicitations. The October Study Tour to Europe was budgeted at $28,055. For the 1958 Crusade campaign, the board unanimously approved the appointments of Gwilym A. Price as chairman of the board, Arthur Page as president, and Eugene Holman as chairman of the executive committee.[2]

New Crusade Films

In June 1957, the Crusade for Freedom planned 400 prints of a 14-minute film about the Crusade for Freedom to be distributed around the country. Arthur Page wrote to CBS president Frank Stanton and explained that the planned 15-minute film *Towers of Truth* was "One of the most important elements of the Crusade's public information activities, as the 400 prints of the new film are expected, as in the past, to be widely shown in all parts of the country — to various civic, luncheon clubs, schools, volunteer Crusade groups and on local television stations."[3]

Television newscaster Walter Cronkite (Figure 23) expressed his willingness to narrate the film but needed the approval of Frank Stanton to do so. Stanton gave his approval for Cronkite but only on his vacation time. Stanton wrote back to Page, "Walter has expressed great enthusiasm for the project and I am sure he will turn in a first-class job."[4] On November 22, 1957, John Patterson wrote to Frank Stanton thanking him for allowing Walter Cronkite to narrate the film and telling him that Cronkite did a "superb job." There was no cost to the Crusade for Cronkite's work, including his traveling to Munich. There was a trade press premiere of the film on November 21, 1955, and Patterson told Stanton:

Figure 23. CBS television news anchor Walter Cronkite at Radio Free Europe in Munich (courtesy of RFE/RL).

> At the showing, the trade press, the Advertising Council people and the Radio Free Europe representatives agreed that the film was both highly professional, and highly effective. RFE likes it so much it is having it dubbed in German and several other languages for showing throughout Europe.[5]

Another film featuring Radio Free Europe planned for distribution was *Lifeline to Freedom*, narrated by journalist and television personality John Daly. The film explained how RFE was maintained and financed as well as who worked for RFE.

Gwilym A. Price

In July 1957 Gwilym Alexander Price, president of Westinghouse Electric Corporation, which happened to provide electronic equipment for Radio Free Europe transmitters, became the 1958 national chairman of the Crusade for Freedom. President Eisenhower wrote a congratulatory letter to Gwilym Price on July 11, 1957:

> The Crusade for Freedom has long enlisted my support. Together with Radio Free Europe and the Free Europe Committee, these provide the peoples of Eastern Europe with truth, which is basic to the building of a just and peaceful world.
> Through the Crusade for Freedom millions of our citizens have voluntarily helped to finance Radio Free Europe's broadcasts. The stirring events of the last year are proof that the spirit is alive in the hearts of peoples everywhere and receptive to message of Radio Free Europe.

I am glad to learn you have accepted the national chairmanship of the 1958 Crusade for Freedom. Now, in asking others to assist you, I hope you will tell them of my deep and continuing interest in the Crusade, a private enterprise, which serves the cause of freedom with truth and power.[6]

In July 1957, Crusade president Arthur W. Page sent out a multi-page report to Crusade supporters entitled "The Growth of the Crusade for Freedom and Radio Free Europe." In the report introduction, Page wrote,

> The past seven years—1950–1957—have, indeed, been extremely fateful ones in the struggle for freedom.... But the choking grip of the iron claw has not been able to kill its victim's desires to know the truth; neither has it been able to keep the truth from reaching them.
> This report, then, is the accounting of the Crusade for Freedom's stewardship: a report of how a small kernel of truth has flourished through seven years of tragic world turmoil until it has become the major source of news for millions, the bright contact between the free and the enslaved. To the millions of Americans who have supported the Crusade since its inception, as individuals, members of organizations, and as corporate owners, must go the credit for the swelling volume of truth piercing the Communist-controlled countries.[7]

Page's presidential report went into full details of the growth of Radio Free Europe, including radio set statistics in East Europe and photographs of the RFE transmitting sites and headquarters building in Munich. There was an illustrated description of how the radio signals were sent from Germany to Portugal for re-transmission to the "Target Countries" behind the Iron Curtain.

Crusade for Freedom executive vice-president John Patterson wrote a letter to Earl Newsom on July 25, 1957, in which he gave an overview of the 1956 Crusade, noting, "We wound up well ahead of last year financially—in fact not too far behind the Crusade's best year of 1954." He went on,

> From the point of view of public participation, however, it was the best ever. Apart from the fantastic coverage the Advertising Council and our people got in TV, radio and press, public contributions were up nearly twenty percent over last year, and were more than any other year.[8]

Advertising Council Continued Support

At the Advertising Council meeting on August 13, 1957, the Ad Council Campaign Review Committee meeting considered a letter from the Crusade for Freedom requesting advertising support for a short-term Crusade campaign planned for January and February of 1958. John M. Patterson, executive vice president of Crusade for Freedom sent a letter to the Advertising Council, which read in part:

> On behalf of the Crusade I want to thank you for the magnificent support of the Advertising Council, which made this year's Crusade the most successful in our history. Of particular interest to you will be the fact that Crusade's message reached

Only With Your Help Can She Know Truth

Don't Let Lies
Win The Battle For Her Mind!

What goes into little Marinka's mind today will affect you profoundly five or ten years from now. If she learns only the Communist "party line," your future is in danger. But she can learn the truth if you help.

Little Marinka's classes are not at all like those your daughter attends. In civics class, she learns to report on her parents' every "incorrect" political statement. Her geography teacher tells her how American troops "occupy" Western Europe and threaten the borders of her country. And in her Physical Education class, Marinka will be taught how to operate a rifle.

How is she to learn the facts? How will she know we want only peace? The truth can still get through to her. Because Marinka's family and millions of other oppressed people behind the Iron Curtain can still listen to Radio Free Europe. Every day, every hour, the 29 super-powered transmitters of this freedom network are at work, over-powering Red efforts at "jamming," slashing through Red lies, renewing hope that freedom will some day return behind the Iron Curtain.

What you must do:

Radio Free Europe needs your help to stay on the air. It is a private organization supported by the American people. Your dollars are needed to help operate its transmitters, pay for equipment, supplies, announcers and news analysts. Freedom is *not* free! Send your truth dollars *today* to Crusade for Freedom, care of your local Postmaster.

FREEDOM IS NOT FREE!
Your dollars are needed to keep RADIO FREE EUROPE on the air!

This monitoring receiver costs thousands of dollars. Yet it can wear out . . . must be replaced or repaired at great cost. You must send your dollars to keep Radio Free Europe operating!

Without your help, his voice is stilled. Your truth dollars pay the salaries of dozens of announcers like him. They broadcast the truth in five languages up to 20 hours a day. Are you giving?

It costs $1 a minute to put freedom on the air. Yes, one dollar "buys" one minute of broadcasting time on the 29 truth transmitters of Radio Free Europe. Keep them on the air with your truth dollars!

Send your truth dollars to

CRUSADE
for
FREEDOM
Care of your local Postmaster

← **NOTE TO PUBLISHER:**
May we suggest that you insert the address of the bank in your state which is receiving Crusade for Freedom contributions. Please consult the enclosed list for the appropriate names and addresses.

(SPONSOR)

NEWSPAPER MAT AD NO. CF-112-58—1000 LINES (5 columns x 14¼ inches)
ALSO AVAILABLE: AD NO. CF-116-58—600 LINES (4 columns x 10¾ inches)

more people in America than ever before, and that as a result individual contributions are up almost 20 per cent over last year.[9]

The Campaigns Review Committee voted to recommend approval of support for Crusade for Freedom for the eighth consecutive year. The Advertising Council chose the theme "Freedom is not free" for the 1958 Crusade campaign as one of its campaign slogans. Another one was "One dollar buys one minute of time on the 29 truth transmitters of Radio Free Europe." The Advertising Council estimated that $5 million would be the value of its free advertising support for the Crusade campaign.

Advertising Campaign

One Ad Council newspaper slogan was "Don't Let Lies Win the Battle for Her Mind!" The advertisement (shown in Figure 24) had a photograph of a small girl named Marinka who was sitting in a classroom with an open book, and it began with "Only with Your Help Can She Know Truth":

> What goes into little Marinka's mind today will affect you profoundly five or ten years from now. If she hears only the Communist "party line" your future is in danger. But she can learn the truth if you help.
> How is she to learn the facts? ... The truth can still get through to her. Because Marinka's family and millions of other oppressed people behind the Iron Curtain can still listen to Radio Free Europe.

The advertisement also had a small photograph of Radio Free Europe's monitoring equipment with the text, "Freedom is not free. This monitoring receiver can wear out, must be repaired at great cost. Send your dollars. Keep Radio Free Europe operating." Another small photograph in the same ad showed RFE's antenna towers with the text, "It costs $1 a minute to put freedom on the air."[10]

The prevailing print media theme in the 1958 Crusade advertising was "FREEDOM IS NOT FREE! Your dollars are needed to keep RADIO FREE EUROPE on the air." One 1958 Crusade campaign newspaper and magazine advertisement contained the phrase, "Don't Let Freedom be CUT OFF THE AIR!" This one showed a cable to a Radio Free Europe microphone being cut by a pair of pliers, as seen in Figure 25. The text read, in part, "Can you imagine it: A policeman's wary eye following you wherever you go ... your neighbor's ear anxiously pressed to your door, listening for the slightest slip of your tongue ... a loud speaker 'serenading' you all day with warnings, instructions, propaganda lies?"[11]

"He Knows Freedom Is Not Free! Do you?" read another advertisement,

Opposite: Figure 24. "Don't Let Lies Win the Battle for Her Mind." Newspaper Advertisement used in 1957–1958 newspaper campaign (courtesy of Advertising Council).

Don't Let Freedom Be Cut "OFF THE AIR"!

Your Truth Dollars Are Needed Today!

Can you imagine it: A policeman's wary eye following you wherever you go . . . your neighbor's ear anxiously pressed to your door, listening for the slightest slip of your tongue . . . a loud-speaker "serenading" you all day with warnings, instructions, propaganda lies?

70,000,000 people behind the Iron Curtain will be buried under this avalanche of oppression unless you help. For, word of freedom can only come to them one way: over the radio, from stations like those of Radio Free Europe. Every day, every hour, the 29 super-powered transmitters of this freedom network are at work, overpowering

"jamming" from Red stations, slashing through Red lies, renewing hope that freedom will some day return to the peoples behind the Iron Curtain.

Why your help is needed

But Radio Free Europe needs your help to stay on the air. It is a private organization supported by the American people. Your dollars are needed to help operate transmitters, pay for equipment, supplies, announcers and political analysts. Don't let freedom be cut "off the air"! Send your truth dollars today to Crusade for Freedom, care of your local Postmaster.

FREEDOM IS NOT FREE!
Your dollars are needed to keep RADIO FREE EUROPE on the air!

Send your truth dollars to

CRUSADE
for
FREEDOM

Care of local Postmaster

(SPONSOR)

NEWSPAPER MAT AD NO. CF-111-58—1000 LINES (5 columns x 14½ inches)
ALSO AVAILABLE AD NO. CF-118-58—600 LINES (3 columns x 7½ inches)

which showed a photograph of a man, indentified as Bela Varga, with a tear drop under his left eye. Monsignor Bela Varga was previously identified as one religious leader, who was quoted in the Advertising Council's 1952-1953 Crusade campaign.[12] The advertisement also had three small photographs that showed "broadcasting tubes wear out fast ... help us buy more," one of a technician in Munich with, "Your truth dollars pay the salaries of dozens of technicians like him," and a third which showed antenna towers with, "Your dollar pays for one minute of broadcasting time." The same photograph and similar text were used in the February 1958 issue of *Reader's Digest*.

The Advertising Council sent out a master campaign kit in 1958 to "Crusaders all over the country" to help them understand how the Ad Council information could best be put to use. Bob Keim, Account Executive of the Advertising Council, announced that the kits would achieve three results:

1. Familiarizes the public with the fact that this year's campaign is underway,
2. Explains the campaign's purpose and nature, and
3. Appeals for truth dollars in support of Radio Free Europe.[13]

The kit detailed the mailing activities of the Advertising Council that resulted in more than "$5,000,000 in donated space and time":

Newspaper: ads sent to 1,651 dailies and 4,500 weeklies
Business papers: business ads were sent to 736 business papers
House magazines: mailed to 3,000 house magazines.
Radio: mailed to all radio stations, including two sets of spot announcements
Television: five filmed commercials and written spot announcements to all program directors.[14]

1957 European Study Trip

Sixty "Trippers" went on the 1957 Study Trip to Europe, October 11–21, 1957. Some of those who made the trip were John S. Gleason, national commander, American Legion; Mrs. Pat Kelly, national president, American Legion Auxiliary; Mrs. William Mason, national president, National Council of Negro Women; George Christopher, Mayor of San Francisco; I.W. Garek, vice president, B'nai B'Rith; Robert P. Keim, Advertising Council; Mrs. R.I.C. Prout, president, General Federation of Women's Clubs; and Richard L. Roudebush, commander in chief, Veterans of Foreign Wars, USA.

Another "Tripper" was Herman W. Steinkraus, president of Bridgeport Brass Company and the Connecticut state Crusade chairman. After his return, the *Bridgeport Sunday Post* on October 27, 1957, featured a detailed article about Radio Free Europe, the Crusade, and his participation in the Study Trip:

Opposite: Figure 25. "Don't Let Freedom Be Cut 'OFF THE AIR.'" Illustrated newspaper advertisement used in 1957-1958 Campaign (courtesy of Advertising Council).

"Steinkraus Lauds Work of Radio Free Europe." Steinkraus was quoted as saying, "The Americans who operate Radio Free Europe are under the impression that the American public does not really understand the important work they are doing. Since the American people will soon be called upon to give as generously as they can to keep this important vehicle operating in the cause of freedom."

Prior to the trip, press releases on the individual "Trippers" were sent to local newspapers with information about the person and the reasons for the trip. A second release was sent to local newspapers on the day the "tripper" left for Europe. Many of the "Trippers" were photographed sitting with a sheet of paper behind a microphone with the words RFE and Crusade for Freedom clearly visible to the newspaper reader. Herman Steinkraus was shown in the *Bridgeport Sunday Post* on October 17, 1957, behind the RFE microphone, "Making Crusade Broadcast." Another "Tripper" was William J. Morrissey, *Independent Press-Telegram* circulation director, whose photograph appeared in a short item in the *Independent Press Telegram* on October 6, 1957, announcing his impending departure to Europe, etc. The newspaper on October 20, 1957, then carried a front-page report "Crusader at Work" showing him at the Munich RFE studios sitting behind the RFE microphone: "In Munich, Germany, William J. Morrissey of Long Beach broadcasts from Radio Free Europe headquarters a friendly message to the captive people behind the Iron Curtain."

Lions Clubs

Dudley (Dud) L. Simms from Charleston, West Virginia, went to Europe as a representative of the Lions Clubs, with a membership of 600,000 in 84 countries in 1957. Simms was the 1958 designated president of 9,000 Lions Clubs in the United States. After his return from the European Study Tour, his photograph with the caption "Crusader at Work" appeared in the local newspaper on October 18, 1957.[15] In December 1957, Simms was quoted in a newspaper article about his experiences in Europe: "We know the RFE is getting through because the Russians are spending millions in their attempt to jam the RFE broadcasts.... A dollar donation to the Crusade for Freedom is a mighty force against Russian shackling of millions of captive people."[16]

Television

Crusade executive vice president John Patterson sent a letter to Arthur Page on December 11, 1957, in which he wrote about the use of Educational Television (ETV) and the Crusade's public information work. The Crusade had commissioned a study by William A. Wood, Columbia University School of

Journalism. Patterson attached a copy of a summary report by William Wood, part of which read:

> Organizations like Crusade for Freedom, anxious to supplement their public appeals with augmented efforts in the area of public education, should take educational television seriously. It can be a vehicle for them. ETV has reached a point where people with an educational job to do should consider it as a subject for action.[17]

February 28, 1958, was "Crusade for Freedom Day" on the Mutual Broadcasting System television network with 18 different spot announcements that were prepared by the Radio-TV Section of the Crusade for Freedom. Popular radio and television shows on the other major television networks also carried spot announcements. "Television home impression" is a term representing the number of times that one television message is seen in one home. From December 29, 1957 to January 11, 1958, the estimated number of television home impressions for Crusade of Freedom messages was 8,300,000.[18]

Allen Dulles to Eisenhower

There was another White House luncheon for leading corporate supporters of the Crusade for Freedom on November 12, 1957. Director of Central Intelligence Allen Dulles wrote to President Eisenhower on November 16, 1957, concerning the upcoming Crusade luncheon and developments at Radio Free Europe. The letter clearly shows the CIA relationship to both RFE and the U.S. State Department:

> I sincerely appreciate your willingness, once again, to give the Crusade for Freedom luncheon. This is really a great encouragement for the organization and a key factor in getting the Crusade off to a vigorous start.
>
> The developments following the Hungarian revolt and repression and the more favorable trends in Poland create a great opportunity for Radio Free Europe, but also raises a series of difficult problems. General Crittenberger is doing a highly creditable Job, and we are carefully following from here, in consultation with the State Department, the policy lines and guidance for the themes, which are being played back to the Satellites on the radio and in the Committee's literature.[19]

American Legion Auxiliary

Based on the resolution at its 39th annual convention held in Atlantic City, New Jersey, in September 1957, the American Legion Auxiliary (ALA) agreed to "continue its full and complete support of the Crusade for Freedom in order to give captive countries of East Europe 'daily testimony that their plight has not and will not be forgotten by the Free World.'" Mrs. Helen M. Meyer as "national security chairman" was awarded a prize in recognition of her work for the 1956 Crusade campaign. Local Auxiliary Units were given the following message to use by the press in announcing the local 1958 campaign's Crusade for Freedom Day: "We who live in freedom have an obligation to those who are denied it, and Radio Free Europe was founded on this philosophy that men everywhere are entitled to freedom, including the rights of a free radio and free press."[20]

The Advertising Council sent out 250 copies a Freedom Program kit to the Secretary of the Auxiliary for distribution at the American Legion Auxiliary's President and Secretaries Conference held on November 4, 1957. Similar kits were later sent to ALA campaign directors at the local level. These kits included instructions on "How to Conduct a Successful Crusade for Freedom Project" and a copy of the *Towers of Truth* film.[21]

During Freedom Week in February 1958, Auxiliary Unit volunteers staffed booths with fund containers in convenient locations throughout cities and towns, participated in the door-to-door campaign soliciting funds, and held meetings in Legion halls and in private homes, one of which, in Calumet Park, Chicago, Illinois, witnessed a vote by the Auxiliary members to contribute $5.00 to the Crusade for Freedom.[22] In Anderson, Indiana, the George Hockett Auxiliary Unit 127 held a Freedom Week meeting for soliciting of contributions at the American Legion Post home and Kenneth Gates, Juvenile Department, Anderson Police showed the film *Lifeline to Freedom*.[23]

Federal Service Joint Crusade

January 13, 1958, to February 28, 1958, was a combined fundraising campaign period for Crusade for Freedom, National Health Agencies, and CARE among federal employees and military services. The National Health Agencies were American Cancer Society; American Heart Association; Arthritis and Rheumatism Foundation; Muscular Dystrophy Association of America; National Society of Crippled Children and Adults; National Association of Mental Health; and National Society for the Prevention of Blindness.

The Billboard *Magazine*

The magazine *The Billboard* in 1958 proudly proclaimed itself in its sixty-fourth year to be "The Amusement Industry's Leading Newsweekly." The March 3, 1958, issue had a full-page article entitled "A Report to the Music Industry" that dealt with Radio Free Europe and the Crusade for Freedom. A photograph was included of the Munich RFE headquarters as well as a graphic of the RFE transmitter sites and how programs were broadcast from German and Portugal to East Europe. The article focused on music: "The youth in these countries want to know about and hear the latest American pop, dance and jazz records. And music of all kinds comprises some 15% of broadcast time to each country behind the Iron Curtain."

One of the major features of *The Billboard* was its list of the top selling records in the United States and this was reflected in the article:

> As soon as each issue of The Billboard is received in the New York office of RFE, the Honor Roll of Hits and Most Played by Jockeys charts are clipped and sent, together, the records are broadcast, with explanatory commentary, on the various programs devoted to this material.
>
> So, while we here in the U.S.A. are busy making, distributing and selling records, the Crusade for Freedom with its Radio Free Europe stations continues its untiring efforts to bring a continuing flow of unbiased news, truth and music to the 70 million people who live in the five captive countries behind the Iron Curtain.

The article was repeated in the May 5, 1958, issue of *The Billboard.*

Fulton Lewis Battle

For reasons not completely clear, King Features syndicated columnist and radio personality Fulton Lewis, Jr., fought a long media battle against both Radio Free Europe and the Crusade for Freedom that threatened the existence of both organizations. It started on October 2, 1957, when his column headlined "Your R.F.E. 'Truth Dollars.'" After examining RFE's policy on broadcasts about Yugoslavia and Communist party leader Tito, Lewis wrote, "In short, the 'truth dollar,' and whatever the Central Intelligence Agency (CIA) is contributing out of the Federal Treasury to subsidize the RFE operation are being used to sell the people behind the Iron Curtain on the glories of Tito and his independent Communism, not on Western Democracy." In his nationally syndicated column on November 14, 1957, Lewis wrote, "The C.I.A.— Allen Dulles' cloak and dagger game, the Central Intelligence Agency — is secretly contributing about three-fourths of the money that the Free Europe funds spend but Dulles doesn't want it known."

For the next months, the Crusade for Freedom and Radio Free Europe executives were busy with countering the continuing attacks in Lewis' columns and radio shows. On November 26, 1977, the Crusade for Freedom put out a nine-page statement entitled, "Facts Concerning Charges of Fulton Lewis, Jr." This was the second fact sheet and listed the "charges" and then listed in detail the "facts."[24]

Fulton Lewis broadcast another attack against Radio Free Europe on December 18, 1957, part of which was, "The important consideration is that they collect these huge sums of money ... they will not however make any public accounting of their funds whatsoever. They do not issue any balance sheet, they do not even provide the most skeletal financial statements, and they will not tell you how the money is being used or what it is being spent for, or even how much they take in."[25]

At a "Deputies Meeting" at the Central Intelligence Agency, Thursday, December 26, 1957, DCI Allen Dulles told the group that he would be meeting General Crittenberger, president of the Free Europe Committee (FEC), to "discuss the current series of Fulton Lewis broadcasts in which Mr. Lewis is attacking RFE and Crusade for Freedom."

Also on December 26, 1957, Joseph Grew, executive committee member of the FEC, wrote to General Crittenberger in which he told him that "I have had two long talks with Allen Dulles and while he feels that something must be done to meet Fulton Lewis' attacks, he feels as I do that a somewhat different approach had better be made.... I think that to send a letter protesting Mr. Lewis's broadcasts would be dangerous. He commands a widespread audience and there are many who would resent our intrusion and who would rally to his support.... Mr. Lewis's broadcasts are no doubt harmful to the Committee and to our work, but I think that a protest from us would do us infinitely greater harm."[26]

The Board of Directors Meeting on December 30, 1957, a relatively heated debate focused on the Fulton Lewis attacks. Arthur Page told the board of directors that in the answer to be prepared, they should, "not (1) pick a fight or call him a liar, nor (2) go into details, but just be very general." Page added that he had spoken with Allen Dulles, "who really wanted us to hold off going after Fulton Lewis."[27]

Arthur Page, president of the Crusade for Freedom and chairman of the executive committee of Free Europe Committee, wrote a letter to Fulton Lewis on January 8, 1958. Page sent a copy to CIA Director Allen Dulles; Gwilym Price sent a copy in a personalized letter to all Crusade corporate members, state chairman 1957, Munich Trip Members, and national organizations. Page wrote, in part,

> We do not dispute your right to attack Radio Free Europe and Crusade for Freedom if you are so minded. In the hope that it might be helpful to our national interest, I want, however, to send you this note to testify how those of us who are giving time to these two organizations feel about them.
>
> I do not propose that either the Crusade for Freedom or Radio Free Europe or Radio Free Europe embark on a public quarrel with you in these matters. Any such public wrangling could in no way contribute to the fight against Communism.[28]

Fulton Lewis wrote back to Arthur Page on January 15, 1958, thanking him for his "gracious and high-minded letter." He added,

> I respectfully contend that the mere statement of objectives, and the supplying of funds with which to carry out these objectives, does not constitute accomplishment. The crux of the operation is whether the machinery performs as it should, and whether the results actually attained are the results that were set out to be attained. In this case, it is abundantly demonstrable that exactly the opposite is true.[29]

On February 18, 1958, Allen Dulles wrote to Eugene Holman, chairman of the Crusade's executive committee, "I trust that the Fulton Lewis business has not been too much of a nuisance to you. It seems to me that he is beginning to run out of steam and certainly I would think that his pieces are boring enough to tire any listener. As one of those who had a share in your involvement, I feel a particular debt of gratitude for the stout attitude you have taken. I am confident that all will come out all right in the end."[30]

By February 21, 1958, the number of Lewis' attacks had reached 23. Arthur Page wrote a letter to Frank McClearn, General Manager of King Features Syndicates, with copies to newspapers that carried his column, on that date, part of which read, "Many hundreds of thousands of good American citizens all over the country are giving their time and money to voluntarily support of the Crusade for Freedom. Some of them have written to us, very much puzzled by Mr. Lewis' comments."[31] Lewis' radio attacks against RFE and the Crusade reached 40 by February 20, 1958, and Arthur Page wrote a letter to Paul Roberts, president of the Mutual Broadcasting System, Inc. (MBS), that had the same basic text of the one he sent to Frank McClearn, with the additional comment, "May I request that you send copies of this letter and the fact sheet to managers of all your stations carrying Mr. Lewis' broadcasts."[32]

Congressional Inquiry

Representative Harry G. Haskell, Republican from Delaware, wrote a letter of inquiry on March 17, 1958, to the U.S. State department on behalf of a "constituent" who had read the Fulton Lewis articles critical of both the Crusade for Freedom and Radio Free Europe. William B. Macomber, Assistant Secretary of State, answered with a letter to Representative Haskell dated March 28, 1958, which, in part, read:

> As you know, the Crusade is a private and non-official organization which sponsors the Free Europe Committee and its radio station Radio Free Europe. Because so many of the functions and objectives of the three organizations relate to foreign affairs, the Department of State is generally familiar with their activities. The Department, however, respects and recognizes the right of American citizens to carry out private endeavors such as the mission of the Free Europe Committee and does not, of course, attempt to direct the Free Europe Committee or to interfere in its management.
> The board of directors of the Crusade for Freedom is composed of respected and distinguished figures in America — whose loyalty to the American way of life is beyond question. The Department believes that the Free Europe Committee and Radio Free Europe have made important contributions to carrying the message of freedom to the peoples of Eastern Europe and are decidedly a significant free world force countering international communism.[33]

John Warner, Legislative Council of the CIA, sent a "Secret" memorandum to DCI Allen Dulles on June 16, 1958, in which he summarized the State Department position in similar letter to Congressman John F. Baldwin (R.–California). Warner wrote that "the constituent was persevering and wrote again to the Congressman, who on June 4, 1958, directed a letter to the Federal Bureau of Investigation requesting information whether the operations of RFE have been subversive or have violated laws of this country."[34]

After meeting with representatives of the CIA, FBI Director J. Edgar Hoover wrote to Congressman Baldwin stating that "I must advise that Crusade for Freedom and its radio station, Radio Free Europe, have not been investigated. I have taken the liberty of referring a copy of your letter and its enclosures to another agency of the Government and have been assured that one of its representatives will call on you in the immediate future to discuss your inquiry."[35]

Warner wrote to Dulles that "Under the circumstances it seems necessary that Mr. Baldwin be briefed by the Agency. While it may not be necessary to give him the full extent of CIA participation, nevertheless we should be prepared to answer his questions frankly.... For this purpose, it is recommended that Cord Meyer and myself arrange a meeting to discuss this matter with the Congressman." Dulles agreed and Cord Meyer and Warner apparently met with Congressman Baldwin.[36]

Lewis Visits Radio Free Europe

In September 1958, Fulton Lewis visited Radio Free Europe headquarters in Munich and filed one of his columns from there. He was not less critical as he wrote, "To me, with 35 years of competitive experience in both fields, the whole thing is a ridiculous, wasteful juvenile exhibition of futility to provide jobs for what is mainly a horde of free-loaders." As further evidence of the effect of the Lewis' attacks, the Montana American Legion Americanism Committee adopted a resolution in July 1959 for an "investigation of charges made by Fulton Lewis, Jr., against operation of Radio Free Europe to determine if the Legion should continue support of the program beamed to satellites in Eastern Europe."[37] But by then, without fanfare, the Fulton Lewis media war against RFE and the Crusade for Freedom appeared to simply run out of steam, or Lewis just lost interest in pursuing the subject.

Grass-Roots Activities

The Fulton Lewis battles in his newspaper column and radio programs had an apparent impact on local crusade activities, which were distinctly lower-keyed in 1958 in comparison with previous years.

Governor Muskie

Governor Edmund S. Muskie, whose father was a Polish immigrant and whose mother was the daughter of Polish immigrants, proclaimed "Freedom Week" in Maine February 17–23, 1958. His proclamation read, in part:

> WHEREAS, the people behind the Iron Curtain are entitled to a continuing flow of unbiased news and truth to form sound judgments and to avoid wanton bloodshed, and
> WHEREAS, funds are needed to support the successful continuation of the vital work being done;
> NOW THEREFORE, I urge that all Maine citizens support to the best of their ability this outstanding program for freedom.[38]

Edmund Muskie afterwards became a United States Senator, Secretary of State, and unsuccessful candidate for the U.S. President.

Pennsylvania State University Chapel Choir

The Pennsylvania State University Chapel Choir went on its biennial six-week concert tour of Europe in the summer 1957, including a concert in Munich, Germany, where they also visited Radio Free Europe. Many of the 60 students were featured in local newspapers in Pennsylvania after their return home, including, Carole P. Young, who was featured in the New Castle, Pennsylvania, *News* on September 4, 1957, in an article "Miss Carol Young Aids in RFE Radio Program." She was described as "One of the American College students, contributing to the effort of RFE in carrying the fight of freedom directly into the camp of totalitarian Communism through this College Crusade."

Another student was Penny Robey of Smethport, Pennsylvania, who was similarly identified in the article text under her photograph, part of which read, "Thousands of American students contribute to this effort through the College Crusade, which is beamed via RFE's transmitters to captive nation students who are subject to Communist indoctrination."[39]

Newspaperboys Campaign

Thousands of local newspaper carriers, or newspaperboys, again volunteered their support for the Crusade for Freedom. The national newspaperboy poster, which showed one about to ring a house doorbell with a newspaper, was entitled "He's helping to keep the Freedom Bell Ringing for 79 Million Iron Curtain People." The text read: "This week, when the newspaper carrier rings your doorbell your newspaper boy will ask for your truth dollars to keep Radio Free Europe on the air." The text went with details of how the "truth dollars" would help: "But Freedom is *not* free. Radio Free Europe is a private organization, supported by the American people. Your dollars are needed to pay for Radio Free Europe's equipment, its announcers, and its news staff. So help keep the freedom bell ringing behind the Iron Curtain." The "Freedom Badge" for the 1957 campaign was "a replica of the actual Freedom Bell that hangs in West Berlin. Let is remind you to give generously to keep the spirit of freedom alive behind the Iron Curtain."

Some newspapers postponed the Newspaperboy campaign to April or May 1958 to avoid conflicts with other fundraising activities in February. There was a meeting of 108 newspaper carriers in Mason City, Iowa, on February 10, 1958, in preparation for the local drive. W. Earl Hall, Iowa state chairman, told the carriers, "Because private individuals and groups in every state voluntarily help raise the money, the crusade is truly an effort of private enterprise. It is a popular movement of the American people against the Communist big lie."[40]

Newspapers used the same photograph with other titles for the advertisement text, e.g. "Local newspaperboys join nationwide fight against Communist press. Tomorrow Our Newspaperboys Begin Their Campaign to Enlist Financial Help in the CRUSADE FOR FREEDOM...." The text was different, too: in the Ogden *Standard-Examiner*, for example, there were two additional text lines:

> The power of Truth
> The people living in the Satellite countries are subject to the confusion of Communist propaganda. They must rely on the truth reporting of *Free Europe Press* and *Radio Free Europe* as a scale for measuring *true* values.
> The pattern of Truth
> *Free Europe Press and Radio Free Europe* supply *truthful* news where news of any kind is rare. They supply news that is rigidly tested for its truth ... then reported calmly and thoroughly.[41]

Road to Nowhere

One of the Advertising Council's newspaper advertisements included a photograph that showed a closed border crossing point with the caption, "Beginning of the open road to nowhere." The text read, "This is the beginning of satellite Europe — where truth and freedom are often only empty words. But real truth can pour into these countries over Radio Free Europe to build a spirit of freedom."[42]

Fund Raising Results

The 1957-58 Crusade campaign raised $2,621,160 in private and corporate contributions against expenses of $931,127.[43]

CHAPTER TEN

Truth Broadcasts, Bowling and Harlem Globetrotters

Statue of Liberty Ceremony

The "5th Annual Consecration of Freedom Day" was celebrated on July 1, 1958, in front of the Statue of Liberty on Liberty Island, New York City. The event also celebrated the 74th anniversary of the gift of the Statue of Liberty from France. The celebration, co-sponsored by the Free Europe Committee and the Downtown–Lower Manhattan Association, included a short speech by Arthur Page, among others, in his dual role of chairman of the executive committee, Free Europe Committee, and president of the Crusade for Freedom. He briefly spoke about both organizations:

> Nine years ago several private citizens organized themselves into a committee. It was, at that time, the stated policy of the United States government to encourage the people of Eastern Europe to regain their freedom. That is still the policy of the Government.
>
> The objective of the Free Europe Committee was to do what private citizens could do to encourage that policy. This we have done for nine years as well as we knew how, and we expect to continue to do so until the captive nations are free to choose their own governments and pursue their quest of happiness in their own way.[1]

Regarding the Crusade for Freedom, Page said, "In these nine years, through the efforts of the Crusade for Freedom, millions of Americans have given their support to the Free Europe Committee and its objectives. The Crusade has helped millions of Americans to understand the aspirations and hope of the captive nations. And in these years the captive people have demonstrated that neither by threats, propaganda, not by instruction of the young can the Soviets destroy the cravings of these people for liberty."[2]

American Legion Support

The annual convention of the American Legion was held in Chicago on September 1–4, 1958. On September 4, 1958, the American Legion adopted a resolution that included a pledge to continue its long-standing support of the Crusade for Freedom. The resolution, in part, read:

> WHEREAS, the President of the United States and many of our leaders continue to support and commend the Crusade for Freedom and Radio Free Europe for their major and effective role in combating this communist Propaganda, and
> WHEREAS, Radio Free Europe's broadcasts offer these enslaved millions daily testimony that their plight has not, and will not be forgotten by the free world, and
> WHEREAS, the continued effectiveness of the Crusade for Freedom depends on the increased financial and moral support of the American people.... Now be it resolved that the American Legion ... pledge to continue its full and complete support of the Crusade for Freedom.[3]

On October 9, 1958, the Crusade for Freedom released a letter "to the American Citizen," under the signature of Gwilym A. Price, who had previously made a trip to Munich and written about his first-hand experiences at Radio Free Europe. In his letter, Price identified CBS President Frank Stanton and David Sarnoff, Chairman of the Board of RCA, as agreeing with him concerning how impressive Radio Free Europe was. Price wrote, "The urgent, continuing need of the people of East Europe for unbiased news and information is undeniable, as is the fact that RFE is fulfilling this need effectively and efficiently." He added, "I consider it a privilege therefore to be identified with the effort to raise money needed to assure the continuance of this vital operation."[4]

Typical Listener Letter

A letter from a Polish woman was identified as one that Radio Free Europe typically receives and was used by some newspapers in early September in the United States:

> In you we find great moral support. You teach us to look into the future calmly and sensibly and prevent the world from forgetting that we are still waiting for full and real freedom. You are playing a great historic role, the importance of which no one today is able to sufficiently comprehend and appreciate.[5]

Truth Broadcast Doubts

In October 1958, John Patterson, Executive Vice President of the Crusade, had meetings with various persons in Washington, DC, including Cord Meyer of the CIA. Patterson send a letter to Crusade president Arthur Page on October 6, 1958, which shows the close relationship that continued to exist between the CIA and the Crusade for Freedom and the fact that there was no major emotional impact item for the upcoming Crusade campaign:

> I had several good meetings in Washington last week on Thursday and Friday. The feeling there is that while the idea of the contest is excellent, they wondered

if we could really get it going for this year's campaign. Their feeling is that this is going to be a year where we are not in a position to draw too much attention to ourselves either in Munich or here. My own feeling is betwixt and between. Certainly we don't want to do it unless we can do it well, and it may be that we should start now to have a really first-class campaign for next year and mount the usual campaign for this coming year. Anyway I will discuss the matter further with Allan Wilson today or tomorrow when he returns to New York.

Patterson went on to tell Page that he and Cord Meyer had discussed the planned annual corporate White House luncheon with President Eisenhower as well as the letter drafted by Arthur Page to be sent by Eisenhower to Gwilym Price, Chairman of the Crusade for Freedom.[6]

October Study Trip

Sixty "Trippers" made the annual study trip to Europe in October 1958. One of them was M.M. Hardin, director of Kennecott Copper Company and New Mexico state chairman for the Crusade campaign. Hardin was from Albuquerque, New Mexico and, after he returned to the United States, the *Albuquerque Tribune* newspaper interviewed him. The interview included a photograph, entitled "Brushes the Iron Curtain," of Hardin standing in front of a guard tower along the Czech-German border and speaking into a Radio Free Europe microphone.

Hardin said, "It has been six years since I was in Europe. On my previous trip, I must confess I had a feeling that we were not making friends or accomplishing very much there. However, the contrast between this visit and the prior one was so great that I feel that communism has in a great extent been stopped on its westward march." Referring directly to the Crusade for Freedom and Radio Free Europe, Hardin said, "Any person that has contributed to the Crusade for Freedom or Radio Free Europe can have a feeling that he is fighting communism in a very direct way, even though he lives in New Mexico."[7]

Another "Tripper" was Art S. Ehrman, editor of the *Eagle* publication for the Fraternal Order of Eagles. After his return to the United States, he spoke before various Eagle groups, including one in Auburn, New York, on January 28, 1959.

He published a detailed first-person account of his European experiences in the February 1959 edition of the *Eagle* entitled, "Operation Truth: For the Millions Enslaved in Iron Curtain Countries RFE Offers Truth and Hope." The magazine's front cover showed him standing under the now familiar guard tower along the Czech-German border and speaking into a Radio Free Europe microphone held by an unidentified RFE person. Ehrman described his visit to the border: "It is hard to describe the eerie feeling of standing at the man-determined line which separates the free world from the one in which there is no freedom, seeing guards in the watch tower observing us and taking our pictures. It was hard to imagine that the lovely little creek we stood beside was the difference between liberty and slavery for the people who live on each side of it."

One photograph showed Ehrman in the group of 59 other "Trippers" embarking in New York on their way to Europe. Other photographs included RFE'S Munich headquarters building, transmitter site in Holzkirchen, and one of the Iron Curtain with the caption: "Tour members take a last look at the invisible yet sinister line of the Iron Curtain, which separates the Red-dominated countries from the free world."

Ehrman wrote, "For Crusade-supported RFE is the voice of the free world going to these captive peoples, letting them know that in this however imperfect planet, there are still places where people may be free, where there are no masters, no slaves." He informed the *Eagle* readers, "It also brought home ever more strongly an appreciation of the need for continuing activities like Radio Free Europe.... Crusade for Freedom is worth every bit of support we can give it."

Betty Shapiro, B'nai B'rith Women national Citizenship and Civic Affairs chairman, was another 1958 "Tripper." In her article published in February 1959 edition of *B'nai B'rith,* she was seen sitting behind RFE microphone with a large Crusade for Freedom poster behind her. She detailed her "whirlwind trip," including the visit to the Czech-German border: "I saw the Iron Curtain.... Here I was representing the only Jewish organization in a group of nearly 60 national leaders who represented all shades of political, economic, civic and religious life." She ended her article with her support appeal: "Here, in the most literal and meaningful sense, is a program financed by the people. I cannot too strongly advocate B'nai B'rith Women's continued support of the Crusade — especially now, during Crusade for Freedom month."[8]

Advertising Council and the Media

In November 1958, directors of the Crusade approved the upcoming contest text for participants to complete the sentence, "As an American I support Radio Free Europe because...." Contributions were not necessary to enter the contest but if the winning participant had contributed one dollar, he or she would win a free trip, along with a family member, to Europe.

There were numerous Crusade for Freedom spot announcements in major network television popular shows such as *Milton Berle* (NBC), *Eddie Fisher Show* (NBC), *Hit Parade* (CBS), *Gunsmoke* (CBS), *Name That Tune* (CBS) and *Lawrence Welk* (ABC). The Mutual Network presented a 15-minute radio show on February 22, 1959, from 12:00 to 12:15 with jazz great Duke Ellington, featuring the Truth Broadcaster Program. As another public service announcement for the 1959 campaign, the Advertising Council sent a text of a one-minute spot announcement of the Truth Broadcast contest to be read over the air:

Help air the truth! Help share the truth! Yes, you can help air the truth to millions of people behind the Iron Curtain! Just write a truth broadcast for Radio Free Europe. You might fly to Europe yourself to put it on the air! It's so easy! Just complete this sentence in 25 additional words or less: "As an American, I support Radio Free Europe because...."

In November 1958, the Advertising Council finalized the entry-blank text and illustrations for the planned "Truth Broadcast" contest that would be distributed as part of the press package in the 1959 active campaign. The suggested message of instructions for announcers, printed with the entry blank, included the phraseology:

- These captive peoples are hungry for the truth.
- Tell them about your desire to help them get the truth.
- Tell them what an important part the truth plays in your own every day life.
- Speak with your heart and your head.

The 1958-1959 Crusade advertising was also sometime alarmist: one advertisement, for example, showed a young girl, presumably in East Europe, sitting behind barbed wire along with a microphone of Radio Free Europe. The slogan was: "Don't let her grow up without hearing the TRUTH!" (See Figure 26.)

A coupon was to be filled out in 25 words or less and the sentence completed "I support Radio Free Europe because..." accompanied the advertisement. One was encouraged to submit as many entries as possible and if "Truth Dollars" accompanied the entry, six selected winners would be sent to Munich to read their winning entry over Radio Free Europe with another family member. If a "Truth Dollar" did not accompany the entry, 200 winners would receive Westinghouse portable radio along with a table-model short-wave receiver. The Advertising Council also recommended the use of sample Truth Broadcasts to tell the listeners, one of which was: "As an American I support Radio Free Europe because I want you behind the Iron Curtain to hear from friends who have access to the truth and want to share it with you."[9]

On January 9, 1959, John Patterson of the Crusade wrote to David Sarnoff, Chairman of the RCA and thus NBC, telling him, "We are not so well covered on radio and TV and I am taking the liberty of asking your help in getting spots." He then asked specifically for popular television stars Steve Allen and Perry Como advising Sarnoff "if they could give us brief personal endorsements, it would make an enormous difference to us."[10] On March 11, 1959, John Patterson sent a letter to Theodore Repplier, president of the Advertising Council, in which he said: "From what the members of your staff tell me, from our field reports, and our own clipping service, it is obvious that never before in the history of the Crusade have the media of this country given us so much support."[11]

On February 5, 1959, Dean Fritchen on the staff of the Crusade for Freedom sent out a memorandum on the subject of "Truth Broadcaster Promotions" to "Those Concerned with the Truth Broadcaster Program." He stated that the

Don't let her grow up without hearing the **TRUTH!**

Radio Free Europe

Now! You can broadcast your ideas
on Truth and Freedom behind the Iron Curtain over

RADIO FREE EUROPE!

For many years, Radio Free Europe has concentrated on telling the truth through the broadcasts of trusted Iron Curtain exiles. Now Radio Free Europe opens its microphones to the Truth Broadcasts of you ... as freedom-loving American citizens.

Now you can send your own Truth Broadcast to captive Europe ... and you may be flown to Europe yourself to broadcast it! Or you may be awarded a Hallicrafters short-wave radio!

Fill out and send in your TRUTH BROADCAST today. Simplicity, sincerity and honesty are important.

You can double your award if you send a dollar with your entry!

Read these rules! See how easy it is to enter!

1. Complete in 25 additional words or less the message starting "As an American I support Radio Free Europe because . . ." Enter as often as you wish, but each message must be mailed separately. They become the property of Crusade for Freedom and will not be returned.

2. Messages will be judged on the basis of appropriateness of thought, clarity, sincerity and originality. The judging will be done by The Reuben H. Donnelley Corporation, in full co-operation with the Free Europe Committee, Crusade for Freedom and The Advertising Council. (Officers and employees of these organizations and their volunteer advertising agencies are not eligible, nor are members of their immediate families.) Your message must be your original work, submitted in your own name. Persons whose messages are selected for broad-

(This program is subject to all governmental regulations.)

cast will be notified in person or by mail by May 15, 1959. If you would like a list of such persons, send a stamped, self-addressed envelope with your entry. The decisions of the judges shall be final.

3. Awards and extra awards are listed elsewhere in this announcement. (Cash equivalents may be awarded at the sponsor's option.) Duplicate awards will be made in the event of ties. It is not necessary for a contribution to accompany your entry to be eligible for an award. However, if your entry is accompanied by one or more Truth Dollars and it is selected, you will receive an extra award.

4. Entries will be accepted only from U. S. citizens.

5. Messages must be postmarked by March 31, 1959, and received by April 10, 1959.

RADIO FREE EUROPE TRUTH BROADCAST

Complete the following sentence in 25 additional words or less: "As an American I support Radio Free Europe because . . ."

_____

_____

_____

To Be Eligible For Awards, Please Fill In Completely:

NAME_____

STREET_____

CITY_____ZONE_____STATE_____

☐ I enclose a contribution of a dollar (or more) to help keep Radio Free Europe on the air. I know I do not need to contribute in order to be eligible for selection as a Truth Broadcaster . . . but I understand that if I do so and my message is selected as one of the six best, I and my family may accompany me to Europe. Or, if my message is among the 200 next best, I will receive a Westinghouse portable radio along with the table-model short-wave receiver.

Mail to Crusade for Freedom, Box 10-F, Mt. Vernon 10, N. Y.

Contributions to Crusade for Freedom have not and will not be used to defray any expenses of this Truth Broadcast Awards Program. Every cent collected by CRUSADE FOR FREEDOM goes to the support of Radio Free Europe.

HELP SHARE THE TRUTH! HELP AIR THE TRUTH!
Send A Truth Dollar To Radio Free Europe!

THIS ADVERTISEMENT SPONSORED IN THE INTEREST OF CRUSADE FOR FREEDOM BY

SPONSOR'S NAME

ADVERTISING COUNCIL PUBLIC SERVICE

NEWSPAPER MAT AD NO. CF-15-59—1000 LINES (5 columns x 14¼ inches)

Do not run these advertisements after March 31, 1959 when competition closes!

Crusade had received up to that date 7,693 "Truth Broadcasts," with an average of $.60 per entry. There was a stock of 156,604 counter cards, 139,215 pads of ballots and 71,638 posters. Radio and television kits had been revised on the advice of the National Broadcasting Company (NBC) and were mailed to every radio and television station in the United States. More than 200 newspapers had requested advertising mats from the Advertising Council, which was "running ahead of last year's Crusade."[12]

Although the 1959 Crusade campaign was still in the middle stages, Crusade president John Patterson, in his letter of March 11, 1959, to Theodore Repplier of the Advertising Council, asked for continuing support in 1960 when he wrote:

> I am writing once more on behalf of the Board of Directors to respectfully request that he Advertising Council renew its support of Crusade for the 1960 campaign. The support of the Advertising Council is vital to Crusade's effectiveness. I know I don't need to tell you of the continuing pleasure I and my staff have in working with the staff of the Advertising Council.[13]

"But not for me"

For the 1959 campaign, the Advertising Council also sent out a two-record set to radio stations: one was entitled "But not for me—Freedom is not free" that contained brief personal appeals in support Radio Free Europe, from musicians and entertainers, Duke Ellington, Arthur Godfrey (Figure 27), Hy Gardner, Judy Holliday, Robert Preston, and Dorothy Collins. It was distributed with a second record, "This Guitar Chose Freedom," that told the story of Hungarian jazz guitarist Gabor Szabo and his escape to freedom in 1956. Television personality Steve Allen was the speaker and Szabo is heard on the record playing songs "I Remember You," "Berklee's Delight," "You Go to My Head" and "Chinatown My Chinatown." The theme of the recording was "How American jazz — stifled behind the Iron Curtain — sounds in a free land."[14]

Reader's Digest *Educational Edition*

John Patterson as president of the Crusade wrote to Arthur Page on March 3, 1959, praising *Reader's Digest* for carrying "what we consider to be one of the most outstanding—and most unusual—contributions we've ever had to the cause of Radio Free Europe.... As a result, this Crusade for Freedom program will not only get extra attention in thousands of schools, but conceivably could be made a regular assignment in many of them."[15]

Opposite: **Figure 26. Illustrated Truth Broadcast newspaper advertisement (courtesy of Advertising Council).**

Figure 27. Television star Arthur Godfrey, a long-time supporter of the Crusade for Freedom, holding a Federal Service Joint Crusade poster, including Radio Free Europe (courtesy of RFE/RL).

Reader's Digest magazine had a readership of 35 million Americans and also published an "Educational Edition" for teachers in March 1958 that was used in approximately 50 percent of high schools in the United States. The *Reader's Digest* section was entitled "Ideas for Talking and Writing: The Play's the Thing." Students were told to first read the advertisement for Radio Free

Europe that appeared on page 249 of the issue and then open for discussion three questions, one of which was "What seems to be the official policy of the United States government towards anti–Soviet uprisings among the captive peoples of Europe?"

Students then were instructed to do research on the question, "What purpose is served by Radio Free Europe? What languages are used for the broadcasts? Is there any way of evaluating the effect of the broadcasts?" Additionally, students were asked to compete in the "Write a Truth Broadcast" contest but even if they did not participate, they should complete the sentence in "forceful words that are precise in meaning." The section ended with the comment to students: "You might also enjoy preparing an imaginary broadcast for Radio Free Europe. Dramatize a scene which you think would convey a true picture of American life."

The Wonderful Thing About Freedom

The April 5, 1959, *This Week* contained an article entitled "The Wonderful Thing About Freedom," which featured photographs of a teacher and students of a fourth grade class in an elementary school in Hewlett, New York. Geraldine M. Rack was the teacher and sent the results of the students' texts of the Truth contest to the weekly newspaper supplement. The editorial comment was: "Some of the most appealing testimonials to freedom we've ever run into were written by the nine-year-old boys and girls on this page." Four of them were printed:

> We are free. Are you? No? Well, try to be free. It is fun. When we fail we try again. You have to do that, too. (Karen)
> Freedom and liberty are so important to all nations and people around the world. Nobody should be deprived of the glorious freedom there can be. (Leslie)
> I would like to see Europe a free country like America and not bothered by the "Iron Curtain," with plenty of food, too. (Michael)
> I would like all people to know that, where America is not perfect, at least we try to correct our mistakes by law and practice. (Susan)

Change of Incorporation Certificate

The original certificate of incorporation for the National Committee for Free Europe contained this sentence:

> No part of the activities of the corporation shall be the carrying on of propaganda or otherwise attempting to influence legislation.

On March 12, 1959, the Board of Directors of the Free Europe Committee changed that by adding the work *substantial* to the sentence:

No substantial part of the activities of the corporation shall be in the carrying on of propaganda or otherwise attempting to influence legislation.[16]

Eisenhower Endorsement

The annual Crusade corporate luncheon with President Eisenhower was held in December 1958. He told those at the luncheon that he hoped that it would continue be an annual affair of his successor, too.[17] George Kinney, Radio Director of the Advertising Council, sent out a Radio Fact sheet to local Crusaders, including a written statement written under the name of President Eisenhower.

> The Communists have isolated their people to keep them from ever hearing the truth — to create a vacuum in their minds, which will absorb lies because there is nothing else for them to seize upon. The only way to frustrate this evil manipulation of human minds and emotions is to supply the truth which gives the oppressed people a measuring stick to lay against each lie that is told to them ••• Radio Free Europe is supplying the truth. Men and women who might otherwise have succumbed to the philosophy that it is good to be slaves still keep alive the spark of freedom in their hearts ••• This work serves not only the nations we seek to help — it serves the best interests of the United States....
>
> Since the Crusade for Freedom began ... I have wholeheartedly endorsed its concept and its activities. More than ever before contributing to the Crusade is an effective way for every American to reassert his belief in the indivisibility of human freedom and in the right of peoples, wherever they may live to have governments of their own choosing.[18]

Radio Free Europe Christmas Messages

Newspapers around the United States in December 1958 carried a photograph of 7-year-old Irena Dubicka of Brooklyn, New York, behind a Radio Free Europe microphone recording a "greeting to the children of Poland on behalf of youngsters in America" that would be broadcast by RFE on Christmas Eve as part a special holiday program. Additional programs to Poland included a broadcast by the Polish Boy Scouts in New York and a Polish Choir in London. RFE broadcast folklore, carols, and interviews with Christmas shoppers in London and New Work —"A potent reminder of the good things to buy in the capitalist countries." Listeners in Hungary heard folk songs, a children's play from the Hungarian High School in Munich, and a special Christmas play performed by émigré actors in New York. Bulgarian émigrés in New York recorded old folklore and Christmas songs that were broadcast to Bulgaria.[19] RFE also broadcast a special Christmas program entitled "Greetings to Jammers." President Eisenhower's annual Christmas message was broadcast over Radio Free Europe and the Voice of America to the countries behind the Iron Curtain and was not jammed.[20]

Corporate Solicitation Luncheons

The Crusade's corporate solicitation luncheon in Baltimore, Maryland, was held on January 19, 1959, with Gwilym A. Price as the speaker. The General Motors Company sponsored another solicitation luncheon for 41 guests in Detroit on January 26, 1959, with the president of Republic Steel Corporation as the keynote speaker. Lockheed Aircraft Corporation hosted a luncheon on February 4, 1959, in Atlanta, Georgia, for 50 guests. There were also Crusade fund solicitation luncheons in February in Miami, Florida; Birmingham, Alabama; Newark, New Jersey; Pittsburgh, Pennsylvania; Richmond, Virginia; Seattle, Washington; Boston, Massachusetts; and Honolulu, Hawaii. Luncheons in March were held in Dallas and Houston, Texas.

1959 Newspaper Campaign

Ted Bates and Company, New York, handled the advertising campaign and Leslie R. Shope, manager of advertising and press relations of the Equitable Life Assurance Society, coordinated the nation-wide volunteer work for the campaign. As the "volunteer coordinator," Leslie Shope sent the following letter newspapers around the country:

> This year's Crusade for Freedom Campaign marks the first time in Advertising Council history that a public service campaign has offered an awards program to the public. Ted Bates and Company has created the enclosed material as our voluntary advertising agency on this campaign.
>
> Its purpose is twofold: one — to increase public understanding of, and moral support for, the work of Radio Free Europe; two — to obtain truth dollars to keep this important anti-communist network on the air, broadcasting truthful news and information into the satellite countries of Eastern Europe. All contributions of truth dollars go in their entirety to Radio Free Europe.
>
> This campaign will enable your readers to help a highly important cause, and at the same time give them the opportunity to earn valuable awards. This appeal should be attractive to potential sponsors of these advertisements.
>
> Free mats will be rushed to you if you'll return order form on the back page without delay.
>
> May we rely on your support for this unique and essential undertaking?

This Week

The *New York Herald Tribune* nationally syndicated weekly newspaper supplement *This Week*, edited and published by William I. Nichols, was printed in over 30 newspapers, with a circulation of 13,000,000.[21] A long-time supporter of the Crusade for Freedom, Nichols had taken on the role of editor and publisher in 1943. At the December 14, 1947, seventh annual ceremony commemorating the 186th anniversary of the bill of rights, Mount Vernon, New York, St. Paul's church, Eastchester, Nichols said, "There were now wide areas behind the iron curtain where truth was blacked out by government censorship and the secret police." He outlined four steps to counter this:

1. The government must provide an adequate United States information program ... only Government activities as the Voice of America could hope to pierce the iron curtain.
2. During the current dollar shortage, the government should find ways to help private enterprise to carry on their overseas information activities.
3. Private enterprise at home can help private enterprise abroad during the dollar crisis by advertising in overseas periodicals.
4. American citizens can spread "sparks of truth" abroad when they send letters, food parcels or clothing packages to individuals overseas.[22]

Magazine Campaign

The January 25, 1959, edition of *This Week* carried a short article by Dean Alfange: "What America Means to Me." Page 4 of the issue had contest information and the blank coupon for the Truth Broadcast contest under the title, "You Can Tell the World." In the contest description one read: "Freedom needs your ideas as well as dollars."

Truth a Weapon the Reds Can't Match

The March 15, 1959, issue of newspaper Sunday supplement *Family Weekly* carried a full-page, first-person report of a visit to RFE in Europe by Charles Ritz, Chairman of the Board, International Milling Company, Minneapolis, Minnesota, who was one of the "Trippers" who went on the European Study tour in the fall 1958. He then featured prominently in the Advertising Council advertisement, which had a photograph that showed him standing under one of the Iron Curtain watch towers along the Czech-German border and giving an interview to a Radio Free Europe reporter. Information about the Truth Broadcast contest was included in the text along with Ritz's personal experiences. The headline was "Truth a Weapon the Reds Can't Match." His report was listed as "An American business leader reports on Radio Free Europe's crusade to pierce the Iron Curtain with Western ideas and news." He wrote, in part:

The goal of RFE is to counter Red brainwashing with truth, the most important weapon in the cold war. Russia can keep newspapers, magazines, and printed news out of the satellite countries, but it cannot effectively shut out the voice of RFE.
Radio Free Europe, we should remember, is supported by the American people through their contributions to the Crusade for Freedom. This is the only source of income for RFE — voluntary contributions from our business firms and ourselves.[23]

Reader's Digest

The *Reader's Digest* contributed free of charge information on the "Write a Truth Broadcast" campaign in the March 1959 Educational Edition that was used in an estimated 50 percent of high schools in the United States, including a teacher's guide. The Teacher's Edition section on Radio Free Europe and the Crusade for Freedom was entitled "Ideas for Talking and Writing."

THE PLAY'S THE THING
TIRED OF THE SAME OLD ROUTINE? This is the time of year to give your school-work a "new look." Dramatization will bring an exciting element to any assignment. And you don't need the talent of a Broadway playwright to learn how to adapt an anecdote, an incident, or, even a complete story to dramatic form. Imagination and ingenuity are important assets to a dramatist. Don't fail to use yours!
DRAMA—in the news...
Read the announcement for "Crusade for Freedom" (p. 249)
FOR DISCUSSION—What recent news events lead us to believe that the spirit of freedom is very much alive in the Iron Curtain countries? What seems to be the official policy of the United States government toward anti–Soviet uprisings among the captive peoples of Europe? What is your personal attitude toward helping such movements?
FOR RESEARCH—What purpose is served by Radio Free Europe? What languages are used for the broadcasts? Is there any way of evaluating the effect of these broadcasts?
SHARE THE TRUTH—Your words may help tell captive Europeans the truth about the free world. Whether or not you actually enter the competition, try to complete the sentence. (1) Jot down ideas that seem important to you. (2) State one idea in forceful words that are precise in meaning. (3) Revise and edit until you have no more than the maximum allowance.
You might also enjoy preparing an imaginary broadcast for Radio Free Europe. Dramatize a scene, which you think would convey a true picture of American life.
These two copies of Reader's Digest carry what we consider to be one of the most outstanding—and most unusual—contributions we've ever had in the cause of Radio Free Europe.[24]

Grass-Roots Activities

Colleges and Universities

By January 1959, the Advertising Council had sent over 700 advertising kits to college newspapers, with an additional 175 Truth Broadcast kit information to colleges and preparatory schools. The Circle K Club of Lakeland College in Plymouth, Wisconsin, positively responded with campus publicity and a contribution to the Crusade. Utah, Montana, and Idaho school administrators approved participation in the "Truth Broadcast" contest with the display of entry cards in classrooms.

Newspaperboy's Crusade

In January 1959, 100,000 newspaperboys from 82 newspapers agreed to participate in the Newspaperboy Crusade campaign. A typical advertisement showed a young boy carrying his newspapers and about to ring a door bell with the text:

> Keep the Truth Alive Behind the Iron Curtain
> Your newspaperboy will ask for your truth dollars to keep Radio Free Europe on the air!
> Here's why you should give:
> Right now — this very moment — Communist lies, distortions and restrictions are working hard — to destroy freedom behind the Iron Curtain. You can help fight these lies! Do it this week by giving to Crusade for Freedom when your newspaperboy asks for your contribution.
> Help share the truth! Help air the truth! Radio Free Europe is a private organization, supported by the American people. Your dollars are needed to pay for Radio Free Europe's equipment, its announcers, its news staff. So help keep the truth alive behind the Iron Curtain. Give your truth dollars to Crusade for Freedom when your newspaperboy calls this week.[25]

Flight No. 447

The Crusade for Freedom national office established a 1959 campaign quota of $10,000 for South Dakota. Harvard Noble was the State Chairman. One of state's local activities was a piloted balloon trip from Sioux Falls, South Dakota, to the East Coast. Ed Yost, who has been flying balloons for 25 years, planned a flight that would begin Saturday night, carry him over Dubuque, Iowa, Chicago, Pittsburgh, and finally land in the New York area Sunday evening. The goal of the balloon flight to the East Coast was to bring attention locally and nationally at each municipality over which the balloon floated. The organizers had estimated a total flight time of about 20 hours to reach the East Coast.[26]

Yost was Raven Industries Operations Manager. Raven Industries had been formed in 1956 by former employees of the General Mills Company balloon program and was involved in the development of high altitude research balloons. The company newsletter reported,

> The balloon was built after working hours by more than a dozen Raven assemblymen. All controls and instruments were likewise built on time donated by the instrumentation personnel and the launching and monitoring were done after hours by the field operations crew. The spirit proved to be contagious and other business firms made substantial contributions in equipment and support.[27]

Saturday evening at Joe Foss Field, searchlights played, sirens blared and a large crowd estimated to be over 1,000 onlookers cheered as Yost, wearing three suits of underwear, fur-lined boots and nylon coveralls, lifted off at 6:30 P.M. in the 50 × 25 foot Raven Industries balloon. State and national flags were visible on the gondola underneath the "inverted tear drop" shaped balloon.

Yost smiled and waved his arms to the crowd from the gondola, which was equipped with a parachute, oxygen, Raven manufactured radio equipment, hot coffee, 15 sandwiches and a red aircraft warning light. A Sioux Falls radio station had begun a marathon at 6 P.M. to collect $5 for each minute for the flight, with proceeds going to Crusade for Freedom.

Yost radioed 40 minutes later that the balloon had leveled off at a height of 8,000 feet, and he had crossed over into the neighboring state of Minnesota. The balloon traveled only about 130 miles eastward before freezing rain and snow forced Yost to end the trip by landing at the Herbert Larson farm near Amboy, Minnesota. He afterwards said, "I could see the light on at the Larson place although it was after midnight. It looked like a nice place so I decided to put down there. The Larsons were a bit surprised. But they certainly were hospitable. Mrs. Larson fried some eggs and put the coffee pot on the stove. The bed they fixed for me was a lot more comfortable than the four by five, one foot deep gondola I was riding."[28] Raven Industries sent a truck to Ambroy, Minnesota, and Yost returned to Sioux Falls Sunday with the balloon equipment.

Raven replaced its normal commercial newsletter in April 1959 with one devoted to the balloon launching, including a full-page fact sheet about Radio Free Europe and Crusade:

> In this issue we'd like to replace the customary description of commercial products with a plea for YOUR support of the Radio Free Europe "Crusade for Freedom" program. To assist in evaluating the worthiness of this cause here are some facts:
> Individuals and companies in America donating truth dollars are the only source of support of the program. As a civilian corporation, Radio Free Europe can ignore the niceties of diplomacy, call a spade a spade, and carry on an active, unrelenting campaign to combat the communist big lie. Send in your contributions now.[29]

Even though the balloon flight plan was not successful in reaching its final goal of landing on the East Coast, the Crusade campaign benefited from newspaper coverage around the country.

Ogden, Utah

Ogden, Utah, was very busy for the 1959 Crusade campaign. The local newspaper ran this advertisement and listed the upcoming activities in Ogden:

> *Pierce the Iron Curtain with the truth!*
> The Crusade for Freedom campaign in Weber County is now in full swing and will continue through the middle of March. The drive is nationwide, and Utah has set its goal for $15,000.
> Numerous activities are being promoted here to raise money to carry on this project.
> Among them will be —
> A Crusade for Freedom bowling tournament under direction of the three local

bowling alleys with Lynn Foley, chairman, assisted by Max Kosof, Robert Farmer, and Joe Barney.

The "Freedom" committee March 19, will sponsor an appearance in Ogden, of the Harlem Globe Trotters at Ben Lomond High School.

The American Legion Baker-Merrill Post No. 9 and Auxiliary, will conduct a canvass of the business district for donations and a "white elephant" sale.

A turkey shoot under direction of Roy Jaycees with Don Shreck in charge is scheduled.

The newspaper boys, under direction of Eliot Sampson, chairman, will make a door-to-door campaign to subscribers of *The Ogden Standard-Examiner*, and other projects are being planned.

This is the fifth year for the Crusade for Freedom drive, which was first sponsored here by *The Ogden Standard-Examiner*. After the first, two years, other organizations came into the sponsorship.

In 1959 there were three bowling alleys in Ogden Utah. The three agreed to support the Crusade for Freedom by holding a "bowling joust" from February 16, 1959, to March 15, 1959. On February 18, 1959, the *Ogden Standard-Examiner* newspaper quoted Sid Weese, chairman of the Crusade campaign in Weber County, who said, "The Trotters have been turning them away everywhere and my advice is to get your tickets early." The newspaper proudly reported on March 18, 1959, that forty newspaperboys would be guests of the Crusade for Freedom at the game because "of their fine work in making their quota in the Crusade drive." The newspaper listed six international vaudeville acts, which also would be part of the evening's entertainment program, including the "Farius duo and trio from Cuba in two different acts of roly poly and equilibristic wizardry." Weekly update reports of the tournament leaders were published in the local newspaper. By the time the "joust" had ended, 1064 two-person teams had entered and $250 was contributed to the Crusade for Freedom. The *Ogden Standard-Examiner* estimated that "if the event was carried out on a nationwide basis and all bowlers contributed their support as did the keglers in Ogden the Crusade for Freedom would derive over a half a million dollars.[30]

Ogden, Utah, not only witnessed a bowling tournament but also Harlem Globetrotters–Washington Generals basketball game at the Ben Lomond High School on March 19, 1959.

Results of Fund Raising

The 1958-1959 Crusade gathered $2,534,297 in private and corporate contributions against expenses of $917,974.[31]

CHAPTER ELEVEN

Concluding the
Crusade for Freedom

VFW and Crusade for Freedom

At the 60th Annual Convention of the Veterans of Foreign Wars of the United States (VFW), in August 1959, held in Los Angeles, California, the following resolutions, among others, were passed by the attendees:

WHEREAS, the Crusade for Freedom and the Radio Free Europe operations against the Communist tyranny are in accord with the long established Veterans of Foreign Wars policy to fight Communism with every weapon available, now, therefore

BE IT RESOLVED ... that we commend highly the purposes and work of the Crusade for Freedom and its Radio Free Europe, and that we urge our members and all other loyal American citizens to extend their support of the continued effective anti–Communist campaigning.[1]

Jewish War Veterans

At their 64th National Convention, the Jewish War Veterans of the United States also passed a resolution endorsing the Crusade for Freedom in support of Radio Free Europe, which read in part,

WHEREAS, Americans, through the operation of Radio Free Europe, have been able to pierce the Iron Curtain, and thereby bring truth and hope to the captive peoples and thus stiffen their resistance to Communist tyranny, and

WHEREAS, the effectiveness of Radio Free Europe depends for continuance upon the whole-hearted support of the American people of the Crusade for Freedom

NOW, THEREFORE, BE IT RESOLVED that the Jewish War Veterans of the United States of America ... endorse the Crusade for Freedom and urge patriotic Americans to act against Soviet oppression by supporting Radio Free Europe.[2]

Change of Articles of Incorporation

At the Annual Meeting of the Members of the Free Europe Committee, Inc., held on Friday, October 2, 1959, at 11:00 A.M., it was proposed that

> To act upon a proposal of the Board of Directors (appended hereto) to change the purposes and powers of the Corporation by amending the second paragraph of Sub-Section (c) of Article Second of the Certificate of Incorporation to read as follows:
>
> "No *substantial* part of the activities of the Corporation shall be the carrying on of propaganda or otherwise attempting to influence legislation." (Emphasis supplied to show change intended.)
>
> Instead of
>
> "No part of the activities of the Corporation shall be the carrying on of propaganda or otherwise attempting to influence legislation."
>
> To elect Directors to hold office until the next annual meeting or until their successors shall be elected in their stead. To appoint auditors to make an examination of the accounts of the Corporation for the fiscal year ending June 30, 1960.

Khrushchev Visit

In September 1959, Soviet Premier Nikita Khrushchev visited the United States. He spent 13 days traveling around the country: New York City, Los Angeles, San Francisco, Iowa, Pittsburgh and Washington DC. In New York City, on September 17, 1957, there was a rally at Carnegie Hall protesting his visit to the United States. The rally was erroneously billed as being sponsored by Crusade for Freedom. Crusade for Freedom headquarters had to put out a disclaimer notice to the press on that day: "The Crusade for Freedom is not sponsoring any rally or demonstration regarding the Khrushchev visit."[3]

On October 8, 1959, Crusade for Freedom sent out a notice to Crusade supporters giving some details of how the Radio Free Europe handled the Khrushchev visit:

> From the moment of his arrival until the moment of his return, Mr. Khrushchev's activities were the subject of on-the-spot reportage by an accredited RFE correspondents traveling with the press party.... The RFE stations were able to present a rounded picture of the Khrushchev visit — a picture that included the boos, the pickets and signs encountered along the way, as well as the applause; the coolness of the Washington and New York receptions; the hostile questions at various meetings. In short, all the things which the Soviet and satellite press and radio were carefully leaving out of their coverage.
>
> We can take real pride in the service rendered to the captive peoples by Radio Free Europe in these extraordinary times.[4]

On November 9, 1959, William Lydgate of the public relations firm Earl Newsom & Company sent a memorandum to Messrs. Jolly and Morris of the same firm on the subject of fund-raising procedures for the Crusade for Freedom. Lydgate wrote, "Most of the funds are collected from corporations. There are some individual gifts but they are not large in total."

Eisenhower Letter to Murphy

W.B. Murphy, president of Campbell Soup Company since 1953, was elected chairman of the board of Crusade for Freedom in October 1959 and assumed his position in November. Gwilym A. Price became Chairman of the Executive Committee and John Patterson remained as president. On November 19, 1959, a letter over the name of President Eisenhower was sent to chairman Murphy with the message:

> The Crusade for Freedom is part of America's historic championship of human liberty.
> Its mission is two-fold. It reminds us of the deadening restrictions of the the individual imposed by those political systems, which cannot tolerate freedom. Through its support of Radio Free Europe it helps to assure the people of the satellite countries that their aspirations for truth and justice find strong support in our land.
> In the past the Crusade has been nobly led by Lucius Clay, Henry Ford II, Eugene Holman and Gwilym Price. I am delighted to learn that you will succeed Mr. Price in the Chairmanship.[5]

The November 30, 1959, Crusade for Freedom press release announced the Murphy selection as chairman of the board and presented biographical data and quoted from the Eisenhower letter. General Crittenberger resigned as president of Radio Free Europe and was replaced by Archibald S. Alexander, former Undersecretary of the Army, on February 1, 1960.

CIA and RFE Differences of Opinion

On January 11, 1960, there was a "heated" discussion involving Cord Meyer of the CIA and C.D. Jackson, in the presence of Allen Dulles and others concerning Radio Free Europe. Jackson wrote a spirited letter the next day to Cord Meyer that included,

> While it is possible for you and your boss, depending on your estimates of the international situation at any given moment, to turn the FEC/RFE spigot on and off as far as the Americans are concerned, the exiles need more than this to keep them functioning happily — in this the synonym for "effectively." ... I don't believe that in all history any men marched to successful battle chanting "Don't rock the boat." Any yet that seems to be today's operative slogan.
> You may counter by saying that I am all wet, that actually the slogan is the very valid one of "hope."
> Here I in turn must counter by saying that hope was the controlling word from 1950 to 1956. But when October-November 1956 came around, which as far as the

Hungarians and the Poles were concerned represented the climax of "hope," with the results we all know—and repeat for good and sufficient reasons—that word "hope" took a terrible beating, a beating from which it has not yet recovered.[6]

Cord Meyer answered on January 24, 1960, which read, in part,

> Don't be sorry because I was not upset, only a little heated, for which I should do the apologizing. On the other hand where there is no controversy there is no life.
> Allen and I had a very good talk with Beverly Murphy, the head of the Crusade, after his inspection tour of both Lisbon and Munich. He is very much impressed by the ability, determination, and morale of the outfit. He declined the usual VIP tour of Munich and instead spent a good deal of time individually with the exile desk chiefs.
> Specifically, they are worried about the present and future attitudes towards RFE of the West German government and people. In an atmosphere of detente they wonder how long the West Germans will be willing to permit RFE to function from German soil.
> Hope to see you again soon. I don't know what we would do without your continued support.[7]

White House Meeting

Crusade Chairman Murphy made an inspection trip to Portugal and Munich to review Radio Free Europe's operations. President Eisenhower sent out an invitation on February 5, 1960: "I am asking a few people most concerned with Radio Free Europe and the Crusade for Freedom to meet with me at 11:00 A.M. February 16, 1960, at my office at the White House to discuss plans for this year."[8]

The White House meeting took place as scheduled to discuss Murphy's findings, as well as the Crusade for Freedom's fund raising. Those in attendance were President Eisenhower and Messrs Murphy, Holman, Price, Alexander, Newsom, Page, Stanton, Allen Dulles and General Andrew J. Goodpaster, who apparently took notes.

Murphy reported that he had asked the language service chiefs of RFE, "What would happen if there were no Radio Free Europe, i.e., if it were to terminate?" The answer was, "Within these countries there would either be an explosion and insurrection or a giving up of any feeling an notion of freedom." Murphy spoke about the upcoming Crusade campaign, including a series of luncheons, and asked for Eisenhower's continued support for them—perhaps in a form of a message to each luncheon chairman. Eisenhower told Murphy he would send a letter reaffirming his support of the Crusade and a message to each luncheon chairman.

Eisenhower told the group that, "After many years spent in international affairs he has concluded that the greatest thing is to create an informed public opinion. This requires that the problems be simplified and clarified, so that people can inform themselves on these issues." The meeting ended after President Eisenhower told the group that he greatly appreciated the work they were doing.[9]

On February 19, 1960, President Eisenhower sent his promised letter to Chairman Murphy, in which he referred to Murphy's inspection trip:

> It was most encouraging to hear the report of your inspection tour of Radio Free Europe's facilities in Lisbon and Munich. I have long been interested in this work—and in the whole program of Crusade for Freedom. Truly millions of people behind the Iron Curtain, with their hopes—indeed their trust—in freedom, have these many years taken heart from the work of Radio Free Europe.
>
> The fact that Radio Free Europe through Crusade for Freedom, with the support of American citizens and organizations across the land, increases its effectiveness behind the Curtain. It clearly demonstrates our people's respect for the power of truth and their willingness to work for its advancement.
>
> We have an important stake in this year's Crusade campaign. I hope the 1960 appeal will receive a broad and generous response.[10]

Advertising Council's Media Message

Ten million dollars was again the stated goal of the 1960 Crusade campaign. Ostensibly to try and reach this goal, the Advertising Council launched another major media campaign, including these instructions to radio stations:

> The Crusade seeks the widest possible participation of the American people, so that they may communicate their friendship, sympathy and moral support to the Soviet captives behind the Iron Curtain.
>
> *SUMMARY—WHAT TO TELL YOUR AUDIENCE*
>
> Describe the continuing propaganda assault of Communism against the free world and recall that Radio Free Europe, a private, non-profit, citizen sponsored organization has for 10 years been bringing the truth to the nations behind the Iron Curtain.
>
> Explain the importance of preventing the 76,000,000 people of these nations from becoming robots of Soviet aggression.
>
> Urge every American to support the Crusade for Freedom and point out that Truth Dollars sent to CRUSADE For FREEDOM c/o their local postmaster are essential to keeping RFE on the air. Radio Free Europe is dependent upon the contributions of the American people for its continued operation.

Broadcasters for Radio Free Europe

A closed circuit half hour television program "They Speak for Freedom" took place on Tuesday, March 29, 1960, in New York City. It was intended for radio and television broadcasters around the United States. Those participating included Donald H. McGannon, chairman of Broadcasters for Radio Free Europe, president of Westinghouse Broadcasting Company, and host of the program;

W.B. Murphy, Crusade for Freedom; Joseph Koevago, former Mayor of Budapest; Leonard Goldenson, chairman ABC network; Robert Sarnoff, chairman, NBC; Frank Stanton, president, CBS; Martin Block, ABC disk jockey; Arlene Francis, radio and television actress; and Howard K. Smith, CBS Washington news correspondent. The purpose of the program was to "commemorate the tenth anniversary of Radio Free Europe."

After being introduced by McGannon, Crusade chairman Murphy said,

> Last January I was privileged to visit Radio Free Europe headquarters in Munich and in Lisbon. After a day or two there a kind of cold shiver goes down one's back. You know there's a vicious cold war going on. You come away with a tremendous feeling of respect for the job Radio Free Europe is doing.

A short but detailed film about Radio Free Europe was then shown. Murphy continued, "All of this costs money. It must be private money. Radio Free Europe is not a government operation. It's a private, non-profit organization supported by American citizens and corporations."

Robert Sarnoff was introduced and he said, "We broadcasters are called upon day-in-and-day-out to serve many good causes and I think we do a pretty good job of it.... Of all the public service efforts that claim our support, Radio Free Europe is the only one which itself is an arm of broadcasting. Now let's show what kind of a job broadcasting can do in this country to raise funds that make this extraordinary service possible."

Frank Stanton then added, in part, "The strength of Radio Free Europe derives from its expression of a free people's concern for entrapped fellow human beings across the seas.... Nothing is more important about Radio Free Europe than that it reflects the convictions of as many American people as hear about it.... I hope that all of us will take the opportunity seriously to do all that we can to inform our listeners and viewers about Radio Free Europe."

McGannon then explained about the upcoming Crusade campaign, including the Radio Free Europe kits, a "do it yourself campaign kit especially prepared for broadcasters. In it you'll find spot announcements, live tapes, films, telops, scripts, discs, the whole works."

He then introduced Howard K. Smith, who said, "I've been privileged to be able to report on that story over the years and I hope I will be able to continue to report it in the future. For every mention of RFE's activities is a contribution to the kind of world we want and the kind of world I'm persuaded most other people want. As newscasters, we want to do all we can to support Radio Free Europe."

McGannon concluded the show with, "Well, that the story. We've talked about Radio Free Europe and what it does, how it does it and what we can do to help it. Now it is time for everyone here, every broadcaster in the business to speak up.... We want you to use on your stations the radio and television material, which will be sent to you very shortly. We want you to put on a saturation campaign during the period of our special drive — April 24th through May 8th. Let's show the people behind the Iron Curtain the way we feel about freedom of speech, free journalism, free radio and free television. Speak up America!"[11]

One-Minute Radio Spot

The Broadcasters for Radio Free Europe sent out the following text of a one-minute spot announcement, with voicing instructions, to radio stations:

ANNOUNCER
(LOUD VOICE OR ON ECHO:) Freedom is not free! Freedom is not free!
(IN STRAIGHTFORWARD, CONVERSATIONAL MANNER:) Yes, *freedom is not free.* Seventy-six million oppressed people in the satellite countries behind the Iron Curtain know that. They'd love to be able to buy their freedom back. But their money can't buy Freedom for them any more. *You* can do something about it. You can help keep the spirit of freedom alive in these people. You can help Radio Free Europe stay on the air! With your help Radio Free Europe's twenty-eight truth transmitters can slash through the Iron Curtain, uncover Red lies, destroy Red plans to crush freedom. Why must you help? Because Radio Free Europe is supported by the American people. Your contributions pay for Radio Free Europe's equipment, announcers, and news analysts. Remember ... Freedom is not free! Freedom is not free! Keep Radio Free Europe on the air! Send your contributions to Crusade for Freedom, care of your local postmaster.

Ten Years of RFE Broadcasting

July 4, 1960, was the tenth anniversary of Radio Free Europe broadcasts. The July 1960 newsletter to Crusade for Freedom and RFE supporters covered this in detail, including a contribution written by Free Europe Committee president Archibald S. Alexander. He wrote, "RFE exists as a symbol of protest against this Communist arrogance and makes it protests in practical ways." He explained,

RFE breaks the monopoly of information which the satellite rulers would otherwise have and brings to the captive peoples behind the Iron Curtain news of what goes on in the free world, and discusses common problems with them.[12]

Former President Harry S Truman was interviewed on a WCBS television show marking the 10th Anniversary of RFE's broadcasts. During the interview, Truman said,

Radio Free Europe very properly came into being as a private operation privately sponsored by contributions of millions of Americans from all walks of life as an expression of their concern for the plight of the the people in the captive nations.
The reasons for the need of Radio Free Europe are as vital today as they were in the beginning and I think even more so.
Share our precious gift of truth and freedom with the less fortunate people behind the Iron Curtain — by your support of Radio Free Europe.

Newspaperboy Campaign

The sixth annual newspaperboys drive was set for "Freedom Collection Day." Badges were again worn and the collection envelopes read, "I am proud to join the Crusade for Freedom." The advertisement showed a boy walking in the direction of the reader, wearing a relatively large badge with the Freedom Bell and holding a collection envelope. The text read, "Open YOUR Door and Your Heart When Your Newspaperboy Calls on Freedom Collection Day." In Idaho, for example, readers were told by Crusade state chairman W.C. Kyle, "When your newspaperboy calls, give generously to the Crusade for Freedom and help win the battle for men's minds by fighting communism with the weapon they dread the most — the truth. Give the gift of free men and women.... Give the truth."[13]

Truth Broadcast Contest

The 1960 Crusade had a "truth message" contest, also referred to as "truth-cast" and "truth broadcast" contest. Crusade Chairman William Murphy was quoted as calling the Truth Message program, "One way the individual citizen can take an active part in the fight against Communist aggression."[14] The Advertising Council's campaign, in cooperation with the Newspaper Advertising Executive Association, included the contest entry blank along with photographs, one showing a young girl and man standing in front of a propaganda poster in Poland as an example of how the Communist regimes especially targeted "children in Red-occupied Europe." The advertisement went on, "There's a desperate battle going on in the captive countries behind the Iron Curtain. It's a battle for men's minds, for the very survival of their hopes for the future."[15]

Another ad began with the question: "What is our best weapon against Communism? The answer was, "Our best weapon is the truth. The Communists fear the truth because they know it could destroy them. Now you can hit them where it hurts — with the truth! With your own truth!"

The entrant was to complete the sentence: "I believe the most important thing people behind the Iron Curtain countries should know is...." The deadline for the contest submission was April 30, 1960. The 1960 contest did not ask for one dollar per entry to be considered for one of the free trips to Munich to Lisbon, Paris, and Munich; 50 would receive the *Encyclopedia Britannica*, and 200 would receive Hallicrafter short wave radios.

The American Hotel Association (AHA) had mailed 68,000 entry blanks and other written materials (weighing over two tons) about Radio Free Europe to approximately 5,800 hotels of the Association. Vernon Herndon, president of the AHA, who earlier had been on a "study tour" of Radio Free Europe, said, "The Truth Broadcast program is supported by people of the greatest integrity and is aimed at bringing the truth about the American way of life to people behind the Iron Curtain. I thoroughly subscribe to its objectives."[16]

The March 1960 issue of *Reader's Digest* carried a free advertisement that included a photograph of Nikita Khrushchev, with the message:

> *IF YOU DISAGREE WITH MR. KHRUSHCHEV ...*
>
> > Capitalism is a worn-out old mare while Socialism is new, young and full of
> > energy
> > The so-called free world constitutes the cruel exploitation of millions ... for
> > the enrichment of a handful...
> > Now it is American imperialism which is forcing its way ... to world domination
> > Your grandchildren will live under Socialism in America.
>
> *Here's how to put your beliefs to work*
>
> If you lived behind the Iron Curtain, you would have to "eat" words like those above about the United States. But you can help give people throughout Europe a better diet of truth and freedom-in your own words.
>
> And you may go to Europe to broadcast them personally!
>
> Enter the 1960 RADIO FREE EUROPE Truth Message Contest. Just write what you think people in Communist countries should know about America or freedom. Winning messages will be beamed over Radio Free Europe to millions who want to hear what you, as an American, have to say.

Letters from Behind the Iron Curtain

The 1960 newspaper campaign conducted by the Advertising Council and prepared by the Ted Bates & Company, Volunteer Advertising Agency, had one slogan, "Answer this call for help from behind the Iron Curtain" with excerpts of letters written to RFE from a listeners in Poland, with the phrases "Keep broadcasting the Truth," "Radio Free Europe gives us hope for a better future," and "God Bless You America. Thank you for keeping our hope for freedom alive with Radio Free Europe." An excerpt of a letter from Romania was quoted in one newspaper ad: "Radio Free Europe encourages us to live...." The February 29, 1969, issue of *Time* magazine, for example, carried an Crusade for Freedom advertisement, which also continued the decade-long Cold War rhetoric:

> This is one of the many letters smuggled our from behind the Iron Curtain that prove the importance of RADIO FREE EUROPE in the battle of men's minds. The battle of Communist lies against the truth.
>
> This is your battle, too! Your own freedom is endangered, for if Communist lies stay unanswered, if the truth does not get through, the Reds will have won a decisive victory in the Cold War.
>
> You can help by keeping the strong, crystal clear voice of RADIO FREE EUROPE broadcasting the truth to combat Communist lies.
>
> You must help! RADIO FREE EUROPE is a private organization that depends on your dollars to pay for equipment, announcers, and news analysts necessary to combat Communist lies.
>
> GIVE THE GIFT OF FREE MEN AND WOMEN ... GIVE THE TRUTH!

Freedom Mobile Trailer

In March 1960, a mobile trailer was underway with display information about Radio Free Europe: In Danville, Virginia, included in the trailer display there was a hollowed-out sofa that had been used by a Czech father to smuggle his wife and two children out of Czechoslovakia. Another display was a working model of the Iron Curtain, with watchtowers, border guards, plowed strips, electrified barbed wires, and land mines. There was also broadcast equipment that could be used by local radio stations for programs originating from the traveling exhibit. Visitors to the trailer also could sign the Freedom scroll, fill out the Truth Broadcast entry forms, and make "free-will" contributions to support Radio Free Europe. The company USFY furnished the trailer at no cost and the Virginia Highway Users Association transported it around the commonwealth.[17]

Nixon Luncheon

Continuing the tradition of business lunches with government personalities in behalf of the Crusade for Freedom, on March 16, 1960, Vice President Richard Nixon, in place of President Eisenhower, gave a short speech about the Crusade for Freedom at a small luncheon at the Bankers Club of America in New York. Four members of the Free Europe Committee, six members of the Crusade for Freedom, twelve representatives of business, and four officers of the government attended the luncheon.

Financial Problems

John Patterson as President of Crusade for Freedom wrote a letter to Arthur W. Page, Crusade Board of Directors, on May 11, 1960. He attached an agenda for the upcoming Executive Committee meeting scheduled for May 17, 1960. Patterson told Page that "actual money raised by the campaign will top — and this is optimistic — $100,000.... With money and pledges in we are something under $300,000 behind this period last year. I am extremely hopeful that we will end up doing at least as well as last year."[18]

At the May 17, 1960, Executive Committee meeting, there was considerable concern about the future of fund raising with a recommendation that Executive Committee members Murphy, Alexander, Newson, Page, Stanton, and Patterson "meet as soon as possible with the chief sponsor (CIA)." Murphy had explained in the memorandum attached to the original agenda notice, "While a budget equal to this year's has already been promised for the fiscal year starting in June, I do not think the money should be advanced unless the sponsors are fully aware of the situation."[19]

Fund Raising Name Change

There was a tentative agreement of the Crusade for Freedom executive committee at their May 17, 1960, meeting to change the name of Crusade for Freedom to Radio Free Europe Fund, effective July 1, 1960. The reasons given were: "Besides being a more honest and explicit name, it eliminates some of the confusion which has plagued the public about what the differences are between Crusade, RFE, and Free Europe Committee."[20] It also was agreed at the May 17th Meeting that "during the first year our letterheads and campaign material will show immediately under the new corporate title 'Radio Free Europe Fund,' our old name (Crusade for Freedom)."[21] That meant all stationary, newsletters, etc., would change the heading from "Crusade for Freedom, Inc. In Support of Radio Free Europe" to "Radio Free Europe Fund (Crusade for Freedom, Inc.)."

The committee also agreed that the 1960-1961 campaign should

1. Obtain strong White House endorsement and sponsorship.
2. Continue to go after large corporate gifts, but expect them to drift downward.
3. Make intense effort to increase the number of corporate gifts from the 1100 level to double or more. However, expect that most of these corporate gifts will be in the $500 to $2,000 range.
4. Repeat the concentrated TV and radio campaign but hold it earlier in the year, possibly February.
5. Attempt to obtain up to eight regional vice chairman, who will be important in the business world and real workers.

The Broadcasters for Radio Free Europe campaign was declared a disappointment because of the low financial returns but "it was the consensus that the educational value had been stupendous and the fringe benefits probably far larger than can be counted in terms of money received."[22]

One Billion Home Impressions

While contributions to the Crusade were falling, it was not from want of trying or public awareness. At the Crusade for Freedom Board of Directors meeting held on June 2, 1960, Arthur H. Wilson, Vice President of the Advertising Council, reported on the results of the 1959-1960 Crusade campaign. Wilson said that the advertising campaign "had had the largest response in Crusade's history. This extended to all media, with the possible exception of newspaper lineage." Wilson reported that there were 365 million home impressions on television and, if combined with the Broadcasters for Radio Free Europe home impressions, there was an "unbelievable total of one billion impressions by the end of June."[23]

1960-1961 Crusade Preparations

At a special meeting of members of the Crusade for Freedom on June 2, 1960, Earl Newsom reported that the "Truth Broadcast" campaign "had not been as successful as had been hoped and should be dropped."[24] In July 1960, Crusade chairman W.B. Murphy announced that, starting with 1960-1961, all fund-raising activities would take place in name of the Radio Free Europe Fund rather than Crusade for Freedom. "The new campaign name has been adopted," Murphy said, "to make it easier for the public to associate the fund with the important work it supports."[25]

Khrushchev's Second Visit to USA

On Sunday night, October 9, 1960, during his second visit to the United States, Soviet Premier Nikita S. Khrushchev was interviewed on a WNTA television program *Open End*, moderated by television producer David Susskind. There were protests before the show with picketers marching before the United Nations building, where the interview took place.

Regular television commercial advertising was unexplainably replaced with those of broadcast appeals for Radio Free Europe, including newsreel scenes of the Iron Curtain and a film scene of a Communist soldier or secret policeman smashing a radio set.[26]

The program was live but was aired on a delayed basis over more than 250 TV and radio stations. Hundreds of viewers of the show telephoned the studio to protest Khrushchev's appearance on national television. But other callers complained about spot announcements during the program that praised the work of Radio Free Europe. At one point in the show one of Khrushchev's aides passed him a note telling him of the Radio Free Europe spot announcements. Reportedly, Khrushchev "just got rigid" with anger and through his interpreter he asked, "How dare you?" and stood up to leave. Susskind stopped him, and the interview then continued with both men standing. Khrushchev regained his composure and said, "Well, do anything you like. We will win. We will win."[27]

According to a UPI report published on October 11, 1960, Khrushchev recalled that an aide handed him a note during his Sunday television appearance to tell him commercials for Radio Free Europe were being broadcast during station breaks: "I spoke to my partner (moderator David Susskind) about it. I told him what you are trying to do — you are trying to stick a pinprick into an elephant — a mighty elephant, the Soviet Union."

On October 16, 1960, an announcer of the television station noted, "Many viewers had questioned the propriety of the Radio Free Europe announcements.

While we believe the content of these announcements, an eloquent plea for free speech, is worthy of exposure on our radio and TV stations, we wish to express our regret at their unfortunate placement on the particular program on which Mr. Khrushchev was a guest."[28]

One of the Advertising Council's Fact Sheets on the 1961 fund-raising campaign mentioned the Khrushchev televised interview:

> During the Khrushchev visit to the United States, Soviet authorities did not call off the jamming efforts directed against RFE, although the jamming of some western broadcasting services into the Soviet Union was temporarily suspended. In spite of the unrelenting Soviet attempts to jam RFE broadcasts, the true facts on the Khrushchev visit got through to the satellite peoples over RFE.

The May 1961 issue of *Reader's Digest* contained a full page produced by the Advertising Council in behalf of Radio Free Europe Fund that continued the cold-war rhetoric of the 1950s:

> "Your Children will grow up under Communism!'" says Nikita Khrushchev.
> Will the Soviet threat come true? Will your grandchildren salute the Soviet flag? Forget God? "Never" you say. But are you sure? How can you oppose Communism? One sure way is to help Radio Free Europe.
> Surely your heart tells you to give something so that our children — and all children — shall live in freedom throughout the world.
> Give Now To ... Radio Free Europe
> The American People's Counter-Voice to Communism.

1960 "Trippers"

The 1960-1961 fund raising campaign, now under the name Radio Free Europe Fund, continued with Advertising Council support. "Trippers" went to Europe in October 1960 for the seventh consecutive year (Figure 28), including Abbot Washburn who originated the Freedom Bell concept, and who participated in a rededication of the Freedom Bell by the "Trippers" on October 24, 1960. Berlin Mayor Willy Brandt gave each "Tripper" a small replica of the Freedom Bell. Another "Tripper" was Eleanor Lansing Dulles, sister of CIA Director Allen Dulles and former U.S. Secretary of State John Foster Dulles. The story was covered in 500 newspapers in the United States.

One of the 1960 "Trippers" was E.K. Hartenbower, general manager of television station KCMO in Kansas City Missouri. After the return of Hartenbower, his television station produced a half-hour documentary film, "The Eagle Cage" about the trip, "This film's anti–Communist perspective compares east-west freedoms, or the lack thereof. Scenes show a U.S. tour group at the East German border, and stress the importance of Radio Free Europe."[29]

Figure 28. "Trippers" in Berlin with Mayor Willy Brandt in October 1960 (courtesy of RFE/RL).

Support from President Kennedy

Newly elected president John F. Kennedy wrote a letter to Murphy on January 31, 1961, in which he said, "For many years I have been convinced that Radio Free Europe is a most valuable undertaking and that it is important that the American people should continue to contribute to its financial support.... I congratulate you and your associates on the devotion and energy that you as private citizens have given to this endeavor and wish you success in your current fund-raising effort. I hope that Americans in all walks of life will contribute to this important cause."

At his press conference on March 8, 1961, in the U.S. State Department auditorium, President Kennedy began with this announcement and appeal:

> First, I want to say a word on behalf of Radio Free Europe, which is now making its annual appeal for support from all of our citizens. For more than ten years this enterprise has been reaching out to people in Europe, Eastern Europe, with truth and devotion to liberty as its message. While this radio is at work, with listeners numbering in the millions, the competition of ideas in these countries is kept alive.

The individual Americans, by giving to Radio Free Europe, may be sure that they are bringing a beacon of light into countries to which millions of us are tied by kinship, and whose hope for freedom all of us must share

This is a peaceful concern but a firm one. Radio Free Europe needs and deserves our generous help.[30]

Chairman Murphy's report of the 1960-1961 campaigns was presented in June 1961. Murphy reported, "The 1960-61 Radio Free Europe Fund Campaign presents a curious mixture of rose and gray." He explained,

The rosy side is that thanks to a brilliant, award-winning advertising promotion job by the Advertising Council, and the truly extraordinary efforts of the Broadcasters for Radio Free Europe, Radio Free Europe probably enjoys today more understanding and enthusiastic acceptance throughout the country than it has had for a good many years.

On the gray side, large corporate contributions continued to decline. While our friends remain faithful to us, they are giving smaller amounts ... by nearly two hundred thousand dollars.[31]

The Crusade for Freedom Is No More

Although the name of the fund raising campaign was changed, it was not until December 20, 1962, at a special meeting of Radio Free Europe Fund (Crusade for Freedom, Inc.) members that the corporate name was legally changed from Crusade for Freedom, Inc., to Radio Free Europe Fund, Inc:

This change of name has been under consideration by the Board of Directors for some time and it is believed that the proposed change will more closely associate the activities of the corporation with those of Radio Free Europe, and thereby be beneficial in the procurement of contributions for the support of Radio Free Europe.[32]

The sole item discussed and resolved at that meeting was the corporate name change, with appropriate notice of changes to the articles of incorporation with the State of New York.

The Central Intelligence Agency supported the Radio Free Europe Fund until 1968, for a total support to both the Crusade for Freedom and the Radio Free Europe Fund of $16,474,731. The CIA stopped its support for the fund raising after the 1967 public revelations of its connection to RFE. The CIA also continued supporting Radio Free Europe until June 30, 1971, by which time its total support was $306,849,269.59.[33]

Appendix A:
National Committee for a
Free Europe Press Release

National Committee for a Free Europe, Inc.
350 Fifth Avenue   New York 3, New York

Bryant 9-3563

NEWS RELEASE

April 26, 1950

Immediate Release

DeWitt C. Poole, president of the National Committee for Free Europe announced today that General Lucius D. Clay has accepted the chairmanship of a Crusade for Freedom to be launched under the sponsorship of the National Committee.

The Crusade, in which every American citizen will be invited to participate, will carry our message of freedom and friendship to the oppressed and threatened people overseas and give the lie to Kremlin propaganda that our goal is world domination and war.

Announcement of the Crusade, which has been in development stages since Feb. 1, 1950, follows closely on the recent appeals by President Truman and Secretary of State Acheson, before the American Society of Newspaper Editors, for a stepped-up Campaign of Truth, in which private citizens would join the government in the battle for men's minds.

The National Committee for a Free Europe, an organization of private citizens, was formed in June of 1949 to give aid and asylum to exiled leaders from the prisoner countries of Central Europe, and to make use of their abilities to carry the story of freedom to their own peoples behind the Iron Curtain. It is establishing its own broadcast facilities, "Radio Free Europe."

In accepting the chairmanship of the Crusade for Freedom, General Clay stated he would devote the next several weeks in perfecting a nation-wide organization, after which the complete program of the Crusade will be presented to the public. He issued the following statement of purpose:

> The soul of the world is sick, and the peoples of the world are looking to the
> United States for leadership and hope.

They are looking to us for leadership in a great moral crusade — a crusade for freedom, friendship and faith throughout the earth.

If we are to prove equal to this desperate need, each U.S. citizen must feel a personal responsibility. We cannot leave the job to government alone.

Our nation is the symbol of these fundamental principles to liberty loving men and women everywhere. Today these principles are being denounced and reviled. We have been fighting a holding action in the cold war — in the contest of ideas between our way of life and totalitarianism — and we have suffered serious setbacks.

In the five years since the United Nations Charter proclaimed the determination of all nations to "reaffirm faith in fundamental human rights and in the dignity and worth of the human person," we have seen the most highly organized and widespread campaign *against* human right and fundamental freedom that the world has ever known.

What an inspiration of hope and encouragement it would be to oppressed peoples everywhere if millions of Americans would voluntarily join in a great moral crusade, would accept the challenge of personal leadership and pledge themselves to work steadfastly and firmly until the tide of the cold war is turned and world peace with individual freedom again becomes a possibility.

Such a "spiritual airlift," originating in the heart-country of liberty, would be the first step in putting *freedom on the offensive.*

In the conviction that countless citizens throughout our country would welcome the opportunity to participate in such an effort, representatives of all the major groups of American life are joining forces to initiate the Crusade for Freedom ... a movement of United States citizens *resolved to strengthen the free peoples of the earth* in the struggle of world peace based on individual freedom and human decency — and *resolved to carry our message of American friendship and goodwill to men and women everywhere.* The National Committee for a Free Europe is acting as sponsoring agency to bring this movement into being.

It is with a great deal of humility that I have accepted responsibility as national chairman of the Crusade, for I am convinced that upon its success could well depend the prevention of World War III.

I am convinced there is nothing that American citizens so united cannot accomplish in such an effort. We are the greatest, most enthusiastic nation of salesmen in the world. In the cause of freedom and friendship we have the greatest product in the world to sell. With characteristic energy, resourcefulness and imagination our people will somehow get the message of truth through the Iron Curtain.

The Crusade committee will actively seek from citizens and groups of citizens throughout the country new ideas and new ways of getting the facts of freedom and friendship across to the peoples overseas. It will mobilize and coordinate all effective methods for doing this job, and undertake to find the resources to translate them into action.

The Crusade will give all of us an opportunity to help counteract the constant claims that our aim is world domination and war ... and, at the same time, assure the victims of tyranny that we, to whom liberty has meant more than to any other people, will not forsake them.

Ours will be a Crusade of the people. We will depend largely for financial support upon small contributions from many hundreds of thousands of individual citizens. By their broad support, the American people will demonstrate their united determination that freedom shall not die.

Appendix B:
Dwight D. Eisenhower
Labor Day 1950 Speech

Launching the Crusade

From Denver, Colorado, General Dwight D. Eisenhower launched the Crusade for Freedom on Labor Day, 1950. We present his notable speech, which was broadcast that evening over all major radio networks.

FELLOW CITIZENS:

Americans are dying in Korea tonight. They are dying for ideals they have been taught to cherish more than life itself. But it will be written and said tonight in Warsaw, in Prague, in Moscow, that they died for American imperialism.

Unfortunately, millions of people will believe this devilish libel against American soldiers, who have taken up arms in defense of liberty a second time in a tormented decade. Those millions will hear no other version but a hissing, hating tirade against America. We think it incredible that such poison be swallowed; but those people, behind and beyond the iron curtain, have seen so much political wickedness and cold blooded betrayal, such godless depravity in government that they find it harder to believe in our peaceful intent and decent motives than in the calculated and clever lies that communism is spreading every hour, every day, through every broadcast and newspaper that it controls.

This slander against our purposes and our men in Korea is merely one example of the campaign of hatred that is being waged against America and freedom around the globe.

We face not only ruthless men, but also lies and misconceptions intended to rob us of our resolution and faith within, and of our friends throughout the world. Communists teach that America is a vicious enemy of humanity. They have embarked upon an aggressive campaign to destroy free government, as in the young republic of Korea; because regimentation cannot face the peaceful competition of free enterprise.

The Communist leaders believe that, unless they destroy our system, their own subjects, gradually gaining an understanding of the blessings and opportunities of liberty, will repudiate Communism and tear its dictators from their positions of power. They know that, for the mass of humanity, America has come to symbolize freedom, opportunity, and human happiness. They have a mortal fear

211

that this knowledge will penetrate eventually to their own people and others in the world.

Communistic aggression, inspired by fear, carries with it the venom of those who feel themselves to be inferior. This accounts for the depth of their hatred, and the intensity of their thirst for power! To destroy human liberty and to control the world, the Communists use every conceivable weapon: subversion, bribery, corruption, and military attack. Of all these, none is more insidious than propaganda. Spurred by this threat to our very existence,

I speak tonight about the Crusade for Freedom.

This Crusade is a campaign sponsored by private American citizens to fight the big lie with the big truth. It is a program that has been hailed by President Truman, and others, as an essential step in getting the case for freedom heard by the world's multitudes.

Powerful Communist radio stations incessantly tell the world that we Americans are physically soft and morally corrupt; that we are disunited and confused; that we are selfish and cowardly; that we have nothing to offer the world but imperialism and exploitation.

To combat these evil broadcasts the government has established a radio program called the Voice of America, which has brilliantly served the cause of freedom, but the Communist stations overpower it and outflank it with a daily coverage that neglects no wave length or dialect, no prejudice or local aspiration. Weaving a fantastic pattern of lies and twisted fact, they confound the listener into believing that we are warmongers, that America invaded North Korea, that Russia invented the airplane, that the Soviets unaided won World War II; and that the secret police and slave camps of Communism offer humanity brighter hope than do self-government and free enterprise.

We need powerful radio stations abroad, operated without government restrictions, to tell in vivid and convincing form about the decency and essential fairness of democracy. These stations must tell of our aspirations for peace, our hatred of war, our support of the United Nations and our constant readiness to cooperate with any and all who have these same desires.

One such private station — Radio Free Europe — is now in operation in Western Germany. It daily brings a message of hope and encouragement to a small part of the European masses.

The Crusade for Freedom will provide for the expansion of Radio Free Europe into a network of stations. They will be given the simplest, clearest charter in the world: "Tell the truth."

For it is certain that all the specious promises of Communism to the needy, the unhappy, the frustrated, the downtrodden, cannot stand against the proven record of democracy and its day-by-day progress in the betterment of all mankind. The tones of the Freedom Bell, symbol of the Crusade, will echo through vast areas now under blackout.

In this battle for Truth, you and I have a definite part to play during the Crusade. Each of us will have the opportunity to sign the Freedom Scroll. It bears a declaration of our faith in Freedom, and of our belief in the dignity of the individual who derives the right of Freedom from God. Each of us, by signing the Scroll, pledges to resist aggression and tyranny wherever they appear on the earth. Its words express what is in all our hearts. Your signature on it will be a blow for liberty.

My great friend, General Lucius Clay, one of our outstanding Americans, is directing the Crusade for Freedom. Your contribution, great or small, will help him provide the means of bringing the truth to a region vital to America's welfare.

Most of us have been enjoying a long weekend terminating in this day dedicated to free American labor. How depressing it is to realize that on this Labor Day, 1950, one-third of the human race works in virtual bondage. In the totalitarian countries, the individual has no right that the state is bound to respect. His occupation is selected by his masters, his livelihood is fixed by decree, at the minimum which will give him strength to work another day.

Because representative labor leaders of America know the record of Communism in beating down labor, they have long been in the forefront of those fighting the spread of this vicious doctrine. But Communism goes further than the exploitation of labor. Unless the individual accepts governmental mastery of his life and soul, he can be convicted without trial; he can be executed without the right of appeal; he can be banished to live out his life in a slave camp.

This is what the Soviet planners contemplate for all the world, including America.

We must meet this threat with courage and firmness. Unless we look, with clear and understanding eyes, at the world situation confronting us, and meet with dynamic purposes the issues contained therein, then we will lose the American birthright. The system of government established by our forefathers will disappear. The American record, from Washington to the day of disaster, would be only a blank page in history.

We, American citizens, can assure that this will never happen to us if the fervor of our devotion to freedom and country is equal to the seriousness of the threat. Amid these dangers, personal participation by each in public deliberation and activity is necessary to our safety. Each must make it his responsibility to see that we remain strong morally, intellectually, materially. Our material strength must comprise a healthy, developed and prosperous population, high productivity, financial stability, and such military power as can meet aggression on respectable terms.

The die has been cast in Asia, but we are in no limited conflict. Free Europe, struggling for moral and economic recovery, is still a tempting target for predatory military force. We must give real support to all aspects of the military aid program and re-examine, at once, our troop strengths in critical areas.

All this means that we must resolutely tighten our belts, both nationally and individually. We must insist upon facing up to the task of paying for the accomplishment of these vital measures, else the Soviets will take heart from their success in bringing us further inflation and closer to economic ruin.

We must have efficiency and economy in all governmental expenditures; and we must concentrate all our resources to assure victory in this bitter and probably prolonged struggle! Until it is won we must practice Spartan frugality in all nonessential matters, so that we may make the greatest possible contribution to the defense of our way of life. All lesser considerations must wait. We cannot tolerate politics as usual any more than we can tolerate business as usual. Ladies and gentlemen — we must get tough — tough with ourselves!

Success in such national crises always requires some temporary and partial surrender of individual freedom. But the surrender must be by our specific decision, and it must be only partial and only temporary. And it must be insured that, when the crisis has passed, each of us will then possess every right, every privilege, every responsibility and every authority that now resides in an American citizen. It would do no good to defend our liberties against Communistic aggression and lose them to our own greed, blindness, or shiftless reliance on bureaucracy and the federal treasury.

In the dangers and trials ahead, our ultimate security lies in the dynamic purpose, the simple courage, the unshakable unity of the United States and the free

world, a unity that depends upon common understanding of and common venera-
tion of freedom. But these can live only where there is access to the truth. This
truth becomes our most formidable weapon, a weapon that each of us can help
forge through the Crusade for Freedom.

And let us never forget that for those who have lost freedom there is no price or
cost or sacrifice that can even faintly reflect its value. It is still the core of America s
boundless heritage. It will remain so for as long as we plain American citizens are
ever ready to guard it with vigilance and defend it with fortitude and faith.

As an old soldier, I thank you very sincerely for your participation in this great
Crusade.

Appendix C:
Crusade for Freedom
Articles of Incorporation
(October 20, 1950)

Certificate of Incorporation
of
Crusade for Freedom, Inc.

Pursuant to the Membership Corporations Law
of the State of New York

We, the undersigned, all being of full age and at least two-thirds of us being citizens of the United States, and at least one of us being a resident of the State of New York, desiring to form a corporation pursuant to the provisions of the Membership Corporations Law of the State of New York, hereby certify as follows:

FIRST: The name of the proposed corporation shall be CRUSADE FOR FREEDOM, INC.

SECOND: The purpose for which the Corporation is to be formed is: To aid the cause of freedom and liberty in Europe and elsewhere by furthering and promoting the dissemination of information designed to alert public opinion in the Untied States and abroad to the perils faced by freedom and liberty from aggressive and imperialistic Communism and totalitarianism in their various forms; to solicit and obtain funds for these general purposes; and to give financial support to activities and organizations dedicated to the same cause.

No part of the activities of the Corporation shall be the carrying on of propaganda or otherwise attempting to influence legislation.

In pursuance of and not in limitation of the general powers conferred by law and the objects and purposes herein set forth, it is expressly provided that the corporation shall also have the following powers:

To do all such acts as necessary or convenient to aid the objects and purposes herein set forth to the same extent and as fully as an natural person would or might do, and as are not forbidden by law or this certificate of incorporation or by the by-laws of the Corporation.

As a non-profit corporation, none of the income of which shall incur to a member, to purchase, receive by deed, gift, devise or bequest, hold, mortgage, lease, sell or otherwise require or dispose of such real or personal property and rights as may be necessary for the purposes of the Corporation, in assurance with the provisions of the Membership Corporation Law.

In general, the Corporation shall have and may exercise all power conferred upon it by the laws of the State of New York now or hereafter in effect.

The Corporation is not organized for pecuniary profit, and no part of its income shall incur to the benefit of any member as such.

THIRD: The territory in which the operations of the Corporation are principally to be conducted is the United States of America.

FOURTH: The principal office of the Corporation will be located in the borough of Manhattan, City, County, and State of New York.

FIFTH: the number of directors of the Corporation will not be less than three or more than fifteen.

SIXTH: The names and places of residence of the persons to be the directors of the Corporation until its first annual meeting are as follows:

Allan W. Dulles	239 East 61st Street New York 21, NY
Charles Maechling, Jr.	2 Stuyvesant Oval New York 9, NY
Vincent A. Rodriguez	8 East 86th Street New York 21, NY

SEVENTH: Of the persons hereinabove named as directors at least one is a citizen of the United States and a resident of the State of New York.

IN WITNESS WHEREOF, we have made, signed and acknowledged this certificate this 20th day of October, 1950.

(signatures) Lucius D. Clay
Allen W. Dulles
Adolphe A. Berle, Jr.
Frank Altschul
DeWitt C. Poole

Appendix D:
Costs and Contributions

Comparison of Central Intelligence Agency Funding, CIA Contributions to
Crusade for Freedom, and Crusade for Freedom Costs and Contributions

Known Central Intelligence Agency Funding
to National Committee for a Free Europe
and Free Europe Committee to 1960

FY 1949	$69,000,000.00
1950	3,108,968.73
1951	8,681,715.50
1952	16,164,867.25
1953	14,871,703.51
1954	12,230,764.38
1955	11,728,850.01
1956	12,299,669.29
1957	14,430,322.30
1958	10,103,301.32
1959	13,480,187.36
1960	13,190,405.72
Total	$130,359,755.37

Known CIA Contributions to
Crusade for Freedom, Inc., and
Radio Free Europe Fund, Inc.

FY 1951–52	$2,343,534
1953	793,528
1954–55	1,747,500
1956	1,070,167
1957	1,000,000
1958	1,000,000
1959	925,000
1960	900,000

1961	851,200
1962	890,600
1963	913,800
1964	928,920
1965	827,600
1966	812,000
1967	870,000
1968	600,882
Total	$16,474,731

Crusade for Freedom Costs Vs.
Public/Corporate Contributions

	Cost	Contributions
1950	$900,000	$1,317,000
1951 (12 mos to 2/28/52)	2,016,433	1,930,135
1952 (16 mos 3/52–6/53)	917,833	931,952
1953–1954	876,667	3,139,376
1954–1955	922,130	3,019,580
1955–1956	1,062,494	2,927,209
1956–1957	997,381	3,027,960
1957–1958	931,127	2,621,160
1958–1959	917,974	2,534,297
1959–1960	?	?
Total:	$9,542.039	$21,448,669

Sources: *U.S. Government Monies Provided to Radio Free Europe and Radio Liberty, Comptroller General of the United States*, p. 101–102. B-173239, Washington, D.C. May 25, 1972. http://archive.gao.gov/f0302/096554.pdf. (Last accessed December 2009)

Comparison sheet of costs and contributions from 1950 to 1958-1959 campaigns. Arthur Page Collection, Wisconsin Historical Society, Madison, Wisconsin.

Appendix E: Chronology of RFE, NCFE, and Crusade for Freedom (1949–1959)

Abbreviations

C. I	Committee I of National Committee for a Free Europe (NCFE)
C. II	Committee II of NCFE
C. III	Committee III of NCFE
CBOD	Communist Bloc Operations Division of NCFE
CF	Crusade for Freedom
CFA	Committee for a Free Asia
DER	Division of Exile Relations of NCFE
DIC	Division of Intellectual Cooperation of NCFE
EC	Executive Committee
EEAL	East European Accessions List
EPOD	Exile Political Organizations Division of NCFE
FE	Free Europe, Inc.
FEC	Free Europe Committee, Inc.
FECS	Free Europe Citizens Service
FED, Ltd.	Free Europe Division, Ltd. of NCFE
FEER	Free Europe Exile Relations of NCFE
FEOP	Free Europe Organizations and Publications
FEP	Free Europe Press
FEUE	Free Europe University in Exile in France
FWOD	Free World Organizations Division of NCFE
GA	General Administration
IDF	International Development Fund
MELP	Mid-European Library Project
MESC	Mid-European Studies Center in France
NCD	National Councils Division of NCFE
NCFE	National Committee for a Free Europe
PSPD	Publications and Special Projects Division
RARET	Sociedate Anonima de Radio Retransmisso in Portugal
RFA	Radio Free Asia
RFE	Radio Free Europe

RFE/RL	Radio Free Europe/Radio Liberty
RSP	Research and Publications Service of NCFE
RSPD	Research and Publications Service Division
WEAC	West European Advisory Committee of Free Europe Committee
WEOD	West European Operations Division

1949

May 11	Certification of Incorporation was filed under the name "Committee for Free Europe."
May 17	Filed name change—"National Committee for Free Europe."
June 2	NCFE Discussed formation of three operating committees: Committee I—Intellectual Activity (C. I) Committee II—Radio and Press (C. II) Committee III—American Contacts (C. III).
June 16	NCFE—The executive Committee of the Board of Directors (EC) is formed, along with the Committee on advertising.
July 7	NCFE—The powers of the Executive Committee established "to exercise the powers of the Board when the Board is not in session."

1950

January 19	NCFE—Formed fund raising committee. Members include: Allen Dulles, Lucius Clay, and DeWitt Poole.
March 16	NCFE—Advertising Committee disbanded. Its remaining budget given to The Fund Raising Committee.
	C. II—Robert Lang sent to Europe to purchase equipment and organize foreign personnel for the creation of a radio station.
April 11	NCFE—Filed name change: "National Committee for a Free Europe."
April 13	C. I—Formed the Mid-European Studies Center (MESC) to aid the publication of materials pertaining to or written by exiles.
	A Board of Review formed to select individuals for research grants. Members include: The Director of MESC, the President or Vice President of the National Councils Division, and a member of Committee 1.
	NCFE—A National Council Division (NCD) formed to conduct relationships with the National Committee, exile individuals, and exile and related organizations and publications to develop and keep records on exiles, their organization and their publications in *any* part of the world.
	C. II—Budget for Radio increased to cover the costs of three shortwave transmitters. "At first planned to use leased facilities in Europe similar to buying of radio time on commercial networks in the U.S."
April 21	NCFE—Budget for FY 1950–51 Committee I MESC $395,000

Committee II/RFE	$2,158,000	
Committee III	$138,000	
NCD	$1,055,790	
General Administration	$494,620	
Crusade for Freedom	$190,300	(remaining portion of six-month budget already approved)
Total	$4,432,430	

NCFE — Maynard Barnes sent to Europe to investigate opening of European Office.

May 18	Contracts for Liberty Bell and replicas.
July 20	C.I — Name changed to the Division of Intellectual Cooperation.
August 24	NCFE — Certificate of Incorporation amended to widen the roles of the various committees.
September 28	RFE — Approval given for the building of a medium wave transmitter in Holzkirchen, Germany.
	CF — Decision to incorporate the Crusade as a separate membership Corporation.
October 24	RFE — Lang requests more money to continue project of German and second-line facilities. Mention of possible sites for secondary sites includes North Africa, Israel, Ireland, and Portugal. State Department negotiated with the U.K. regarding this matter.
November 15	RFE — The aims and objectives of RFE are presented by Poole and Altschul. Board approved the installation of two shortwave transmitters at Biblis, Germany.
December 7	C.I — Resolution establishing Committee I is rescinded.
	DIC — Created to find employment for exiles, contracts for research material, pay stipends, provide tuition and living expenses for exile students, and encourage intellectual efforts. MESC will operate under this division. A.A. Berle selected to serve as Chairman.
	RFE — Approved the construction of a power installation at Holzkirchen, as well as a monitoring and receiving station at Schleissheim, Germany.
December 21	RFE — State Department approved NCFE negotiations with the Portuguese for second-line facilities.

1951

January 16	NCFE — Position of Vice-Chairman of the Board of Directors is created. D.C. Poole is elected.
	RFE — Approved the construction of studio and offices in Munich. Authorized a cash advance of $200 to each employee in case of emergency evacuation.
January 16	RFE — Information Gathering Center is to be enlarged.
February 15	RFE — Portuguese authorities approved in principle NCFE's plans for building a second-line facility.

Lang reported that RFE could be on the air in Germany by May instead of September if additional funds were available. Board agreed.

MESC — Board directs MESC to prepare textbooks to be used immediately after the liberation of Eastern Europe.

March 22   MESC — Dr. Levering Tyson is appointed Director.

April 12   RFE — Portuguese company formed to manage the construction and running of the second-line facilities in Portugal. (4.10.51) to be known as the Sociedate Anonima de Radio Retransmissao (RARET).

May 17   NCFE — Poole reports the creation of a University in Exile (FEU) at Strasbourg, France. Royall Tyler sent to negotiate the opening of a NCFE branch office in Europe.

June 7   RFE — RFE awarded the Peabody Award.

NCFE — Position of Comptroller established.

July 19   NCFE — Opened office in the LsSalle Apartment Hotel in Washington, DC.

NCD — Authorized the NCD to create and support consultation panels for three Baltic States. Also approved in principle the purchase of limited number of foreign periodicals as a method of support.

August 2   MESC — W. Dean resigns as Director of MESC. No replacement is to be found until a survey of the center can be completed with the intention of enlarging MESC's scope.

C. III — Board agrees to discontinue Committee III ASAP. Lecture program to be abolished. Its publishing and pamphlet operations to be transferred to the DIC.

FEUE — Informal agreements with the French authorities achieved. Grounds and staff should be ready be 11.1.51.

RFE — Question of Hungarian Programming to be studied August 23

RFE — Hungarian Broadcasting Review Committee submitted a favorable report re initiating Hungarian broadcasting. The EC approves Program.

MESC — MESC begins scholarship program for exile students who formally state their intention to return to their native countries after liberation.

MESC receives approval for their Eastern European List — Library of Congress Project at a cost of $29.

September 20   MESC — Members of the MESC's Board of Review amended to read Director of the Division of Intellectual Cooperation. The President of NCFE, or the Vice President in charge of the NCD, and Mr. A.A. Berle.

October 19   NCFE — Poole tenders his resignation no later than 4.1.52 as Vice President of the Board and the President of FEUE.

| | Discussed Operation Santa Claus, which involves the sending of penicillin and other drugs by balloons to behind the Iron Curtain. |

November 27   RFE — RFE reached an agreement with the Austrian Government regarding the removal of interference from broadcasting channels, at a cost of $339,000.

CF — Adopted policy that all Crusade Funds to be used only for the purchase of land, buildings, and equipment acquired by it only for RFE. This action to bring NCFE's policy in line with the publicity statements being made by the Crusade.

December 20   NCFE — Budget.

General Administration	$1,040,188
Radio Free Europe	
NYC Office	$2,455,000
Germany	$4,442,295
Portugal	$638,000
(RFE Total)	$7,535,895
Division of Intellectual Cooperation	$812,788
National Councils Division	$1,406,221
American Contacts (7/51–10/51)	$38,085
Research and Publications Services	$358,253
TOTAL OPERATING EXPENSES	$11,191,430

The NCFE also supported additional approved projects totaling $607,935 and the FEUE Project amounting to $421,000.

1952

January 3   MESC — Enlarged the authority of the Board of Review (Executive Memorandum, Series A. No. 1-10/17.51) to review all special compensation problems of exiles and to determine on an individual basis the nature if such.

The members of the Board of Review amended to read: Chair, A.A. Berle; Vice-Chair, F.R. Dolbears or his deputy, Levering Tyson or his deputy, and Spencer Phenix or his deputy.

RFE — Lang reported that Polish programming would require a capital outlay of $786,238.62, and that if begun as planned on 4.1.52 operating cost would run $169,800 through 6.30.52. Board agreed to program.

February 7   NCFE — Washington office to be closed ASAP, but not considered a permanent move.

March 13   RFE — U.S. officials to delay entry in Turkey, and Turkish Projects for at least two weeks.

March 27   RFE — German officials agreed to issue the necessary licenses for RFE operation after the end of the occupation.

RFE — Outlined the financial relationship and accounting procedures between RARET and NCFE.

April 17   NCFE — Agreed that all possible pressure should continue until Washington officials promise appropriate provisions for the care or removal of NCFE employees in Germany, as well as the staff and students in Strasbourg.

It was determined that the termination of IRO activities and the continued escape of individuals from behind the Iron Curtain — "presumably encouraged to make the effort as a result of RFE's programs." NCFE should provide some sort of exile assistance programs.

May 22   RFE — Board approved the sale of the Lampertheim station to the American Committee for the Liberation of the Peoples of Russia, Inc. for $85,000.

NCFE — Admiral Millar submitted the proposed budget for FY 1952-1953 totaling $25,111,417.68.

June 16   MESC — Mr. Phenix is directed to draft a resolution defining the authority of the Board of Review.

NCFE — Approved the proposed budget for FY 1952-53, which included expenditures for the installation of broadcast and program facilities in Turkey, the extension and enlargement of the work in Europe of exile committees for the benefit of persons escaping from behind the Iron Curtain, and increased support for exile groups in the U.S.

July 17   NCD — Board approved $1,733,306 in FY 1952-1953 for the NCD, which is to cover four additional staff members, the moving of all exile organizations to NYC, relocating the Baltic panels in one central location, and the publication of the *Baltic Review*.

NCD — Dolbears recommends that the name of NCD be changed to the Division of Exile Relations (for the history of NCD see page 3 of 7.17.52).

RFE —(Research and Publication Service, which began in FY51-52)

Approved RFE budget for RPS — the majority of which is given over to the publication of *News from Behind the Iron Curtain*.

RFE — Approved RFE budget of $13,632,432. Discussion was raised over the estimate of the London-Paris program. Mr. Lang said that such an office was necessary to ensure that the Munich programs do not get sterile.

September 4   NCFE — Resolved to put before the members of the Corporation a NCFE name change to Free Europe Committee, Inc. The reasons for this are listed on page 9.

Approved a revised budget for FY 1952-1953 of $18,000,000 instead of $18,908,923. The reductions occur in the GA's of RFE's budgets.

DIS — Approved resolution defining the authority of the MESC's Board of Review.

November 25   RFE — Appointed committee to discuss the problems RFE is having in Germany.

Approved the Condon signing lease for installation near Cham, Germany.

December 11   RFE — Gave Condon the authority to sign lease and the construction contracts for the Moorsburg monitoring site.

FEUS — Approved in principle the construction at Robertsau and the location of a second unit at Saarbrucken.

December 31   RCFE — Board agreed upon new guide lines for MESC's Board of Review regarding the stipends given "charity" cases.

Approved policy statement, which lists NCFE's radio endeavors first, then NCFE's efforts to promote understanding among the captive peoples of Eastern Europe of "the important part they can play together with their free neighbors in eliminating causes of war and in furthering the establishment of a durable people's peace in Central and Eastern Europe." (See pages six, seven, and eight of 12.31.52.)

1953

January 28   RSPD — Samuel Walker, Director of RSPD, outlined a publications project, which will use the printed word as a means of communicating with people in Eastern Europe. A pilot project was approved for early spring of 1953.

February 19   DER — DER's refugee program given the authority to open a dollar account in Paris. Associated with the account are S. Phenix, F.C. Augustine, R.L. Bull, A.C.J. Sabalet, R. Sears, and R. Taylor.

NCD — Board adopted policy that all stipend payments made by NCFE to individuals of National Councils, except charity cases, would be discontinued effective the day NCFE's ceases to acknowledge such a group to be functioning effectively.

RSPD — RSPD is placed under the direct control of the president. Prior to this it had been under the control of the now defunct Editorial Board of the DIC.

RFE — Board agreed to send representatives to Turkey to discuss the setting up of a broadcasting station on Turkish soil.

NCFE — Board rescinded Executive Memorandum, Series A. No. 1-3, which covered the reorganization of the operating division.

Given the consent of the State Department and the German government, NCFE will consider Eastern Germany a "de facto" satellite state and within the scope of NCFE's activities.

March 17   RFE — Condon discusses negotiations with the Federal Ministry of the Interior in Bonn for the legal recognition of NCFE as a foreign membership organization.

CF — Heritage Foundation is to manage the Crusade's campaign for FY 1953-54. NCFE'S only responsibility would be to check advertising for accuracy.

	MESC — MESC redefines its emphasis from a make-work program for exiles to a qualified research program.

MESC — MESC redefines its emphasis from a make-work program for exiles to a qualified research program.

GA — Created new budget account entitled "Meritorious Exile Support." Budget outlays for FY 1953-54 would be $115,000.

April 21 NCFE — Proposed Budget for FY 1954-55:

Operating
Exile Relations	$1,683,612
Intellectual Cooperation	$1,321,714
Research and Publications	
Service	$702,160
General Administration	$1,082,107
Radio Free Europe	$11,173,748
Free Europe in Exile	$813,590
TOTAL	$16,776,931

Capital
Radio Free Europe	$1,559,275
TOTAL OPERATING	
AND CAPITAL	$18,336,206

May 19 RFE — The possibility of live broadcast from Portugal was discussed and dismissed at the same time.

The State Department approved the negotiations with Turkey for a broadcast station.

June 6 DER — Authorized opening a dollar account in Frankfurt, Germany to be used by the Free Europe Citizens Service, a NCFE refugee program.

de Neufville requested $80,000 to research a proposed Federation of Europe. In addition, he recommended that DER's budget be given $185,000 to provide for a conference. The board approved in principle assuming the State Department's approval was forthcoming.

July 14 RFE — Discussion of Operation Prospero.

NCFE — Given recent developments in the USSR and satellite states, board agreed in principle that a Strategy Board should be formed to coordinate all the divisions. Under this group would be a panel of division chiefs who would meet frequently. de Neufville was appointed to serve as executive secretary for both.

October 2 RFE — Board approves formation of panel of 38 American Area Policy Specialists to act as consultants for RFE.

DER — de Neufville outlined progress in Federation of Europe Project. 9 panels formed, which will carry out the plan for collaboration between Eastern and Western Europe after liberation.

December 17 FEP — "News Behind the Iron Curtain" to be put on subscription basis. A free German edition was also going to be printed.

1954

February 15	NCFE — Approved creation of four new vice president positions. Elected Messrs. Lang, Tyson, Walker, Yarrow.
March 4	NCFE — Resolved to change NCFE's name to Free Europe Committee, Inc. (FEC).
March 15	FEP — Board approves Operation Veto, scheduled for the end of April.
April 19	DIC — Board of Review reiterates the guidelines of eligibility for financial assistance to meritorious exiles to counter adverse propaganda, to discharge a debt of gratitude of the U.S., and to reward for distinguished service to the nation.
	RARET — Due to uncertain future in Portugal, Board asked for resignations of Messer's. Phenix, Thomas, Caesar and Lolliot, together with two Portuguese Directors most closely associated with these four from the board of RARET.
June 28	FEP — Operation Focus tentatively scheduled for September.
September 20	RFE — Turkish Project well received by officials. Board approves preparation of movement of a mobile transmitter to Turkey from Cham, Germany.

FEC — Committee for Divisional Directors agreed:

a. Policy Planning Advisor — continue to be lodged in the post of Counselor in the office of the President.

b. Labor Advisor also continues to be part of office of the President.

c. Public Relations — consolidation of such posts into one, again in the office of the President.

d. DER — Federation of Europe Project to be discontinued.

e. Free Europe Citizens Service — to be transferred with that of DER to the GA at a reduced scale of operation.

f. DER's purpose is to strengthen friendly relations with exile councils and committees and to support a limited number of exile activities in cooperation with RFE and FEP.

g. DIC to discontinue as a division.

h. FEUE — in future all decisions made by the Board of Trustees would be final and not subject to the approval of the FEC's Board.

November 15	FEC — Total operating and capital budget for FY 1954-55: $14,965,352.

Operating

General Administration	$1,122,760
Exile Relations	$1,050,000
Intellectual Cooperation	$519,445
Free Europe Press	$1,379,163
Radio Free Europe	$9,277,353
Total Operating	$13,550,851

Capital
Radio Free Europe — New	$124,609
Radio Free Europe — 1953-54	$1,080,161
Total Capital	$1,204,770

Special Projects
FEUE	$900,000
Mid-European Law Project	$176,104
East European Accessions List	$145,492
Georgetown University Project	$40,000
Total Special Projects	$1,162,664

December 20   FEP — Hungarian protests Operation Focus. State Department rejects complaint.

1955

January 25   FEUE — Main activities of FEUE being moved from Strasbourg to Paris.

April 24   FEC — State Department requests that FEC support the newly formed Romanian National Committee in terms of stipends, office costs, and travel expenses. To not do so would be "detrimental to the national interests."

FEC — Budget for 1955-1956
Operating Costs	$14,378,355
Capital-RFE	$426,509
Total Budget	$14,804,864
Total Special Projects	$948,477

May 24   RFE — Turkish Project — the basic legislation preliminary to granting a license to FEC was passed.

October 27   RFE — Turkish Project — Arthur Page "had a talk with sponsor in order to obtain a clarification of sponsor's views with respect to the Turkish contract and project. He reported that the sponsor had indicated that the necessary funds to finance the Turkish operations were just not available and that consequently the signing of said contract at this time would have to be postponed indefinitely. He also stated that in the opinion of other friends any delay in the signing of this contract or in negotiating another would not disturb our present friendly relations with the Turkish government."

1956

18   FESC — Due to increased redefection activities, FESC is replaced under the jurisdiction of the DER.

DER — DER's name changed to Free Europe Exile Relations (FEER).

15   FEP — West German government informally requested an end to balloon activities in response to USSR pressure. FEC decided to await a formal request before responding.

Vaclav David, Czech Foreign Minister, sent a statement to Secretary General of the United Nations alleging that FEC's balloon activities violated Chicago Convention on Civil Aviation of 1944. A reply was sent to these accusations.

2   RFE — Granted an additional $5,152,000 in funds to cover the opening of a London office, and beefing up transmitters in Portugal. Necessary due to increase in sunspot activity, which will allow the USSR to jam more effectively.

18   FEP — Balloon safety features installed will cut next year's deliveries by 10 percent.

November 27 FEP — Agreed to temporary suspension of balloon operations to avoid any affront to German government at a time when anti–Adenauer Germans and others are raising incitement charges against RFE.

RFE — In response to incitement charges, an investigation indicates that RFE has scrupulously followed policy lines laid down in 1949 to the present.

FEP — Began a mailing project when censorship was relaxed in Poland. It is being done through European publishers without any attribution to RFE or FEP.

FEUE — Requested a loan of $500,000 to undertake a program of emergency Hungarian support. Repayment would be obtained from sponsor.

1957

January 8   FEC — Number of directors increased from 15 to 20.

February 18 FEC — Requested all department heads to examine staff for "welfare" cases and to submit a report. Hoped to relocate such individuals outside the organization.

FEP — Balloon site at Fronau to be closed.

RFE — Pressure was being exerted on RFE to leave Vienna in order to maintain neutrality vis-à-vis the Hungarian refugees.

March 28   FEP — All balloon sites have now been deactivated.

April 8   FEC — FY 1957-58 Budget

RFE Operating Budget	$9,744,644
RFE Capital Budget	$275,622

FEC — President reports that the Committee is supporting 100 to 150 exiles who are contributing little. Other means of support should be found but not without FEC retaining overall control of exiles.

RFE — In order to streamline activities, all news departments are to pool their efforts in serving the FEP. The news offices in Frankfurt, Germany, and Salonica, Greece, to be closed.

July 8   FEP — Balloon operations completely suspended. Proposed a new FEP publication entitled "Panorama" that would depict life in the West and would be distributed to the Captive European nations.

September 5   FEC — President commented on FEC's expansion of areas of interest to Asia, Africa, and South America. He stated that there was no restriction in the Charter that limited its activities to the five captive European countries.

October 2   FEC — President reported that in an effort to solidify Hungarian exile leadership, a declaration of Unity and Purpose is to be signed by all the leaders of the separate Hungarian groups no later than 10.31.57.

November 27   RFE — "Friends" request that a panel of Americans review scripts before and after broadcast.

1958

January 10   FEC — President hoped to reduce the FY 1958-59 budget by one million dollars. He recommended that the HELP and EEAL projects be transferred out of FEC.

               RFE — German authorities take issue with security clearances of RFE employees. It would be discussed with "Friends" in Munich.

April 8   FEC — Board agreed in principle to the creation of a West European Advisory Board.

October 3   RFE — Consideration given to broadcasting to Baltic States, due to reduction of Voice of America coverage.

               FEC — Advisory Group of the FEC to survey the need for increased FEC activity in Latin America.

November 10   FEC — FEC functions of planning, publicity, review of program research and evaluation, analysis, and guidance consolidated under the direct supervision of the President.

               Issued the first issue of a confidential Monthly Report covering the FEC's activities for September.

1959

March 12   FEC — Board agrees on the following change to the Charter:

               "No *substantial* part of the activities of the Corporation shall be the carrying on of propaganda or otherwise attempting to influence legislation."

               From

               "No part of the activities of the Corporation shall be the carrying on of propaganda or otherwise attempt to influence legislation."

               RFE — Decides not to pursue Baltic Broadcasting.

               FEC — Initial meeting of the West European Advisory Committee tentatively scheduled for middle of May. This committee sprang out of the contact with the Council of Europe.

April 14   FEER — Board approved a merger of FEER and FEP effective 7.1.59 due to duplication of effort in East-West Contacts Project and the Free World Areas Project, as well as in the publication and administrative fields.

FEC — West European Advisory Council (WEAC) is approved by the State Department for May 18 or May 20.

June 18   FEER-FEP — Board approved the move of the FEER-FEP headquarters from Paris to London.

October 7   FEC — President informed the meeting of the change of method of financing the FEC's activities, effective 8.1.59. The Crusade funds would now be used to fund RFE and other FEC activities. Board rescinded resolution adopted in 1954.

Source: Unattributed document in the RFE/RL Collection, Hoover Institution, Stanford, California.

Chapter Notes

Preface

1. *Cold War Radio: The Dangerous History of American Broadcasting in Europe, 1950–1989* (McFarland: Jefferson, NC, 2009).

2. Memo from Deputy Director, Plans, Thomas Karamessines, to Director of Central Intelligence, Richard Helms, November 13, 1968. Central Intelligence Agency (CIA), Freedom of Information Act Electronic Reading Room (last accessed December 2009).

3. The reader is directed to the home page of Radio Free Asia, http://www.rfa.org, for more details (last accessed December 2009).

4. There are two excellent insider studies of Radio Liberty: Gene Sosin, *Sparks of Liberty: An Insider's Memoir of Radio Liberty* (Pennsylvania University Press, 1999), and James Critchlow, *Radio Hole-in-the-Head. Radio Liberty: An Insider's Story of Cold War Broadcasting* (Washington, D.C.: The American University Press, 1995). A somewhat older but well researched book is Joseph Whelan, *Radio Liberty — A Study of Its Origins, Structure, Policy, Programming and Effectiveness*, Library of Congress, Congressional Research Service, Washington, D.C., 1972.

5. Charles Taylor Papers, Library of Congress, Washington, D.C.

Introduction

1. Jean Smith, *Lucius D. Clay: An American Life* (New York: Henry Holt & Co., 1990), p. 566.

2. A photocopy of this directive can be found in Michael Warner, ed., *CIA Cold War Records: The CIA under Harry Truman*, "Psychological Operations, NSC 4-A" (Washington, DC: CIA, 1994), pp. 175–177. Also, see Document 253, "Memorandum from the Executive Secretary (Souers) to the Members of the National Security Council," NSC 4-A, Washington, December 9, 1947, in Foreign Re-

lations of the United States, 1945–1959, *Emergence of the Intelligence Establishment*, http://www.fas.org/irp/offdocs/nsc-hst/ and http://www.state.gov/www/about_state/history/intel/index.html (last accessed December 2009).

3. *Ibid.*

4. Michael Warner, p. 216.

5. *Emergence of the Intelligence Establishment*, Document 269.

6. *Ibid.*

7. *Ibid.*

8. National Security Council Directive on Office of Special Projects, NSC 10/2, Washington, June 18, 1948. The full text of this directive can be found in Michael Warner, ed., *op. cit.*, pp. 213–216 and *Emergence of the Intelligence Establishment*, Document 206.

9. *Ibid.*

10. *Ibid.*

11. VOUSA was Voice of USA later to become Voice of America. *Foreign Relations of the United States, 1948*, Eastern Europe: The Soviet Union, Volume IV, Department of State, Washington, D.C., p. 425.

12. *Ibid.*, p. 426.

13. For full details of Wisner's experiences in Romania, the reader is directed to Evan Thomas, *The Very Best Men: Four Who Dared: The Early Years of the CIA* (New York: Simon & Schuster, 1995).

14. "RFE was one of the projects in which Dulles was especially interested...," Wayne G. Jackson, CIA Historical Staff, Allen Welsh Dulles as Director of Central Intelligence, 26 February 1953 — 29 November 1961, Volume III, Covert Activities, July 1973, p. 102

15. Evan Thomas, p. 61.

16. Memorandum from the Director of the Policy Planning Staff (Kennan) to the Under Secretary of State (Lovett), Washington, June 30, 1948. *Emergence of the Intelligence Establishment*. Document 294.

17. Memorandum from the Assistant Director for Policy Coordination (Wisner) to Direc-

tor of Central Intelligence Hillenkoetter, in Foreign Relations of the United States, 1945–1950, *Emergence of the Intelligence Establishment.* Document 306.

18. Hillenkoetter's Memorandum for the Record, 4 August 1948, in Warner, *op cit.*, p. 217.

19. Memorandum from the Assistant Director for Policy Coordination, Central Intelligence Agency (Wisner) to Members of His Staff, Washington, June 1, 1949, *Emergence of the Intelligence Establishment.* Document 310.

Chapter One

1. RFE/RL Collection, Hoover Institution, Stanford, CA.
2. *Ibid.*
3. *Ibid.*
4. Telegram from Acting Secretary of State Webb to Certain Diplomatic Offices, Foreign Relations of the United States, 1949, Volume V, p. 290.
5. *Ibid.*, footnote by historian.
6. Charles Taft Collection, Library of Congress, Washington, DC. Charles Phillip Taft, one of the first members of the NCFE, was the son of President William Taft and a member of the Cincinnati, OH, City Council and was Mayor of Cincinnati 1955–1957. He was the Ohio Chairman of the Crusade campaign.
7. Arthur W. Page Collection, Wisconsin Historical Society, Madison, WI.
8. CIA FOIA Document released in October 1992 (last accessed August 2009). Dulles's letter of August 5, 1949, to Senator Flanders was not released. Electronic Reading Room.
9. *Ibid.*
10. Sig Mickelson, p. 21.
11. Richard Harris Smith, *OSS: The Secret History of America's First Central Intelligence Agency,* 1972, p. 95. For details of some of his heroic actions in World War II, see Sonay Jason, *Maria Gulovich, OSS Heroine of World War II: The Schoolteacher Who Saved American Lives in Slovakia* (Jefferson, NC: McFarland, 2008).
12. Letter DeWitt Poole to Allen Dulles, August 13, 1949, Dulles Collection Princeton University Archive.
13. Charles Taft Collection, Library of Congress.
14. Letter from DeWitt Poole to Allen Dulles, October 13, 1949, Dulles Digital Collection. Princeton University Digital Archive.
15. *Ibid.*
16. *Ibid.*
17. CIA FOIA Document, Electronic Reading Room.
18. *Analysis and Plan of Fund-Raising for the National Committee for Free Europe,* John Price

Jones, Inc. December 1949, Wisconsin Historical Society, Madison, WI, Box 71, Arthur Page Collection.
19. *Ibid.*
20. *Ibid.*
21. RFE/RL Collection.
22. Attachment to a letter dated January 26, 1950, from DeWitt Poole to Arthur Page. Arthur Page Collection.
23. RFE/RL Collection, Hoover Institution.
24. *Ibid.*
25. Sig Mickelson, pp. 52–54. Nate Crabtree went on to publish a history of the Freedom Bell with photographs as *The Story of the World Freedom Bell* (Minneapolis: Nate Crabtree, 1951).
26. DeWitt Poole to Lucius Clay, February 24, 1950, RFE/RL Collection, Hoover Institution.
27. John Burton Letter, February 28, 1950. RFE/RL Collection.
28. CIA FOIA Document, Electronic Reading Room.
29. Minutes of Board of Directors Meeting, March 16, 1950. RFE/RL Collection.
30. NCFE Annual Meeting Minutes, Arthur Page Collection.
31. *Ibid.*
32. John Woolley and Gerhard Peters, The American Presidency Project [online]. http://www.presidency.ucsb.edu/ws/?pid=13768. (Last accessed August 2009).
33. Press Release, RFE/RL Collection. Hoover Institution.
34. RFE/RL Collection.
35. John Woolley and Gerhard Peters, The American Presidency Project [online].
36. RFE/RL Collection.
37. *Ibid.*
38. Memorandum of Conversation, by Mr. Claiborne Pell of the Office of Eastern European Affairs. May 4, 1950. *Foreign Relations of the United States, 1950. Central and Eastern Europe, the Soviet Union, Volume IV (1950)* (Washington, DC: U.S. Government Printing Office, 1950), pp. 19–20. http://digital.library.wisc.edu/1711.dl/FRUS.FRUS1950v04 (last accessed August 2009).
39. Crusade for Freedom, Progress Report No. 2, RFE/RL Collection, Hoover Institution.
40. Arthur Page Collection.
41. RFE/RL Collection, Hoover Institution.
42. *Ibid.*
43. Dulles Collection, Princeton University Digital Archives.
44. Memorandum from the Assistant Director for Policy Coordination (Wisner) to Director of Central Intelligence Hillenkoetter. *Foreign Relations of the United States, 1945–1950, Emergence of the Intelligence Establishment* (Washington DC: U.S. State Department, 1996). Document 306.

45. RFE/RL Collection.
46. *Time,* July 17, 1950.
47. *Evening Times,* Cumberland, MD, Wednesday, July 13, 1950, p. 4.
48. Cord Meyer, *Facing Reality: From World Federalism to the CIA* (New York: Harper & Row, 1980), p. 112. In the 1950s, Cord Meyer was the CIA Chief of the International Organization Division, which had administrative oversight of Radio Free Europe and Radio Liberty, among other organizations. In his published memoirs there is a full chapter on RFE with detailed information on his and the CIA's role in Hungary.
49. Cold War Broadcasting Impact Report on a Conference organized by the Hoover Institution and the Cold War International History Project of the Woodrow Wilson International Center for Scholars at Stanford University, October 13–16, 2004.
50. RFE/RL Collection.
51. *Ibid.*
52. Progress Report No. 4, from General Adcock to the NCFE Board of Directors. RFE/RL Collection.
53. RFE/RL Collection.
54. Frank Altschul Letter to Allen Dulles, August 21, 1950, with 15-page report August 15, 1950, Allen Dulles Digital Collection, Princeton University.
55. See Chapter 3 on the development of Radio Free Asia.

Chapter Two

1. Dwight D. Eisenhower Memorial Commission, Eisenhower's Speeches, Crusade for Freedom, Denver, Colorado, September 4, 1950. http://www.eisenhowermemorial.org/speeches (last viewed December 2009).
2. Martin J. Medhurst, Eisenhower and the Crusade for Freedom: the rhetorical origins of a Cold War campaign, *Presidential Studies Quarterly* 27, no. 4, 1997.
3. Allen W. Dulles Papers, Princeton University Digital Files, Subseries 4D, General, English, 1942–1974, Doc 19500911_0000030165. pdf http://arks.princeton.edu/ark:/88435/st74 cq497 (last accessed December 2009).
4. Nate Crabtree, *The Story of the World Freedom Bell* (Minneapolis, MN: Nate Crabtree, undated), p. 43.
5. Crusade Chairman, Arthur W. Page Collection, Wisconsin Historical Society, Madison, WI, Box 72.
6. The "Freedom Scrolls" in original envelopes and boxes remain enshrined in the Freedom Bell tower vault at the base of the belfry. Visitors to the building can readily see the envelopes and packages containing the scrolls through the vault's glass door.

7. *The Post Standard,* Sunday, October 1, 1950, Syracuse, NY, p. 26.
8. *The Ogden Standard-Examiner,* Ogden, UT, Friday evening, September 29, 1950, p. 9A. The store owner, Lowell R. Boyle, went on to become the industrial division chairman in Ogden, UT, for the 1951 Crusade campaign — Ogden Standard Examiner, September 14, 1951.
9. RFE/RL Collection.
10. Arthur W. Page Collection.
11. *Los Angeles Times,* Los Angeles, CA, August 26, 1951, p. B-2.
12. Wanger Collection, Box 7, Folder 38, June–August 1950.
13. *Ibid.*
14. *Los Angeles Times,* Los Angeles, CA, September 29, 1950, p. A1.
15. Martin Bernstein, *Walter Wanger: Hollywood Independent* (Minneapolis: University of Minnesota Press, 2000), p. 268.
16. *Ibid.,* p. 270.
17. Wanger Collection.
18. Wanger Collection, Box 6, Folder 39.
19. *The Lowell Sun,* Lowell, MA, Saturday, September 9, 1950, p. 5.
20. NCFE Executive Committee Meeting Minutes, October 5, 1950. RFE/RL Collection.
21. RFE/RL Collection.
22. Wanger Collection, Box 6, Folder 39.
23. *Ibid.*
24. *Ibid.*
25. Memorandum for Mr. Poole from Frederick Osborn, Subject: Empire State Ceremony, September 28, 1950, RFE/RL Collection.
26. Press Release Crusade for Freedom, October 10, 1950.Wanger Collection, Box 6, Folder 39.
27. *Ibid.*
28. RFE/RL Collection.
29. *Ibid.*
30. *Advertising Council News,* October 1950.
31. DeWitt C. Poole to Allen Dulles, September 28, 1950, CIA FOIA, Electronic Reading Room.
32. *Ibid.*
33. NCFE Meeting Minutes, RFE/RL Collection.
34 RFE/RL Collection.
35. Letter from DeWitt Poole to W. H. Jackson, October 25, 1950, CIA FOIA, Electronic Reading Room.
36. RFE/RL Collection.
37. Frank Wisner, Memorandum for: Deputy Director of Central Intelligence, Subject: Radio Free Europe, 22 November 1950. CIA FOIA, Electronic Reading Room.
38. RFE/RL Collection.
39. Wanger Collection, Box 6, Folder 40. Also, comparison sheet of costs and contributions from 1950 to 1958-1959 campaigns, Arthur Page Collection.

Chapter Three

1. Letter from Dulles to the Board of Directors of the NCFE. CIA FOIA, Electronic Reading Room. W.H. Jackson would resign at DDCI in August 1951 to be replaced by Allen Dulles, and when Dulles became Director of Central Intelligence, Frank Wisner became his DDCI.

2. Secret Report Attachment to Memorandum by the Undersecretary of State for Public Affairs (Edward W. Barrett) to Deputy Secretary of State (Mathews, January 24, 1951, *Foreign Relations* 1951 IV), pp. 1206–1208.

3. Memorandum Allen Dulles, Deputy Director, Plans to Frank Wisner, Assistant Director, Policy Coordination, January 11, 1951. CIA FOIA, Electronic Reading Room.

4. *San Mateo Times*, San Mateo, CA, May 16, 1951, p. 3.

5. *Prospectus*, Committee for a Free Asia, Inc., May 1951. RFE/RL Collection, Hoover Institution.

6. *Ibid.*

7. For details of the construction, testing, and first operations of the Holzkirchen transmitter, see Charles E. Ruckstuhl, "The Beginning of Electronic Warfare: Piercing the Iron Curtain," *World and I*, October 2003.

8. *Chronicle-Express*, Pann Van, NY, May 17, 1951, p. Six-A.

9. *Chronicle-Express*, May 31, 1951, p. 1.

10. *Los Angeles Times*, Los Angeles, CA, August 26, 1951, p. B-2.

11. *Time*, September 1, 1951.

12. *The Daily Review*, Pan Van, NY, September 4, 1951, p. 9.

13. *Kokomo Tribune*, Kokomo, IN, October 17, 1951, p. 16.

14. Hearst Newsreel, News of the Day 23, no. 200. http://history.sandiego.edu/GEN/qt/coldwar/1951reagan480.html (last accessed November 2009).

15. From a Chronology outline found in the RFE/RL Collection.

16. Drew Pearson, "The Washington Merry-Go-Round," October 28, 1956.

17. *Ibid.*

18. *Ibid.*

19. *Front Page News*, Department of Public Services, August 14, 1950.

20. Drew Pearson, "Washington Merry-Go-Round," August 13, 1951. Bell Syndicate, Inc.

21. "Washington Merry-Go-Round," August 17, 1951.

22. "Washington Merry-Go-Round," August 25, 1951.

23. *Chronicle-Express*, Page Seven-A.

24. Pearson, August 17, 1951, and Alan Michie, p. 137.

25. Crusade for Freedom, "Minutes of a Special Meeting of the Board of Directors," September 30, 1952. RFE/RL Collection.

26. *Joplin Globe*, Joplin, MO, September 25, 1951, p. 1.

27. *Foreign Relations*, 1951 IV, p. 1270.

28. National Archives, Maryland, CIA-RDP 80R01731R00310018031-9.

29. Nancy Bernhard, *U.S. Television News and the Cold War Propaganda, 1947–1960* (Cambridge: Cambridge University Press, 1999), p. 47.

30. The first transcontinental television program, carried by 94 stations, was west coast to east coast on September 5, 1951, when President Truman addressed the nation from San Francisco, during the international conference to sign the peace treaty with Japan.

31. Description of Sullivan is from Lawrence R. Samuel, *Brought to You By: Postwar Television Advertising and the American Dream* (Austin: University of Texas Press, 2003), p. 82.

32. *San Mateo Times*, San Mateo, CA, Monday, September 24, 1951, p. 15.

33. *San Antonio Express*, San Antonio, TX, Thursday, September 4, 1951, p. 6.

34. *The Daily Review*, Oakland, CA, Friday September 7, 1951, p. 9 and *New York Times*, September 9, 1951.

35. *The Daily Oklahoman*, Oklahoma City, Tuesday, September 25, 1951, p. 7.

36. *Nevada State Journal*, Reno, NV, Sunday, September 16, 1951, p. 9.

37. *Ibid.*

38. *Nevada State Journal*, Sunday October 21, 1951, p. 19.

39. *The Marion Star*, Marion, OH, October 20, 1951, p. 10.

40. Quoted as printed in *Foreign Relations 1951 IV*, pp. 1415–1416.

41. *Chronicle Telegram*, Elyria, Ohio, Thursday, October 4, 1951, page 8.

42. "Freedom Balloons Carry True Story of Train Escape," *Chronicle-Express*, Penn Van, NY, October 4, 1951.

43. *Foreign Relations*, op cit.

44. *Nevada State Journal*, Reno, Nevada, Sunday, September 16, 1951, p. 9.

45. UP report in *Stars and Stripes* newspaper, Saturday, November 17, 1951, p. 2.

46. "Ideas Asked How to Pierce Iron Curtain," *The Daily Review*, Oakland, CA, Friday, September 8, 1951, p. 12.

47. *Ibid.*

48. "South Carolina Town Debunks Propaganda," *The Post-Register*, Idaho Falls, ID, Friday, August 3, 1951.

49. *The Burlington* (NC) *Daily Times-News*, Tuesday, September 4, 1951.

50. *The Stars and Stripes*, Monday, February 3, 1952, p. 5.

51. *Florence Morning News*, Florence, SC, Monday, December 31, 1951, p. 2.

52. *New York Times*, October 3, 1951.

53. *Popular Science*, October 1951, p. 24.

54. A copy of this advertisement by the Madison Community Advertising Fund is in the Arthur Page Collection.

55. *The Daily Inter Lake*, Kalispell, MT, September 20, 1951, p. 1.

56. *The Independent Record*, Helena, MT, October 4, 1951, p. 5.

57. *The Daily News*, Huntingdon and Mount Vernon, PA, October 31, 1951, p. 11.

58. *The Pinedale Roundup*, Pinedale, WY, September 27, 1951, p. 1.

59. *Alton Evening Telegraph*, Alton, IL, September 25, 1951, p. 1.

60. Minutes of NCFE Meeting January 18, 1952, RFE/RL Collection.

61. Accountant's Certificate from the firm Haskins & Sells, CPA, June 27, 1952. RFE/RL Collection, Hoover Institution.

62. Minutes of NCFE Meeting September 4, 1952, RFE/RL Collection. Comparison sheet of costs and contributions from 1950 to 1958-1959 campaigns, Arthur Page Collection. Support from CIA taken from *U.S. Government Monies Provided to Radio Free Europe and Radio Liberty*, Report to the Committee on Foreign Relations, United States Senate, Washington, DC: Comptroller General of the United States, May 25, 1972. Appendix II, p. 101. http://archive.gao.gov/f0302/096554.pdf (last accessed December 2009).

Chapter Four

1. The CIA International Operations Division reportedly gave the Congress of Cultural Freedom $130,000 in support. Frances Stonor Saunders, *The Cultural Cold War: The CIA and the World of Arts and Letters*, p. 117.

2. Notes of the October 1952 board of directors meeting, RFE/RL Collection, Hoover Institution, Stanford, CA.

3. Minutes of Special Meeting, January 16, 1952, RFE/RL Collection.

4. Memorandum for the Files, November 23, 1951, *Foreign Relations, 1950–1955* (U.S. Government Printing Office, Washington, 2007). Document 94.

5. *Ibid.*

6. *Oakland Tribune*, Oakland, CA, December 20, 1952, p. 1.

7. RFE/RL Collection.

8. *Foreign Relations, 1951*, Vol. IV, Document No. 658, pp. 1315–1316.

9. Memorandum of Conversation, Washington, D.C., January 17, 1952, "Meeting to Discuss the Crusade for Freedom held in Mr. Barrett's Office," *Foreign Relations, 1950–1955* (U.S. Government Printing Office, Washington, 2007). Document 100.

10. *Ibid.*

11. Minutes of the NCFE Board of Directors Meeting, January, 21, 1952, RFE/RL Collection.

12. *Ibid.*

13. Arthur Page Collection, Wisconsin Historical Society, Madison, WI.

14. Letter from Abbott Washburn to Fred Smith, March 3, 1952, Arthur Page Collection.

15. Page Collection.

16. *Ibid.*

17. *Crusade for Freedom 1952, Notes on a Program*, RFE/RL Collection.

18. Noel Griese, *Arthur W. Page: Publisher, Public Relations Pioneer, Patriot* (Tucker, GA: Anvil, 2001), p. 368.

19. RFE/RL Collection.

20. Letters from Robert D. Jordan, RFE/RL Collection.

21. *Ibid.*

22. Copy of letter in the RFE/RL Collection.

23. DeWitt Poole died on September 3, 1952. The NCFE Board Meeting on September 4, 1952, expressed the Board's feelings on the death of Poole and the minutes were sent to Poole's widow as a show of sympathy. RFE/RL Collection.

24. RFE/RL Collection.

25. Rion Bercovici, Crusade for Freedom Press Release, RFE/RL Collection.

26. Crusade for Freedom Press Release, RFE/EL Collection.

27. Advertisement Council Archives, University of Illinois Urbana-Champaign, IL.

28. Crusade for Freedom Press Release, October 21, 1952, RFE/RL Collection.

29. Crusade for Freedom Press Release, October 25, 1952, RFE/RL Collection.

30. *The New York Times* published the full text of Eisenhower's radio speech, for example, on November 12, 1952. Transcript of radio program in RFE/RL Collection.

31. *Ibid.*

32. Undated Advertising Council "Report of Crusade for Freedom Campaign 1952," Arthur Page Collection.

33. Advertisement Council Archives, University of Illinois.

34. *Ibid.*

35. *Austin Daily Herald*, Austin, MN, December 15, 1952.

36. *Ogden Utah Standard Examiner*, December 9, 1952 p. 12A.

37. Minutes of Campaign Review Committee Meeting, December 17, 1952. Ad Council Archives, University of Illinois.

38. Undated Annex "B" Crusade for Freedom Objectives and "Packaging," RFE/RL Collection.

39. *The Gastonia (NC) Gazette*, Gastonia, NC, December 12, 1952, p. 13. *Statesville Daily Record*, Statesville, NC, Friday, December 12, 1952, p. 1.

40. *The Charleroi Mail*, Charleroi, PA, Wednesday, December 24, 1952, p. 5.

41. *Nevada State Journal*, Reno, NV, January 23, 1953, p. 9.

42. *Reno Evening Gazette*, February 9, 1953, p. 15.

43. *Reno Evening Gazette*, April 6, 1953, p. 9.

44. Central Intelligence Agency, Freedom of Information Act, Electronic Reading Room.

45. National Archives, College Park, MD, CREST, CIA-RDP80B01676R00400007032-8.

46. A person using the initials REL wrote a note about the phone call on a copy of the letter from Edward Bartelt to General Smith. National Archives, College Park, MD, CREST, CIA-RDP80B01676R00400070032-8.

47. Syndicated column "Washington-Merry-Go-Round," March 13, 1953. Neither Congress nor the media in the United States followed up on Pearson's exposé.

48. Figures taken from the Agenda for Special Meeting of the Board of Directors, April 12, 1955. RFE/RL Collection and from comparison sheet of costs and contributions from 1950 to 1958-1959 campaigns. Arthur Page Collection.

Chapter Five

1. Letter from Lucius Clay to Admiral Miller, President, Crusade for Freedom, January 28, 1953. RFE/RL Collection, Hoover Institution, Stanford, CA.

2. Washburn's resignation letter on The President's Committee on International Information Activities.

3. The Eisenhower letter was apparently never found. See letter from Theodore Mecke, Assistant Manager, General Public Relations, Ford Motor Company to Miss Cathleen Soden, Crusade for Freedom, May 15, 1953. RFE/RL Collection.

4. Minutes of March 17, 1953, Directors Meeting, RFE/RL Collection.

5. RFE/RL Collection.

6. Minutes of the Annual Meeting of the Crusade for Freedom. RFE/RL Collection.

7. *Ibid.*

8. Minutes of April 21, 1953, NCFE Meeting, RFE/RL Collection. The budget was further reduced at the July 14, 1953, meeting to $17,241,652.

9. Copy in the RFE/RL Collection.

10. Minutes of April 21, 1953, NCFE Meeting, RFE/RL Collection. The budget was further reduced at the July 14, 1953, meeting to $17,241,652.

11. *Ibid.*

12. RFE/RL Collection.

13. Arthur Page Collection, Wisconsin Historical Society, Madison, WI.

14. *Ibid.*

15. Report of the President's Committee on International Information Activities, June 30, 1953, "Project Clean Up," p, 1833.

16. Allan A. Michie, *Voices Through the Iron Curtain: The Radio Free Europe Story* (New York: Dodd, Mead, 1963), pp. 136–141.

17. Minutes of July 14, 1953, NCFE Meeting, RFE/RL Collection.

18. Foreign Relations, 1942–1954, Volume VIII, Note No. 4, p. 106.

19. Richard M. Fried, *The Russians Are Coming! The Russians Are Coming!: Pageantry and Patriotism in Cold-War America* (New York: Oxford University Press, 1998), p. 48.

20. Carl Koch would later be arrested in Czechoslovakia, when he was on a private visit, and later released to return to Germany.

21. "Czechoslovakia: The Wonderful Machine," *Time*, August 3, 1953.

22. *Ames Daily Tribune*, Thursday, September 11, 1953.

23. *Council Bluffs Iowa Nonpareil*, Council Bluffs, IA, January 8, 1954, p. 14.

24. AP item quoted in *The Era*, Bradford, PA, January 22, 1954, p. 10.

25. *Albuquerque Journal*, Albuquerque, NM, January 22, 1954.

26. *The Charleroi Mail*, Charleroi, PA, January 30, 1954.

27. *New Castle News*, February 23, 1954, p. 1. The Freedom Tank was eventually put on display at the Ford Museum in Detroit and eventually sold to a Michigan farmer. In August 2010, the author learned that the "Freedom Tank" was originally a German World War II tank and military historian Jim Gilmore had bought it from a farmer. It is in "fair" condition in his collection in Pennsylvania.

28. See Chapter 7 for details.

29. Arthur Page Collection.

30. *Ibid.*

31. *Ibid.*

32. National Archives, College Park, MD. CREST, CIA RDP80R01731R001300220014-3.

33. *Ibid.*

34. *Ibid.*

35. Arthur Page Collection.

36. RFE/RL Collection.

37. Advance Kit Copy, University of Illinois Archives, Urbana, Advertising Council Collection.

38. *Ibid.*

39. Highlights of the Board of Trustees' Meeting, The American Heritage Foundation, November 18, 1953. RFE/RL Collection.

40. *Ibid.*

41. What was discussed remains unknown. National Archives, College Park, Maryland, CREST, CIA-RDP80B01676R00400070025-5.

42. *The Bismarck Tribune*, Bismarck, ND, February 19, 1954.

43. *The Spokesman Review*, Spokane, WA, February 13, 1954, p. 1, including a photograph of the women in the native costumes.

44. *The Bismarck Tribune*, Bismarck, ND, February 6, 1954.

45. Advertisement in *The Bismarck Tribune*, Tuesday, February 16, 1954.

46. *The Bismarck Tribune*, Bismarck, ND, February 18, 1954.

47. *Lima News*, Lima, OH, February 19, 1954, p. 12.

48. *The Cedar Rapids Tribune*, Cedar Rapids, IA, Thursday, February 11, 1954, p. 9.

49. RFE/RL Collection.

50. Total number of equivalent number of homes that could have watched the Crusade for Freedom television spots over the months of the campaign. Approximately 56 percent of American households had television sets.

51. Minutes of the Trustee's Meeting and a copy of the Preliminary Report are in the RFE/RL Collection.

52. Page Collection.

53. *Ibid.*

54. *Ibid.*

55. Thomas D'Arcy Brophy Collection, Wisconsin Historical Society.

56. Page Collection.

57. *Operation VETO. A Combined Political Warfare Operation: The Printed and Spoken Word*, Free Europe Press, Free Europe Committee, New York, Sep. 17, 1954. RFE/RL Collection.

58. *Department of State Bulletin*, June 7, 1954, p. 881.

59. UPS Report, *Stars and Stripes, European Edition*, May 7, 1954, p. 2.

60. "Operation VETO. A Combined Political Warfare Operation: The Printed and Spoken Word," Free Europe Press, Free Europe Committee, New York, Sep. 17, 1954. Copies of the leaflets are included in this report.

61. The American Heritage Foundation received $2,870,042.56 in contributions and Free Europe Committee separately received $269,333.10. Total figures come from a comparison sheet of costs and contributions from 1950 to 1958-1959 campaigns. Arthur Page Collection.

Chapter Six

1. Alan Michie, *Voices through the Iron Curtain: The Radio Free Europe Story* (New York: Dodd, Mead, 1963), p. 104.

2. Michie, pp. 278–279. Cord Meyer, *Facing Reality: From World Federalism to the CIA* (New York: Harper & Row, 1980), p. 120. Full details of the Swiatlo case can be read in L.W. Gluchowski, *The Defection of Jozef Swialto and the Search for Jewish Scapegoats in the Polish United Workers' Party, 1953–1954*, Intermarium, Columbia University electronic journal of modern East Central European postwar history. www.columbia.edu/cu/ece/research/intermarium/vol3no2/gluchowski.pdf-2009-08-20 (last viewed November 2009).

3. Ted Shackley, *Spymaster: My Life in the CIA* (Washington, DC: Potomac Books, 2005), pp. 79–85. Another CIA officer who had the chance to interview Swiatlo, after his arrival in the United States, was Tennent H. Bagley, *Spy Wars: Moles, Mysteries, and Deadly Games* (New Haven, CT: Yale University Press, 2007).

4. Michie, p. 165. A listing of his interviews is available at the Open Society Archives, Budapest, Hungary, HU OSA 300-50-6.

5. Stewart Steven, *Operation Splinter Factor* (Philadelphia: J.B. Lippincott, 1974), p. 208.

6. *Operation SPOTLIGHT: Regime, Press and Radio, Western Press and Radio and Internal Reactions, Feb. 12–Mar 13, 1955*, Free Europe Committee, New York, March 1955, Free Europe Press, both of which can be found in the RFE/RL Collection, Hoover Institution, Stanford, CA.

7. *Ibid.*

8. *The Inside Story of the Bezpieka and the Party: Jozef Swiatlo Reveals the Secrets of the Party, the Regime, and the Security Apparatus*, English translation, p. 2, in RFE/RL Collection.

9. Gluchowski, *Defection.*

10. *Oneonta Star* (New York), January 17, 1956, p. 2.

11. Shackley, *Spymaster*, p. 85.

12. Polish historian Andresz Paczkowski e-mail message. Author's Collection.

13. Minutes of the Special Meeting of the Executive Committee of the Board of Directors of FEC, July 19, 1954. RFE/RL Collection.

14. *Operation Focus, Volumes 1–III, Progress Reports on Operation and Program Summary, Regime Reaction, Refugee Reports, and Leaflet Content* (New York: Free Europe Press, 1954), copies of which are located in the Radio Free Europe Collection.

15. RFE/RL Collection.

16. Earl Newsom Collection, Wisconsin Historical Society, Box 76.

17. December 20, 1954, Free Europe Committee Meeting. RFE/RL Collection.

18. Letter from Lewis Galantiere, Free Europe Committee to Arthur Page, Chairman of the Executive Committee Crusade for Freedom and Director of the Free Europe Committee, December 27, 1954. Page Collection.

19. RFE/RL Collection.

20. *Ibid.*

21. Memorandum from Robert L. Smith to

William Greene, December 3, 1954. RFE/RL Collection.

22. *Journal*, Syracuse, NY, February 22, 1955.

23. National Archives, College Park, MD, CREST CIA-RDP 80B01676ROO400070011-1.

24. Ibid.

25. Free Europe Committee Regular Monthly Meeting, November 15, 1954, RFE/RL Collection. See Appendix E for exact budget figures.

26. Minutes of the Regular Monthly Meeting of the Board of Directors of Free Europe Committee, November 15, 1954. RFE/RL Collection.

27. Free Europe Committee Meeting, February 17, 1955. RFE/RL Collection.

28. Free Europe Committee Regular Monthly Meeting, November 15, 1954.

29. Letter from William A. Greene, National Crusade Chairman, to Arthur Page, Page Collection, Wisconsin Historical Society.

30. Letter from Arthur Page to Gwilym A. Price, Page Collection.

31. Letter from Price to Page, March 7, 1955, and letter from Page to William Greene, March 8, 1955. Page Collection.

32. John T. Woolley and Gerhard Peters, *The American Presidency Project* [online]. Santa Barbara, CA: University of California (hosted), Gerhard Peters (database). http://www.presidency.ucsb.edu/ws/?pid=10408 (last accessed November 2009).

33. Page Collection.

34. *Syracuse Journal*, Syracuse, NY, February 22, 1955.

35. *Crusade for Freedom Newsletter* 3, no. 1, September 15, 1955. RFE/RL Collection.

36. *Idaho Sunday Journal*, February 6, 1955.

37. *Interim Progress Report*, January 18, 1955, Page Collection.

38. *Life* Magazine, February 22, 1954, p. 37.

39. *Bismarck Tribune*, Bismarck, ND, Saturday, February 24, 1955.

40. *Bismarck Tribune*, February 17, 1955, front page.

41. *The Cedar Rapid Gazette*, Friday, July 1, 1955, p. 7.

42. *Reno Evening Gazette*, Reno, NV, Thursday, January 27, 1955, p. 15.

43. *Jefferson City Post Tribune*, Jefferson City, MO, Wednesday, February 23, 1955.

44. Judson Bruce Pearson, Jiri Nehnevajsa, and Rodney D. Elliott, *Message Diffusion Under Uncontrolled Conditions* (University of Colorado Press, 1957).

45. See, for example, *The Ogden* (Utah) *Standard-Examiner*, February 21, 1955, for a copy of this advertisement.

46. *Family Weekly Magazine*, October 3, 1955.

47. *Crusade for Freedom Newsletter*, September 15, 1955.

48. *The Cedar Rapids Gazette*, April 3, 1955.

49. Comparison sheet of costs and contributions from 1950 to 1958-1959 campaigns. Arthur Page Collection.

Chapter Seven

1. Crusade for Freedom, Inc., Board of Directors Meeting, Thursday, April 21, 1955, 3:00 P.M. M — Ford Motor Company Offices, 477 Madison Avenue, Twenty-First Floor. RFE/RL Collection, Hoover Institution, Stanford, CA.

2. Free Europe Committee Summary Memo from Lewis Galanitere to Whitney Shepardson, August 4, 1955. Arthur Page Collection, Wisconsin Historical Society, Madison, WI.

3. Page Collection.

4. National Archives, College Park, MD, CREST, CIA-RDP80B01676R00400007002-1.

5. Ibid.

6. Letter from John De Chant, Vice President of the Crusade for Freedom to Earl Newsom, November 23, 1955, outlining the Nixon dinner agenda. Newsom Collection.

7. Ibid.

8. Page Collection.

9. Note from Arthur Page to Cord Meyer, January 12, 1956. Page Collection.

10. Page Collection.

11. *Austin Daily Herald*, Austin, MN, February 8, 1956.

12. *Montana Standard*, Butte, MT, February 2, 1956, p. 5.

13. The photo of Arthur Wong sending a balloon aloft also appeared on page 4 of the February 14, 1956, edition of the Montana newspaper *The Inter Lake*.

14. *The Independent Record*, Helena, MT, February 12, 1956.

15. *Crusade for Freedom Newsletter* 3, no. 1, September 15, 1955. RFE/RL Collection.

16. *The Cedar Rapids Gazette*, Cedar Rapids, IA, April 28, 1956.

17. *Minnesota Alumni Weekly* 54, no. 6, February 1955, p. 2.

18. *The Daily Inter Lake*, May 3, 1956.

19. *Ames Daily Tribune*, Ames, IA, September 28, 1956.

20. *The Morning Herald*, May 18, 1956.

21. *The Waco News-Tribune*, Waco, TX, May 24, 1956, p. 1.

22. *Cumberland Evening Times*, February 9, 1956.

23. *South Town Economist*, Chicago, IL, November 21, 1956, p. 11.

24. Newsom Collection, Box 57, Folder 3.

25. Ibid.

26. Library of Congress, http://lccn.loc.gov/2001659802 and http://lccn.loc.gov/2001659803.

27. John Woolley and Gerhard Peters, *The American Presidency Project* [online]. Santa Barbara, CA: University of California (hosted),

Gerhard Peters (database). http://www.presidency.ucsb.edu/ws/?pid=10763. (Last accessed November 2009).

28. Minutes of the Executive Committee Meeting, January 13, 1956. Page Collection.

29. Minutes of the Executive Committee Meeting, January 17, 1956, Page Collection.

30. Letter from Arthur Page to Juan Trippe, January 27, 1956. Page Collection.

31. Letter from Robert L. Smith to Earl Newsom, January 8, 1956. Newsom Collection, Box 57, Folder 3.

32. Earl Newsom letter to Arthur Page, March 12, 1956. Newsom Collection.

33. Memorandum to the File from E. K. Meade, Jr., March 7, 1956. Newsom Collection.

34. "Candor" here probably refers to Arthur Page's attempt to remove the Crusade for Freedom and Radio Free Europe from the covert umbrella of the CIA with public disclosure of the true source of most of the funding. See Noel Griese, *Arthur W. Page: Publisher, Public Relations Pioneer, Patriot* (Tucker, GA: Anvil Publishers, 2001).

35. Letter from Earl Newsom to Arthur Page, April 26, 1956. Newsom Collection.

36. Letter from Newsom to Allen Dulles, June 1, 1956. Newsom Collection.

37. The project never reached fruition presumably because of the negative publicity repeating allegations of incitement by Radio Free Europe in the Hungarian Revolution in November 1956. See Chapter 8 for more details.

38. Comparison sheet of costs and contributions from 1950 to 1958-1959 campaigns. Arthur Page Collection.

Chapter Eight

1. Space does not allow for a fuller treatment of the Hungarian Revolution and the role of Radio Free Europe. For one scholar's view, see A. Ross Johnson, *To the Barricades: Did Radio Free Europe inflame the Hungarian revolutionaries of 1956? Exploring one of the Cold War's most stubborn myths*, Hoover Digest, 2007, No. 4. For another scholar's view of the CIA's intelligence failure, see the excellent book by Charles Gati, *Failed Illusions: Moscow, Washington, Budapest and the 1956 Hungarian Revolt* (Stanford, CA: Stanford University Press, 2006). He was able to obtain the following highly-censored but revealing documents under the U.S. Freedom of Information Act from the CIA for his book: (1) *CIA Clandestine Services History, The Hungarian Revolution and Planning for the Future, 23 October–4 November 1956*, Volume I of II, January 1958; (2) *CIA Historical Staff, The Clandestine Service Historical Series, Hungary*, Volume I, [Deleted], May 1972; and (3) *CIA Historical Staff, The Clandes-*

tine Service Historical Series, Hungary, Volume II, External Operations, 1946–1965, May 1972. National Security Archive, George Washington University, Washington, DC. Cord Meyer was, at the time of the Hungarian Revolution, the CIA Chief of the International Organization Division, which had administrative oversight of Radio Free Europe and Radio Liberty. In his memoir *Facing Reality: From World Federalism to the CIA* (New York: Harper & Row, 1980), he presented a full chapter on Radio Free Europe with detailed information on his and the CIA's role in Hungary.

2. U.N. Review. United Nations, *Report of the Special Committee on the Problem of Hungary*, June 20, 1957.

3. *German Foreign Office Review*. The German Foreign Office borrowed a set of RFE recordings for the period from the RFE transmitters in Biblis—the set preserved later in the Federal German Archives—and conducted its own review. Preliminary results were discussed with RFE management in Munich on November 27 (RFE Munich teletype MUN 321, November 27, 1956) and communicated to the U.S. Government via the Bonn Embassy on December 20. (Department of State, *Foreign Relations of the United States 1955–1957*, Volume XXV. Washington, DC: Government Printing Office, 1990, Editorial Note 228, pp. 556–557).

4. As reported in *U.N. Review Report of the Special Committee on the Problem of Hungary*, June 20, 1957.

5. George R. Urban, *Radio Free Europe and the Pursuit of Democracy: My War within the Cold War*. (New Haven and London: Yale University Press, 1997), p. 228. His book contains a detailed chapter review of the Hungarian Revolution based on his access to the full set of recorded programs. For his insightful and contemporary review of Hungary 1956, see his book *The Nineteen Days: A Broadcaster's Account of the Hungarian Revolution* (London: Heinemann, 1957).

6. Arthur Page Collection. Wisconsin Historical Society, Madison, WI. The note was subsequently sent out on January 8, 1957.

7. *Ibid*. The White House meeting was postponed to February 5, 1957.

8. The Washington Merry-Go-Round, "Green Candles in Windows Show Hungary Unrest," *The Constitution-Tribune*, Chillicothe, MO. November 8, 1956, p. 14.

9. Library of Congress, http://lccn.loc.gov/9450922.

10. *New York Times*, January 26, 1977, p. 30.

11. *Ibid*.

12. *Crusade for Freedom Newsletter* 6, no. 9, December 5, 1956. Copy provided by Public Relations Department, General Mills Archive.

13. *Ibid*.

14. *Crusade for Freedom Newsletter* 6, no. 10, February 7, 1957. General Mills Archives, Public Relations Department.
15. Earl Newsom Collection, Madison Historical Society, Madison, WI.
16. Arthur Page Collection.
17. Memorandum from KM to Earl Newsom, January 11, 1957, presented the agreed-upon luncheon schedule.
18. Newsom Collection.
19. See Chapter 7 for list of the large corporate contributions (gifts).
20. *Crusade for Freedom Newsletter*, February 7, 1957.
21. *Ibid.*
22. *Big Spring* (TX) *Herald*, February 4, 1957, p. 5.
23. *Ibid.*
24. *Southeast Economist*, Chicago, IL, February 21, 1957, p. 12.
25. *The News*, Newport, RI, February 4, 1957, p. 14.
26. *Ogden Standard-Examiner*, Ogden, UT, February 14, 1957, p. B-1.
27. *The News-Palladium*, Benton Harbor, MI, February 22, 1957, sec. two, p. 4.
28. *Dodge County Independent*, Kasson, MN, February 14, 1957.
29. *Crusade for Freedom Newsletter* 7, no. 1, July 1957. RFE/RL Collection.
30. *The Progress-Index*, Petersburg Colonial Heights, VA, February 6, 1957, p. 1.
31. *The Independent Record*, Helena, MT, February 10, 1957, p. 1.
32. *Southeast Economist*, February 18, 1957, p. 15.
33. *Southeast Economist*, February 21, 1957, p. 12.
34. *Waco-Herald Tribune*, Waco, TX, March 31, 1957, p. 12.
35. Letter from General Crittenberger to Eugene Holman, December 5, 1956. RFE/RL Collection.
36. Herb Altschull, United Press article, February 16, 1957.
37. Eugene Holman to Willis Crittenberger, Arthur Page Collection.
38. *Syracuse Herald Journal*, Syracuse, NY, February 20, 1957.
39. *Crusade for Freedom Newsletter*, April 1957.
40. *Crusade for Freedom Newsletter*, February 7, 1957.
41. Comparison sheet of costs and contributions from 1950 to 1958-1959 campaigns. Arthur Page Collection.

Chapter Nine

1. Crusade for Freedom Budget for 1958-1959 Campaign dated May 1, 1958. Arthur Page Collection, Wisconsin Historical Society, Madison, WI.
2. Executive Committee Meeting Notes, RFE/RL Collection, Hoover Institution, Stanford, CA.
3. Arthur Page Collection.
4. Arthur Page Collection.
5. Letter from John Patterson to Dr. Frank Stanton, November 22, 1958. Page Collection.
6. Page Collection.
7. Page Collection.
8. Earl Newsom Collection, Wisconsin Historical Society, Madison, WI.
9. *Ibid.*
10. *The Charleston Gazette*, Charleston, WV, Wednesday, February 12, 1958, p. 18.
11. *The Daily Republic*, Mitchell, SD, Friday, February 14, 1958, p. 8.
12. The reader is directed to Chapter 4 for more information.
13. *Crusade for Freedom Newsletter*, March 1958. RFE/RL Collection.
14. *Ibid.*
15. *The Charleston Gazette*, Charleston, WV, October 18, 1957, p. 9.
16. *Charleston Daily Mail*, Charleston, WV, December 18, 1957, p. 17.
17. Page Collection.
18. Crusade for Freedom, Progress Report, March 1958. RFE/RL Collection.
19. Document No. 19571116_0000481633.pdf, Dulles Princeton Digital Collection.
20. *Anderson Daily Bulletin*, Anderson, IN, Saturday, February 1, 1958, p. 2.
21. Crusade for Freedom Progress Report, October 1957. Page Collection.
22. *The Sun-Standard*, Chicago, IL, February 20, 1958, p. 6.
23. *Anderson Daily Bulletin*, Anderson, IN, February 27, 1958, p. 1.
24. RFE/RL Collection.
25. Full transcript of the radio program "Lewis Talks of Radio Free Europe," prepared by Radio Reports, Inc., Newsom Collection.
26. Page Collection.
27. *Comments December 30, 1957, in Board of Directors Meeting*, RFE/RL Collection.
28. Page Collection.
29. *Ibid.*
30. Allen W. Dulles Papers, Princeton University Digital Files, Subseries 4D, General, English, 1942–1974, Document 19580218_00004 81644. http://arks.princeton.edu/ark:/88435/st74cq497 (last accessed December 2009).
31. RFE/RL Collection.
32. *Ibid.*
33. Page Collection.
34. National Archives, College Park, MD, CIA Records Search Tool (CREST), CIA-RDP 80R01731R0002000010053-5.
35. *Ibid.*

36. *Ibid.*
37. *The Independent Record*, Helena, MT, Monday, July 20, 1959, p. 2.
38. *Crusade for Freedom Newsletter*, March 1958, RFE/RL Collection.
39. *McKean County Miner*, Smethport, PA, Thursday, September 5, 1957, p. 1.
40. *Globe-Gazette*, Mason City, IA, February 11, 1958, p. 15.
41. *The Ogden Standard-Examiner*, Ogden, UT, Friday Evening, February 15, 1957, p. 7A.
42. *The Denton Record-Chronicle*, Denton, TX, Sunday, February 10, 1957, sec. 2, p. 9.
43. Comparison sheet of costs and contributions from 1950 to 1958-1959 campaigns. Arthur Page Collection.

Chapter Ten

1. Program of the events of July 1, 1958, is included in the Arthur Page Collection, Madison WI.
2. *Ibid.*
3. *Ibid.*
4. *Ibid.*
5. *Oshkosh Northwestern*, Oshkosh, WI, September 4, 1958, p. 3.
6. Letter from John Patterson to Arthur Page, October 6, 1958. Page Collection.
7. *The Albuquerque Tribune*, Albuquerque, NM, October 31, 1958.
8. *B'nai B'rith*, Vol. VIII, no. 7, February 1959. Arthur Page Collection.
9. *Ibid.*
10. Memorandum from President of the Crusade John M. Patterson to Friends and Supporters of the Crusade for Freedom, April 1, 1959, Page Collection.
11. Patterson to Repplier, March 11, 1959, Page Collection.
12. Earl Newsom Collection, Wisconsin Historical Society, Madison, WI.
13. Page Collection.
14. Library of Congress, http://lccn.loc.gov/200165978 and http://lccn.loc.gov/2001659787 (last accessed December 2009).
15. Newsom Collection.
16. Page Collection.
17. Arthur Page to Joseph Grew, December 19, 1958. Page Collection.
18. Advertising Council, University of Illinois, Urbana-Champaign.
19. *Syracuse Herald American*, Syracuse, NY, December 21, 1958.
20. UP Report quote, for example, in *The Press Courier*, Oxnard, CA, December 26, 1959. "Greetings to Jammers," *Globe-Gazette*, Mason City, IA, December 24, 1959, p. 2.
21. *This Week* would stop publication in 1970.

22. *The New York Times*, December 15, 1947.
23. "TRUTH: A Weapon the Reds Can't Match." *Family Weekly*, March 15, 1959.
24. Patterson to Page, March 3, 1959, Page Collection.
25. *Ogden-Standard-Examiner*, Ogden, UT, February 11, 1959, p. 7A.
26. *The Daily Republic*, Mitchell, SD, Thursday, March 5, 1959, p. 3.
27. *RAVEN newsletter*, no. 5, April 1959.
28. *The Daily Republic*, March 9, 1959, p. 2.
29. *RAVEN newsletter*.
30. *Ogden-Standard-Examiner*, March 31, 1959, p. 3b.
31. Comparison sheet of costs and contributions from 1950 to 1958-1959 campaigns. Arthur Page Collection.

Chapter Eleven

1. Crusade for Freedom Newsletter 9, no. 4, February 1960, p. 8, Arthur Page Collection, Wisconsin Historical Society, Madison, WI.
2. Reprinted in Crusade for Freedom Newsletter, Volume 9, no. 1, February 1960.
3. Earl Newsom Collection, Wisconsin Historical Society, Madison, WI.
4. *Ibid.*
5. Page Collection.
6. United States Declassified Document Reference System, DDRS=2577060001.
7. DDRS=2577100001.
8. Arthur Page Collection.
9. General A.J. Goodpaster, *Memorandum of Conference with the President, February 15, 1960*. DDRS=2316640001-03.
10. Arthur Page Collection.
11. Full transcript in Newsom collection.
12. July 1960 Radio Free Europe Fund Newsletter, Volume 10, no. 1. Page Collection.
13. *The Post-Register*, Idaho Falls, ID, Monday, February 29, 1960, p. 6.
14. *The Cedar Rapids Gazette*, Cedar Rapids, IA, Sunday, February 2, 1959, p. 11.
15. Advertising Council Archives, University of Illinois, Urbana-Champaign, IL.
16. *Crusade for Freedom Newsletter* 9, no. 4.
17. *The Bee*, Dunville, VA, Saturday, March 12, 1960, p. 7.
18. Letter John Patterson to Arthur W. Page, May 11, 1960, Page Collection.
19. Agenda for the Executive Committee Meeting. RFE/RL Collection, Hoover Institution, Stanford, CA.
20. *Ibid.*
21. *Ibid.*
22. *Ibid.*
23. Minutes of Annual Meeting of the Board of Directors of Crusade for Freedom, Inc., June 2, 1960. RFE/RL Collection.
24. Meeting of Special Meeting in lieu of

Annual Meeting of Members of Crusade for Freedom, Inc., June 2, 1960. RFE/RL Collection.

25. By then, the CIA had funded Radio Free Europe with $131,000,000, with an additional $9,600,000 for the operating expenses of the Crusade for Freedom.

26. *Time*, October 24, 1960. Also, Horace Newsome, ed., *Encyclopedia of Television*, 2nd ed., Museum of Broadcast Communications (Chicago, IL: Fitzroy Dearborn Publishers, 2004), p. 2231.

27. John Scali, *Ironwood Daily Globe*, Ironwood, MI, October 10, 1960, p. 5.

28. *Oakland Tribune*, Oakland, CA, Monday, October 17, 1960, p. E-19.

29. Annual Meeting of Board of Directors, President's Report, June 15, 1961. RFE/RL Collection.

30. John F. Kennedy Presidential Library & Museum, News Conference 6. Kennedy maintained the annual presidential luncheon for corporate executives who supported Radio Free Europe.

31. Annual Meeting of Board of Directors, June 15, 1961. RFE/RL Collection.

32. Notice of Special Meeting of Members to be held, Thursday, December 20, 1962. RFE/RL Collection.

33. *U.S. Government Monies Provided to Radio Free Europe and Radio Liberty, Comptroller General of the United States*, B-173239, Washington, D.C. May 25, 1972, pp. 101–102. http://archive.gao.gov/f0302/096554.pdf. (Last accessed December 2009). Also, see Appendix D for more details.

Selected Bibliography

Books

Alexeyeva, Ludmilla. *U.S. Broadcasting to the Soviet Union*. New York: Helsinki Watch Committee, 1986.

Bernhard, Nancy E. *U.S. Television News and Cold War Propaganda, 1947–1960*. Cambridge: Cambridge University Press, 1999.

Bernstein, Matthew. *Walter Wanger: Hollywood Independent*. Minneapolis: University of Minnesota Press, 2000.

Browne, Donald R. *International Radio Broadcasting: The Limits of the Limitless Medium*. New York: Praeger Special Studies, 1982.

Critchlow, James. *Radio Hole-in-the-Head. Radio Liberty. An Insider's Story of Cold War Broadcasting*. Washington, DC: American University Press, 1995.

Foreign Relations, 1950–1955. U.S. Intelligence Community, *1950–1955*, Washington DC: U.S. Government Printing Office, 2007.

Foreign Relations of the United States, 1945–1950, Emergence of the Intelligence Establishment. Washington, DC: U.S. Government Printing Office, 1996.

Fried, Richard M. *The Russians Are Coming! The Russians Are Coming!: Pageantry and Patriotism in Cold-War America*. Oxford: Oxford University Press, 1998.

Griese, Noel. *Arthur W. Page: Publisher, Public Relations Pioneer, Patriot*. Tucker, GA: Anvil Publishers, 2001.

Grose, Peter. *Gentleman Spy: The Life of Allen Dulles*. Amherst: University of Massachusetts Press, 1994.

_____. *Operation Rollback: America's Secret War Behind the Iron Curtain*. Boston: Houghton Mifflin, 2000.

Hersh, Burton. *The Old Boys: The American Elite and the Origins of the CIA*. St. Petersburg, FL: Tree Farm Books, 2002.

Hixon, Walter L. *Parting the Curtain: Propaganda, Culture, and the Cold War, 1945–1961*. New York: St. Martin's Griffin, 1997.

Holt, Robert T. *Radio Free Europe*. Minneapolis: University of Minnesota Press, 1958.

Jackson, Wayne G. *Allen Welsh Dulles as Director of Central Intelligence, February 26, 1953–November 29, 1961*. CIA Historical Study, 1973.

Lendvai, Paul. *The Bureaucracy of Truth: How Communist Governments Manage the News*. London: Burnett Books, 1981.

Liebau, Veronika, and Daum Andreas. *The Freedom Bell in Berlin/Die Freiheitsglocke in Berlin*. Berlin: Jaron, 2000.

Lucas, Scott. *Freedom's War: The American Crusade Against the Soviet Union*. New York: New York University Press, 1999.

Meerloo, Joost. *The Two Faces of Man*. New York: International Universities Press, 1954.

Meyer, Cord. *Facing Reality; From World Federalism to the CIA*. New York: Harper & Row, 1980.
Michener, James A. *The Bridge at Andau*. New York: Random House, 1957.
Michie, Allan. *Voices Through the Iron Curtain: The Radio Free Europe Story*. New York: Dodd, Mead, 1963.
Mickelson, Sig. *America's Other Voice: The Story of Radio Free Europe and Radio Liberty*. New York: Praeger, 1983.
Mosley, Leonard. *Dulles: A Biography of Eleanor, Allen, and John Foster Dulles and Their Family Network*. New York: Dial Press, 1978.
Muravchik, Joshua. *Exporting Democracy: Fulfilling America's Destiny*. Washington, DC: American Enterprise Institute, 1991.
Nelson, Michael. *War of the Black Heavens: The Battles of Western Broadcasting in the Cold War*. Syracuse, NY: Syracuse University Press, 1997.
Osgood, Kenneth. *Total Cold War: Eisenhower's Secret Propaganda Battle at Home and Abroad*. Lawrence: University of Kansas, 2006.
Parta, R. Eugene. *Discovering the Hidden Listener: An Assessment of Radio Liberty and Western Broadcasting to the USSR During the Cold War*. Stanford: Hoover Institution Press, 2007.
Powers, Thomas. *The Man Who Kept the Secrets: Richard Helms and the CIA*. New York: Pocket Books, 1991.
Price, James R. *Radio Free Europe: A Survey and Analysis*. Washington, DC: Congressional Research Service, Library of Congress, 1972.
Puddington, Arch. *Broadcasting Freedom: The Cold War Triumph of Radio Free Europe and Radio Liberty*. Lexington: University of Kentucky Press, 2000.
Report of the Presidential Study Commission on International Radio Broadcasting: The Right to Know. Washington, DC: U.S. Government Printing Office, 1973.
Samuel, Lawrence R. *Brought to You By: Postwar Television Advertising and the American Dream*. Austin: University of Texas Press, 2003.
Saunders, Frances Stonor. *The Cultural Cold War: The CIA and the World of Arts and Letters*. New York: New Press, 1999.
Smith, Jean. *Lucius D. Clay: An American Life*. New York: Henry Holt & Co, 1990.
Sosin, Gene. *Sparks of Liberty: An Insider's Memoir of Radio Liberty*. University Park: Pennsylvania University Press, 1999.
Short, K.R.M., ed. *Western Broadcasting Over the Iron Curtain*. London: Croom Helm, 1986.
Srodes, James. *Allen Dulles: Master of Spies*. Washington, DC: Regnery, 1999.
Starr, Richard F., ed. *Public Diplomacy: USA Versus USSR*. Stanford, CA: Hoover Institution Press, 1986.
Thomas, Evan. *The Very Best Men: Four Who Dared: The Early Years of the CIA*. New York: Simon & Schuster, 1995.
Tyson, James L. *U.S. International Broadcasting and National Security*. New York: Ramapo Press, 1983.
Urban, George R. *The Nineteen Days: A Broadcaster's Account of the Hungarian Revolution*. London: Heinemann, 1957.
_____. *Radio Free Europe and the Pursuit of Democracy: My War Within the Cold War*. New Haven and London: Yale University Press, 1997.
Wall, Wendy. *Inventing the "American Way": The Politics of Consensus from the New Deal to the Civil Rights Movement*. Oxford: Oxford University Press, 2008.
Warner, Michael, ed., *CIA Cold War Records: The CIA Under Harry Truman*. Washington, DC: CIA, 1994.
Washburn. Philo C. *Broadcasting Propaganda: International Radio Broadcasting and the Construction of Political Reality*. Westport, CT: Praeger, 1992.

Wiener, Tim. *Legacy of Ashes: The History of the CIA*. New York: Doubleday, 2007.
Wilford, Hugh. *The Mighty Wurlitzer: How the CIA Played America*. Cambridge, MA: Harvard University Press, 2008.

Other

U.S. Government Monies Provided to Radio Free Europe and Radio Liberty, Report to the Committee on Foreign Relations, United States Senate, Washington, DC: Comptroller General of the United States, May 25, 1972. http://archive.gao.gov/f0302/09 6554.pdf (last accessed December 2009).

Index